365 Ways A Year To Cater To Her

BECAUSE SHE DESERVES YOUR BEST -
NOT OCCASIONALLY, BUT ALWAYS.

DEVOLIS D. NEWBURN

FY CREATIVE MEDIA

© 2025 by Devolis Newburn

All rights reserved. No part of this book may be reproduced, stored in a retrieval system, or transmitted in any form or by any means—electronic, mechanical, photocopying, recording, or otherwise—without prior written permission from the publisher, except for brief quotations used in critical reviews or articles.

Published by **F.Y. Creative Media** www.fycreativemedia.com

ISBN (Paperback): 979-8-9926541-0-3
ISBN (Hardcover): 979-8-9926541-1-0
ISBN (eBook): 979-8-9926541-2-7
ISBN (Audiobook): 979-8-9926541-3-4

Disclaimer:
This book is intended for informational and educational purposes only. The author and publisher are not responsible for any actions taken based on the advice in this book. Readers are encouraged to consult professionals for specific advice tailored to their individual needs.

Cover Design: Dusan Arsenic
Interior Design and Formatting: Smartt Guys design

Library of Congress Control Number: Pending

For permissions, inquiries, or bulk purchases, contact:
connect@fycreativemedia.com

Printed in the United States of America
First Edition: 2025

Publisher's Note:
The publisher is not responsible for websites (or their content) referenced in this book.

To my grandmother, Ethel Fay Young,
The best friend I ever had, my partner in crime,
and my unwavering cheerleader.

You gave me strength, wisdom, laughter, and love in its purest form.
Your grit, wit, and guidance carried me through my darkest days
and reminded me of the man I was meant to be.
From our late-night talks over coffee to the life lessons you taught me,
you are the reason I know how to love and lead with purpose.

Even though you left us in November 2024, your presence remains
a guiding light in my life. This book, this journey,
and this life are all better because of you.
I love you like the air I breathe.

Forever in my heart.

CONTENTS

Introduction — *16*

1. Pray for Her / Speak Positive Energy Over Her Life — *20*
2. The Way to Her Heart? Start in the Kitchen — *21*
3. Capture Your Love Story, One Page at a Time — *22*
4. Start Her Day with Words That Matter — *23*
5. Work On the Shoulders, One Knot at a Time — *24*
6. Serve Up Love, One Dish at a Time — *25*
7. Put Your Heart on Paper — *26*
8. Hide Little Joys for Her to Find — *27*
9. Step Up and Lighten Her Load — *28*
10. Shape Memories with Clay or Color — *29*
11. Seal Her Day with Gentle Affection — *30*
12. Unwind, One Soothing Touch at a Time — *31*
13. Spotlight Her Style with Fashionable Compliments — *32*
14. Hold Her Close and Let the World Fade Away — *33*
15. Chase the Sunset — *34*
16. Lose Yourself in the Stars — *35*
17. Spread a Blanket and Make the Moment Yours — *36*
18. Engrave Your Love in a Timeless Treasure — *37*
19. Celebrate Her in Front of Friends or Family — *38*
20. Curl Up and Let the Story Bring You Closer — *39*
21. Steam Up Your Connection — *40*
22. Exchange Words That Last a Lifetime — *41*
23. Escape Together and Rediscover Each Other — *42*
24. Be Her Rock When the Storm Hits — *43*
25. Run Your Fingers Through Her Hair — *44*

26	Take Her Hand and Walk Beside Her	45
27	Melt Her Stress Away, From Head to Toe	46
28	Binge, Bond, and Blanket Up	47
29	Deliver Flavor and Fun to Her Doorstep	48
30	Call Out the Things You Appreciate About Her	49
31	Laugh, Play, and Tickle Her Heart	50
32	Make Movie Nights Magical with Favorites and Themed Experiences	51
33	Explore Hidden Gems and New Horizons	52
34	Arrange an Indoor Picnic Basket with Her Favorite Foods	53
35	Send Love and Light: Uplift Their Day, One Text at a Time	54
36	Gift Her a Build-A-Bear Filled with Love and Personalized Messages	55
37	Hold Each Other Close and Dance the Night Away	56
38	Make Her Mouth Water with a Delicious Breakfast in Bed	57
39	Create Memories at an Amusement Park or Carnival	58
40	Drop the Scorecard, Embrace the Partnership	59
41	Speak from the Heart: Admire Her Strengths and Virtues Out Loud	60
42	Fresh Sheets, Fresh Start . . . Make the Bed and Win Her Heart	61
43	Take Her Up a Famous Tower for a Romantic View of the City	62
44	Explore the Outdoors Together on a Scenic Bike Ride or Hike	63
45	Give Her a Star and Show Her Your Love is Infinite	64
46	Show Her You Care with a Cozy Cuddle Cushion or Body Pillow	65
47	Let Her Find Comfort Resting Her Head on Your Shoulder	66
48	Make Time for Each Other by Establishing a Regular Date Night	67
49	Experience Musical Magic by Attending a Live Concert	68
50	Bonus: Always Try to Find the Good in Her	69
51	Find Peace in Shared Stillness	70
52	Turn Your Love into a Masterpiece	71
53	Dive into Adventure and Keep It Just Between You	72
54	Speak Volumes with a Gentle Touch	73
55	Master Something New, Hand in Hand	74
56	Step Into Rhythm and Romance	75
57	Make Her Feel Like a Movie Star in the Rain	76

58	Celebrate What Makes Her One of a Kind	77
59	Savor the Moment with Every Soft Kiss	78
60	Blend Work and Bliss with a Spontaneous Escape	79
61	Discover Beauty and Meaning Through Art and History	80
62	Piece Together the Memories You Treasure	81
63	Leave Your Love in Her Ears and Heart	82
64	Hold Her Close with Your Hands and Eyes	83
65	Curate the Music That Tells Her Story	84
66	Sweep Her Off Her Feet with a Surprise Night	85
67	Write Your Love in Recipes She'll Treasure	86
68	Inspire Her with Quotes That Celebrate Her	87
69	Wrap Yourselves in Warmth and Love	88
70	Send Her to Work with Love in a Lunchbox	89
71	Be Her Partner in Style and Support	90
72	Celebrate Your Bond with Coordinated Style	91
73	Celebrate Her Hard Work and Unwavering Dedication	92
74	Keep Your Connection Close, One Hand at a Time	93
75	Bring Her DIY Dream to Life	94
76	Cheer, Laugh, and Bond in the Stands	95
77	Sleep Beside Her, Holding Her Close (Without Wanting Sex)	96
78	Brighten Her Day with Blooms of Love	97
79	Walk as the Sun Paints the Sky	98
80	Capture Your Love in a Jar of Memories	99
81	Put Your Heart into Words She'll Treasure	100
82	Leave Mirror and Fridge Notes That Lift Her Spirits Daily	101
83	Sweeten Her Day with a Delicate Treat	102
84	Turn Everyday Outings into Playful Romance	103
85	Craft a Coupon Book Full of Love and Fun	104
86	Show You've Still Got It by Carrying Her to Bed	105
87	Display Your Love Through Digital Memories	106
88	Honor Every Achievement She Earns	107
89	Share the Beliefs That Shape Your Heart	108

90	Transform Chaos into Calm Together with Care	*109*
91	Explore Unique Eats and Moments	*110*
92	Master the Art of Truly Listening	*111*
93	Heal and Strengthen Through True Forgiveness	*112*
94	Secretly Take Note of Her Clothing and Shoe Styles and Sizes	*113*
95	Offer to Be Her Fitness Partner for Life	*114*
96	Give Her Space to Breathe and Reset	*115*
97	Learn, Laugh, and Create Delicious Memories Together	*116*
98	Massage Her Feet After a Long, Rough Day	*117*
99	Offer to Gently Wash and Pamper Her Body	*118*
100	Bonus: Pour Into Her Spiritually, Take Her to a Religious Service	*119*
101	Sow a Seed into Her Business Idea	*121*
102	Explore the Wonders of Nature Side by Side	*122*
103	Light Up Your Love with DIY Candles	*123*
104	Tell Her Exactly How Much She Means to You	*124*
105	Let Go of Unrealistic Expectations About Her	*125*
106	Teach Her Skills You're Passionate About	*126*
107	Take Her Out for a Game of Mini-Golf	*127*
108	Guard Her Heart with Every Thoughtful Action	*128*
109	Surprise Her with Luxurious, Popular Perfumes	*129*
110	Embark on a Horseback Adventure Together	*130*
111	Gift a Gourmet Food Subscription She'll Love	*131*
112	Celebrate Every Milestone with Praise and Love	*132*
113	Deepen Intimacy Using a Feather and Blindfold	*133*
114	Take Charge of an Unforgettable Date Night	*134*
115	Unwind Together at a Beach or Lake	*135*
116	Prepare a Romantic, Blissful Bubble Bath	*136*
117	Whisper Sweet Words While Kissing Her Neck	*137*
118	Curate a Delectable Cheese and Charcuterie Board	*138*
119	Plan a Fun, Immersive Themed Dinner Night at Home	*139*
120	Build a Blanket Fort for Cozy Connection	*140*
121	Share Your Heart Through Timeless Love Poems or Literature	*141*

122	Experience the Thrill of Racing Go-Karts Together	*142*
123	Sit Down and Uncover Family Histories to Deepen Connection	*143*
124	Make Yourself as Presentable as the Day You Met Her (. . . or Better)	*144*
125	Explore Historical Sites for a Day	*145*
126	Feeling Nostalgic? Play Old Video Game Consoles Together	*146*
127	Celebrate Her Journey of Growth and Transformation	*147*
128	Make a Practice of Holding Her Hand Across the Table at Dinner	*148*
129	That Messy Vehicle of Hers . . . Wash It!	*149*
130	Don't Just Watch . . . Create a Bond . . . Fold Towels Together	*150*
131	Savor Romance at a Scenic Winery	*151*
132	Reassure Her of Your Trust and Faith in Her	*152*
133	Be Her Hero When She's Under the Weather	*153*
134	Plan a Surprise Outing to Her Favorite Makeup Store	*155*
135	Explore Sweet Heaven Together with Chocolate Tasting	*156*
136	Make Her Chocolate or Her Favorite Flavor Covered Strawberries	*157*
137	Encourage Her with Belief in Her Limitless Potential	*158*
138	Offer to Wash, Treat, and Brush/Comb Her Hair	*159*
139	Surprise Her with a Late-Night Cocktail or Mocktail	*160*
140	Attend a Book Reading or Poetry Slam	*161*
141	Design a Custom Map of Your Love Story Locations	*162*
142	Be Specific in Your Compliments About Her Actions or Qualities	*163*
143	Strike a Pose: Try Yoga Together	*164*
144	Create a Recurring Calendar of Event Dates Important to Her	*165*
145	Ride the Rails on a Scenic Train Adventure	*166*
146	Soar, Swing, or Zip? Time for Adventure Date Thrills	*167*
147	Get Her Locked and Loaded on the Gun Range	*168*
148	Set Sail by Renting a Boat for a Day	*169*
149	Snuggle Under the Stars in a Hammock Hideaway	*170*
150	Bonus: Surprise Her with Her Dream Pet	*171*
151	Are You Two Goal Getters? Be Her Accountability Partner	*172*
152	Give Her S'more Love with Cozy Bonfire Nights	*173*
153	Share Love with Forehead Kisses That Warms Her Heart	*174*

154	DIY and Personalize a Personal Craft with Her Name	175
155	Explore Culture and Cuisine at a Festival Together	176
156	Passport to Romance Anyone? Surprise Her with an International Trip	177
157	Boost Her Confidence by Celebrating Her Resilience	178
158	Purchase Her Preferred Feminine Products	179
159	Preventive Maintenance, Sir . . . Her Snacks Matter	180
160	It's a Berry Sweet Idea to Go Fruit Picking Together	181
161	Order Her a Journal to Document Shared Experiences	182
162	Turn the Page by Sharing a Best-Selling Book	183
163	Secure Smiles with Stolen Kisses Throughout the Day	184
164	See Her Heart in Action: Volunteer for Her Passion	185
165	Create a Themed Dress-Up Night for Two	186
166	Hobby Love: Curate a Personalized Gift Box	187
167	Spark Meaningful Conversations by Diving into Her Dreams	188
168	'Seas' the Day by Surprising Her with a Beach Trip	189
169	Be Her Proactive Fixer-Upper Hero . . . Her "Maintenance" Man	190
170	Climb Higher in Your Relationship with Indoor Rock Climbing	191
171	Pamper Her with a Bath Bomb and Essential Spa Kit	192
172	Celebrate Her Continuous Support and Understanding	193
173	Surprise Her with a Visit to a Popular Nail Salon	194
174	Play On: Plan a Couple's Game Night with Her Favorite Games	195
175	Not a Nail Tech? You Are Today… Give Her a Pedicure	196
176	Sip Love Daily by Gifting Her a Custom Mug	197
177	Provide a Safe Space for Her to Share Her Fears	198
178	Hands on the Wheel, and Hers in Yours	199
179	Escape Close to Home with a Nearby Staycation	200
180	Purchase Cooking Utensils with Heartfelt Messages	201
181	Share A Cozy Dream Together and Bond Forever	202
182	Stay Aligned with Love by Booking Her a Chiropractor	203
183	Crack the Code with Escape Room Adventures Together	204
184	Gently Remind and Encourage Her to Prioritize Self Care	205
185	Invest in Yourself Through Counseling	206

186	Pack a Surprise Snack Bag for a Day Out	*207*
187	It's Written in the Stars: Plan a Date Night at a Planetarium	*208*
188	Give Her Sweet Dreams: Gift Comfort with New Bedding	*209*
189	Give Her Grace During Challenging Moments	*210*
190	Plan a Sunrise Romance with a Morning Coffee or Breakfast Date	*212*
191	Seeing Is Believing: Help Her Create a Vision Board	*213*
192	Have Dinner on the Move with a Progressive Dining Delight	*214*
193	Picture Perfect Nostalgia with a Polaroid Camera and Film	*215*
194	Time Travel Together, Recalling and Reliving Special Moments	*216*
195	Create Love by Candlelight: A Romantic Dinner at Home	*217*
196	Bond Over a Thoughtful Scavenger Hunt at Home	*218*
197	Discover Local Gems and Nearby Landmarks Together	*219*
198	Buy Her a Surprise Outfit and Plan a Romantic Friday Date	*220*
199	Embrace Moments That Matter: Show Gratitude for Togetherness	*221*
200	Bonus: Speak with Integrity About Her, Both in Private and Public	*222*
201	Take a Romantic Late-Night Stroll Under the Stars	*224*
202	Plan a Scenic Day Trip with Spontaneous Adventure	*225*
203	Ride Love's Wave by Renting Jet Skis for Two	*226*
204	Reassure Her She's the One, Your Forever Choice	*227*
205	Share Inspiring Quotes and Words of Love That Lift Her Up	*228*
206	Create Playful Fun with a Pillow Fight Royale	*229*
207	Mom's Day Off: Get the Kids to Treat Her Like a Queen	*230*
208	Feed Her Spirit by Bonding, Reading Together from a Spiritual Source	*231*
209	Pockets Full of Love: Hide Sweet Notes for Her to Find	*232*
210	Buy Her a Special Necklace . . . But Make It Fun	*233*
211	Dream Out Loud by Discussing and Building a Vision Together	*234*
212	Create "Treasures of Us" with a Relationship Time Capsule	*235*
213	Be Her Safe Ride Home After a Girls' Night Out	*236*
214	Show Affection in Action by Making Your Love Publicly Known	*237*
215	Draw a Personal Masterpiece of Something Meaningful	*238*
216	Bake a Special Dessert or Sweet Treat for Her from Scratch	*239*
217	Share Love from Above Together on a Helicopter Tour	*240*

218	Show Pride in Your Relationship and Her Role in It	241
219	Make It Picture Perfect by Framing Love in a Surprise Photoshoot	242
220	Convert Her Old Media to Digital Modern Memories	244
221	Give Her Your Undivided Attention During Special Moments	245
222	Write a Love Story Starring the Two of You	246
223	Treat Her to Sips at Sunset with a Personalized Tasting	247
224	Gift Her a Romance Token for Selfless Intimacy	248
225	Learn from Past Mistakes to Avoid Repeating Them	249
226	Cater to Her Through Better Financial Stewardship	250
227	Delight Her with a Day of Saying Yes to Everything She Loves	251
228	Celebrate Her Unique Sparkle and Everything That Makes Her Special	252
229	Score Strikes and Share Laughs During Bowling and Laser Tag	253
230	Shape Beauty Together in a Glass-Blowing Experience	254
231	Help Her Glow with the Ultimate Hydrating Facial Surprise	255
232	Create Lasting Memories Letting Loose at an Entertainment Venue	256
233	Show Her She'll Always Be Your Number One Priority	257
234	Dive Into Her Passions and Empower Her Growth	258
235	Unleash Creativity with a Paint and Sip Night at Home	259
236	Dance to the Rhythm of Love at a Music Festival	260
237	Grow Closer While Building a Terrarium	261
238	Spread Joy Every Day with Words That Affirm Her Worth	262
239	Relax and Connect Over a Game of Billiards	263
240	Feel the Thrill of Love (and Pain) with an Action-Packed Paintball Date	264
241	Slide Into Good Memories with a Day at the Waterpark	265
242	Surprise Her with Comfort-Focused Lingerie or Sleepwear	266
243	Empower Her Leadership Role at Home with Love and Respect	267
244	Brighten Her Day with a Silly Selfie and a Sweet Note	269
245	Bond Over Creativity by Crafting a Homemade Gift Together	270
246	Spark Laughter and Playfulness with a Blindfold Tasting Game	271
247	Chase Adrenaline and Excitement with a Supercar Experience	272
248	Share in Conversations About the Best Parts of Your Childhood	273
249	Hold Her Close During Fireworks or Stunning Scenic Views	274

250	Bonus: Possession Isn't Love—Trust Is Key to a Strong Relationship	*275*
251	Turn Dreams into Reality by Helping Her Fulfill Her Bucket List	*277*
252	Savor the Craft of Local Flavors at a Brewery or Distillery	*278*
253	Laugh and "Howl" Your Hearts Out at a Karaoke Night Together	*279*
254	Be the Rock She Can Rely On	*280*
255	Bond Over Language Learning and Unlock New Worlds Together	*281*
256	Explore New Adventures by Discovering a Hobby You Both Love	*282*
257	Craft Love Together Through Brushstrokes and Clay	*283*
258	Have Saturday Morning Cartoons and Cereal Together	*284*
259	Sip, Watch, and Laugh While People-Watching at a Cozy Café	*285*
260	Strengthen Your Spiritual Connection with Consistent Prayer	*286*
261	Celebrate Her Intelligence and Admire Her Wisdom	*288*
262	Assumptions Make Messes—Ask First, Clean Less Later	*289*
263	Let Loose and Laugh Together at a Comedy Show	*290*
264	Craft Unique Memories While Knitting a Blanket or Scarf Together	*291*
265	Bake Up Flavor with a Homemade Pizza Night	*292*
266	Rejuvenate Her Spirit at a Botanical Garden or Nature Reserve	*293*
267	Set the Mood with a Surprise Sunset Picnic	*294*
268	Celebrate Her Agility and Ability to Wear Multiple Hats	*295*
269	Tackle Procrastination Together by Helping Her Complete a Project	*296*
270	Ignite Her Off-Roading Interests with an ATV Riding Adventure	*297*
271	Surprise Her with a DIY Basket of Snacks She'll Love	*298*
272	Honor Her Inner Beauty and All the Qualities That Make Her Shine	*299*
273	Upgrade Her Ride with Thoughtful Accessories	*300*
274	Relax and Connect While Listening to Music on a Rainy Day	*301*
275	Hit the Bullseye with a Memorable Night of Axe Throwing	*302*
276	Enjoy a Night of Jenga and Drinks Together	*303*
277	Praise Her for Her Willingness to Help Sustain a Peaceful Home	*304*
278	Discover Hidden Wonders While Exploring a Nearby Nature Trail	*305*
279	Preserve Her Culinary Traditions with a Personalized Recipe Box	*306*
280	Celebrate Her Uniqueness by Highlighting What Makes Her Special	*307*
281	Learn How to Eat "Dessert". . . the Right Way	*308*

282	Write a Song for Her . . . and Sing It	309
283	Celebrate Your Love Story by Creating a Movie Reel of Special Moments	310
284	Show Excitement when She Dresses for Special Occasions	312
285	Express Pride in Her Career and Business Achievements	313
286	Never Be the One Walking Farthest from the Curb	314
287	Assess Items That Might be Worn Out and Seek Ways to Upgrade Her	315
288	Plan a "Romantic" Water Day with a Water Fight	316
289	Unwind and Connect with Music and Ambiance at a Chill Lounge	317
290	"You Don't Have to Lie to Kick It"—Lies Break What Love Creates	318
291	Ease Her Week by Preparing Her Clothes Ahead of Time	320
292	Plan a Romantic and Adventurous Ski Resort Weekend	321
293	Team Up for Fun During a Local Group Scavenger Hunt	323
294	Indulge Her in a Dessert-Only Date Night for Pure Sweetness	324
295	Share Youthful Moments Together at a Nearby Car Show	325
296	Drop the Hints—Speak Your Heart Without the Games	326
297	Every Queen Deserves a Fairytale Moment	328
298	Fill a Gratitude Jar Together to Celebrate Shared Moments	329
299	Be Vulnerable About the Things You Struggle With	330
300	Bonus: Physical Abuse Has No Place in Her Life	331
301	Climb a Lighthouse or Scenic Overlook for Stunning Views	333
302	Curate a Sentimental Keepsake Box Full of Memories	334
303	Make Today Count by Achieving What Was Once Out of Reach	335
304	Sweep Her Off Her Feet—Literally—with a Passionate Lift and Kiss	336
305	Share Trust (and Maybe Laughter) by Letting Her Style Your Hair	337
306	Explore an Intimate Store Together for New Adventures	338
307	Include Her in Major Decision-Making Moments	339
308	Improve Your Perspective of Her Capabilities	340
309	Glide Across the Water on a Ferry to a Nearby Island Escape	341
310	Challenge Each Other in a Mystery Ingredient Cooking Showdown	342
311	Discover Ways of Cultivating a New Mindset About Life Together	343
312	Turn Your Evening into One of Discovery with DIY Science Experiments	344
313	Do Something Different and Take a Pottery Class Together	345

314	Wander Through the Beauty of a Botanical Garden or Arboretum	346
315	Build and Fly a Kite Together for a Little Outdoor Fun	347
316	Refresh Her Favorite Sneakers to Show You Care About the Details	348
317	Bounce Into Fun and Soreness at a Trampoline Park Date	349
318	Spice it Up with a Bucket List of Places to Make Love	350
319	Plan a Family Gathering to Reconnect Her with Loved Ones	352
320	Delight Her with Thoughtful Gifts of Her Favorite Girly Essentials	354
321	Remember Diamonds Are Still a Girl's Best Friend	355
322	Uncover Hidden Gems Together at a Local Market or Bazaar	356
323	Paddle Through the Rapids on a Canoe or Kayak Journey	357
324	Step Up—Lead with Love and Confidence	358
325	Roll, Bounce, and Glide Together with a Roller Skating Date	359
326	Grant Her the Gift of a Day of "Nothingness"	360
327	Let Her Sleep in While You Tackle the Morning Chaos	361
328	Surprise Her with a Spontaneous Financial Gift	362
329	Fold Together: Learn the Art of Origami	363
330	Dive into Her World: Learn About What She Loves	364
331	Keep Chivalry Alive: Always Open the Door for Her	365
332	Don't Skimp . . . Give Her the Best in All You Do	366
333	Have a Goofy Night Face Painting Each Other	367
334	Have an Indoor Nerf Gun War Together	368
335	Take a Scenic Drive and Escape into Nature	369
336	Craft Beauty Together: Take a Flower Arranging Class	370
337	Roll and Feast with DIY Sushi Night at Home	371
338	Plan a Special Intimate Night of "Hide 'n Go Get It"	372
339	Create a Popcorn Paradise with Flavored Kernels	373
340	Challenge Her to a Coloring Book Contest	374
341	Learn How to Make Homemade Ice Cream Together	375
342	Relieve Her Stress by Covering a Major Expense	376
343	Keep Her Inspired with a Personalized Magazine Subscription	377
344	Create and Laugh: Produce a Funny Movie Together	378
345	Respect Her Boundaries and Foster a Space of Trust	379

346	Deepen Your Intimacy with the Wisdom of the Kama Sutra	*381*
347	Be Mindful to Get Her the Help She Needs	*382*
348	Preserve Her History: Restore a Treasured Photo	*384*
349	Explore More: Take a Multi-City Flight Together	*385*
350	Bonus: Commit to Being the Best Version of You	*386*
351	Balance the Books of Love and Labor	*388*
352	Gift Her a Personalized Greeting from Her Favorite Celebrity	*390*
353	Support Local Creativity by Attending a Theater Production	*391*
354	Romance on Ice: Go Ice Skating Together	*392*
355	Keep it Simple by Spending Time Feeding Ducks at a Local Lake	*393*
356	Embrace Nature with a Weekend Camping Trip	*394*
357	Chase Serenity by Taking Her to a Waterfall or Natural Springs	*395*
358	Support Her Soul . . . Give Her Spiritual Encouragement	*396*
359	Plan a Day of Extreme Sports (e.g., Skydiving, Bungee Jumping, Ziplining)	*398*
360	She's Gotta Have Bras, Man . . .	*399*
361	Immortalize Her Memories with a Custom 3D Hologram Photo Cube	*400*
362	Keep a Spirit of Gratitude and Continue to Seek Wisdom	*401*
363	Be Willing to Learn How to Love Her . . . According to HER Needs	*403*
364	Bonus: Be Genuine in How You Love Her	*404*
365	Commit to Better Days, a Better Life	*405*
	Conclusion	*406*
	Reflections Journal: Your Journey of Growth and Love	*408*
	About the Author	*410*
	Book Group Discussion Questions	*412*
	Bonus Challenge: Show Your Love in Action	*414*
	Acknowledgments	*415*

INTRODUCTION

What if I told you the secret to a deeper, more fulfilling relationship starts with a single, thoughtful act today? By picking up this book, you've taken a step toward deepening your relationship, growing as a man, and creating lasting memories with the woman you cherish. Thank you for investing in *365 Ways a Year to Cater to Her*. It's my sincere hope that you'll find encouragement, new perspectives, and actionable steps that bring you and your partner closer than ever. I'm grateful for your trust in these pages, and I thank you in advance for sharing this journey with others—whether by recommending this book to a friend or simply by showing up with love in your own relationships.

This book was written with intention, based on years of observing, listening, and learning how to give and receive love in ways that feel genuine and lasting. With each new day, you'll find small yet meaningful ways to strengthen your connection and bring joy to both you and your partner. As we dive in, I want to share where this journey began for me—the early experiences that inspired me to see relationships differently and strive for more in love.

The introduction you're reading now is the longest chapter, and the rest of the book has been written as an easy, enjoyable read to guide you through each step with simplicity and impact. So, if you're ready, I'm ready…let's get it!

Growing up, I saw men in my life largely committed to the roles of protector and provider. They embraced these traditional values wholeheartedly, which meant working hard, keeping the family safe, and putting food on the table. Most of them were strong in faith—many were preachers and pastors, men who could quote scripture and who taught biblical principles with conviction. Yet, I couldn't shake the feeling that something essential was missing in how they loved their wives. The kind of love I saw was often practical and dutiful, but rarely tender or mindful of the woman's heart, mind, or spirit. Romance and thoughtfulness were left out of the picture, and it seemed that affection was reserved only for the occasional holiday gift or special occasion. As a boy, I would listen to love songs and watch music videos of Al B. Sure, Ralph Tresvant, Jodeci, and Babyface, where men expressed adoration and vulnerability. And I wondered: "Why don't I see this around me?" My own mother worked tirelessly to make my father happy, and yet I never saw him return that devotion in the small, thoughtful ways I dreamed of. That realization was the beginning of a lifelong curiosity for me.

I promised myself early on that I'd be different. By the age of thirteen, I had told my mother that if I ever had a wife, she'd receive the kind of love I saw missing in our lives. That determination became personal for me. I wanted to be a man who would stand out—a man who knew not only how to provide and protect but also how to cater to a woman's spirit. I began to learn what this might look like by observing my female friends and listening to their frustrations, picking up on the things they craved but rarely received from the men in their lives. From these conversations, I developed a real understanding of what it meant to be attentive, present, and intentional in a relationship. I taught myself how to wash a woman's hair, learned to give a proper scalp massage, and practiced being proactive with my words and actions. In short, I studied how to make a woman feel valued in ways that went beyond the traditional framework.

The other part of this is the lessons learned. I've had my share of mistakes, challenges, missteps, dumb decisions, and not-so-big big deals in my life of dating and marriage, and looking back, I realize that much of what I thought I understood about love and relationships was only scratching the surface of the deeper truths I would come to uncover. Every misstep taught me something—about patience, humility, communication, and the importance of showing up consistently, even when it felt inconvenient or uncomfortable. Through years of reflection and growth, I've learned to recognize the subtle dynamics that often go unnoticed in relationships: how small, unspoken resentments can erode trust, how failing to listen deeply can create distance, and how genuine vulnerability can disarm even the most ingrained defenses. These lessons didn't come from textbooks or lectures—they came from the lived experience of trial and error, of heartbreak and healing, and of intentionally choosing to become better. It's these hard-earned insights, paired with decades of personal growth and observation, that I bring to this book—not as someone who claims to have all the answers, but as someone who has been in the trenches and knows the value of persistence, reflection, and intentional love.

This book is my answer to what I saw lacking throughout various phases of my life, from childhood to adulthood, and it's written especially for men—men who are married, in committed relationships, or preparing themselves for love, but feeling uncertain about how to truly connect. It's for those who may want a deeper connection with their partner, who want to go beyond basic roles to create moments of real care, understanding, and closeness. It's also for the men who are struggling, who feel stuck in a cycle of relationships that just don't last. With this book, I hope to offer men not only a set of practices but a mindset shift—a new perspective on love as something that requires daily thoughtfulness and self-awareness. I believe deeply that love is in the details, and these pages offer a toolkit to help men find and foster those details, transforming love from a duty into a celebration.

I speak from experience. Nearly all of the practices in this book are ones I've done myself. Some worked beautifully and helped me build meaningful relationships; others fell flat because the recipient wasn't in a place to appreciate them, or because it wasn't the right approach for her. But these experiences taught me that real love is not defined by whether a single gesture is successful—it's defined by consistency, patience, and the willingness to stay true to values that strengthen the relationship over time. As I grew, I saw how these principles not only helped my relationships but also shaped me into a more mindful, centered man.

When you really think about it, we live in a world where relationships are increasingly shaped by societal pressures and online influences, and it's easy to get caught up in harmful narratives about love and partnership. These messages often create confusion and frustration, particularly for young men starting their journey or seasoned men trying to maintain meaningful connections. This book offers a different path—one rooted in understanding, empathy, and thoughtful action.

Some might ask, "Why should I do any of this if she doesn't do anything for me?" It's a valid question, and it reflects a common frustration many men feel when relationships seem one-sided. But here's the truth: great relationships aren't built on keeping score—they thrive on mutual respect, shared effort, and the understanding that love is a choice you make every day.

Studies show that healthy relationships positively impact emotional and physical health. For men, having a supportive partner often leads to better habits, reduced stress, and even longer lifespans. But relationships flourish when both people invest in them, and that starts with setting the tone. By showing consistent care and thoughtfulness, you not only encourage your partner to reciprocate but also create a foundation for a more fulfilling connection. Love is contagious, and often, the effort you put in inspires your partner to meet you halfway—or more.

Whether you're a teenager exploring what it means to love or a seasoned man seeking deeper connection, this book is your guide to fostering meaningful partnerships. It's not about one-sided effort or grand displays—it's about daily acts of kindness, patience, and intention that build trust, appreciation, and closeness over time. And what I want you to gain through this book are qualities that enhance your character—intentionality, empathy, emotional intelligence, and the confidence to lead with care and integrity. From my personal experience, I've found that embracing these attributes not only deepens connection with your partner but also helps you cultivate purpose and self-awareness as a man.

So, why do this? Because a strong, healthy relationship doesn't just benefit your partner—it helps you grow into your best self. It's an investment in your happiness and your capacity for love. Every day you wait is a missed opportunity to build the relationship you deserve. Don't let time or fear rob you of the joy and connection you could create today. Together, let's move beyond quick fixes and fleeting gestures to create connections that last a lifetime.

Ultimately, this book is about fostering growth on every level—emotional, spiritual, and mental. I want men to connect with the highest version of themselves, the one their Creator envisioned, and I want women to know that men who embody this care and respect still exist. By the end of this book, you will have practical tools and actionable insights to transform your relationship, deepen emotional intimacy, and become the partner you aspire to be. It's often easier for a man to change when he gets advice from another man than when he feels pressure to meet a partner's unmet needs. My hope is that, as you read, you'll feel empowered to treat love as an active choice, and to use the guidance here to deepen your connection with a woman in ways that honor her whole self. So let's get started. Your journey to a stronger, more loving relationship begins right now.

Pray for Her / Speak Positive Energy Over Her Life

This, to me, is the most important chapter because if you can't cover her spiritually, everything else will eventually fall out of balance. Praying for her or speaking positive energy into her life creates a foundation that strengthens your bond. While it may feel uncomfortable at first, it's a vital step toward deepening your connection. This simple act shows her that you care for her on a deeper level, not just emotionally or physically, but spiritually as well. When you make this a habit, you're building a strong, lasting foundation for your relationship.

For those who embrace a faith-based approach to life and believe in a higher power, taking the time to pray for your significant other can be a profound way to show love and support. Gently wrap your arms around her and pray for God's blessings over her life, asking for guidance, protection, and success in all her endeavors. This act of prayer can strengthen the spiritual connection between you both and bring her a sense of peace and reassurance.

If you or your partner are atheists, you can still create a similar moment of connection by speaking positive affirmations over her life. Hold her close and express your hopes and desires for her well-being, success, and happiness. Whether it's about her career, personal growth, or everyday challenges, let her know that you believe in her abilities and that you are there to support her every step of the way.

2

The Way to Her Heart? Start in the Kitchen

Cooking her favorite meal is a wonderful way to show you care, demonstrating that you've taken the time to remember what she enjoys and are willing to put in the effort to make her happy. Whether you're a seasoned chef or a kitchen novice, preparing a meal tailored to her tastes shows that you're attentive to her preferences and willing to go the extra mile to make her feel special. The aroma of her favorite dish cooking can fill the home with warmth and anticipation, setting the stage for an unforgettable evening together.

If you're not sure where to start, think back to the moments she's talked about her favorite comfort foods or that special dish she always orders at her preferred restaurant. You don't need to be a professional chef to make this significant—your effort and care will shine through. If you're feeling ambitious, add a little extra touch by finding out her favorite drink pairing or dessert to complete the meal. These small details turn a simple dinner into a gesture she'll cherish.

Beyond the meal itself, this gesture is an opportunity to create a shared experience. Invite her to join you in the kitchen, where you can cook together, or surprise her with a beautifully set table. Either way, the act of cooking for her is a personal and meaningful way to nurture your relationship, bringing satisfaction to you both.

Capture Your Love Story, One Page at a Time

A personalized photo album or scrapbook is a heartfelt way to capture and celebrate the special moments you've shared together. Gather your favorite photos, mementos, and souvenirs, and arrange them in a way that tells the story of your relationship. Whether it's the first picture you took as a couple, a ticket stub from a concert you both loved, or a short note she once wrote to you, each piece adds a layer of meaning to the album.

Taking the time to craft something so personal shows her how much you value your shared experiences. It's a gift that goes beyond the material, offering a tangible reminder of the love and happiness you've built together. Every time she flips through the pages, she'll be reminded of the care and effort you put into creating something uniquely hers—a keepsake that she can treasure for years to come.

4

Start Her Day with Words That Matter

Starting her day with a heartfelt good morning message is a simple yet powerful way to show her that she's the first thing on your mind. Whether you're apart or just getting ready to tackle the day ahead, a kind message can set a positive tone and make her feel loved and appreciated from the moment she wakes up. You might share a sweet memory, an encouraging word, or just confirmation of how much she means to you.

These morning messages don't need to be elaborate or take a long time for you to compose; even a few sincere words can have a lasting impact. Over time, this small daily ritual can become something she looks forward to, a consistent reminder of your love and commitment. It's a beautiful way to keep your connection strong, no matter how busy life gets.

Speaking of a busy life, in the hustle and bustle of daily life, it's so easy to get consumed by the demands of work and the pressures of a demanding profession. For those with particularly busy schedules, finding even a small moment to send a heartfelt message can feel like a challenge—but it's one worth prioritizing. Taking just a few seconds to remind her she's on your mind can make a world of difference, not only for her but for the connection you share. No matter how hectic life gets, this small gesture shows her that, amidst the chaos, she still comes first.

5

Work On the Shoulders, One Knot at a Time

A gentle shoulder massage is a wonderful way to help her unwind and show your care through touch. After a long day, offering to relieve some of the tension in her shoulders can be a deeply comforting gesture. This simple act not only soothes physical stress, but also communicates that you're attuned to her needs and willing to help her relax and feel at ease.

Now, don't get all extra—breathing hard on her or trying to turn this into something it's not. Keep it calm, focused, and soothing. This is about making her feel comfortable, cared for, and free of stress. The more genuine you are, the more she'll appreciate the effort and be able to fully relax.

Taking the time to give her a massage can also strengthen your emotional connection. As you carefully work out the knots and ease her muscles, you create a moment of closeness and intimacy. It's a gesture that speaks volumes, letting her know that her well-being is important to you and that you're there to support her in the most nurturing way.

6

Serve Up Love, One Dish at a Time

Cooking a fancy dinner together is a fun and engaging way to bond while creating something delicious. Instead of going out to a restaurant, bring the experience home by selecting a gourmet recipe that excites both of you. Gather the ingredients, pour a glass of wine, and enjoy the process of preparing the meal as a team. This shared activity turns cooking into a collaborative and intimate experience, where you can laugh, learn, and connect.

As you work side by side in the kitchen, you'll have the chance to communicate, cooperate, and even discover new aspects of each other's personalities. By the way, as a side note, make sure she washes her hands…you know how these women are in the kitchen (sarcastically speaking). Once the meal is ready, set the table with candles and enjoy the fruits of your labor in a cozy, romantic setting. Cooking together not only results in a delicious dinner but also strengthens your relationship through teamwork and shared accomplishment.

While cooking, focus on being present and savoring the experience for what it is—a chance to connect and create something meaningful together. It's tempting to get caught up in who chops faster or whose seasoning stands out, but try not to take things too seriously or turn it into a competition. The real charm lies in the humor of a misplaced ingredient or sneaking a taste of the dish while it's still in progress. Keep the process relaxed and enjoyable, emphasizing the time spent together rather than aiming for culinary perfection. These shared efforts and lighthearted moments are what truly make the experience memorable.

7

Put Your Heart on Paper

Handwritten love letters are a timeless and deeply personal way to express your feelings. In an age dominated by digital communication, taking the time to sit down and write out your thoughts by hand makes your words even more meaningful. Whether it's a long letter recounting the many reasons you love her or a short note tucked into her bag for her to find later, the personal touch of your handwriting adds warmth and sincerity.

These letters become keepsakes that she can treasure and revisit whenever she wants to feel close to you. Writing down your feelings allows you to reflect on what she means to you, and it gives her a tangible reminder of your love that she can hold onto. This simple yet meaningful gesture can strengthen your emotional connection, showing her that your love is something you're willing to put into words and share in a heartfelt, enduring way.

8

Hide Little Joys for Her to Find

Surprising her with small gifts left in unexpected places is a sweet and thoughtful way to show her that you're thinking of her throughout the day. It could be a little something she loves, like her favorite candy tucked into her bag, a cute trinket left on her nightstand, or even a coffee waiting for her in the fridge. These little surprises can brighten her day and remind her that you're always finding ways to show your love and appreciation.

The key here is the element of surprise. It doesn't have to be expensive or elaborate; what matters is the thought behind it. Whether it's something that makes her smile or helps ease a stressful day, these small gestures show that you're paying attention to the little things that make her happy. They create moments of joy and connection, no matter how busy life gets.

By leaving these gifts in places where she'll stumble upon them unexpectedly, you're creating pockets of happiness in her daily routine. It's a way of keeping the romance alive and showing her that you care, even in the smallest of ways.

Step Up and Lighten Her Load

Taking over her chores or tasks for a day is a considerate and practical way to show your appreciation for all she does. Whether it's doing the laundry, grocery shopping, or handling the dishes, stepping in to ease her responsibilities can provide her with much-needed rest and relaxation. It's a gesture that goes beyond words, demonstrating your willingness to support her and make her day a bit smoother.

This act of service not only helps her out but also shows that you're attentive to her needs and understand the effort she puts into maintaining your shared life. It's a way of saying, "I see you, and I value what you do." By taking on her responsibilities for a day, you're giving her the gift of time—time to relax, pursue a hobby, or simply unwind, knowing that you've got everything under control.

The key here is to be proactive—don't wait for her to display the Bat Signal or drop hints about needing help. Step up and take initiative before she even has to ask. Pay attention to the tasks she juggles daily, and think about what you can take off her plate without needing a reminder. Whether it's tidying up the house, running errands, or managing dinner prep, your willingness to act without prompting speaks volumes. It shows her that you're not just aware of her efforts, but you're also committed to being a true partner in every sense of the word.

10

Shape Memories with Clay or Color

Taking a pottery or painting class together is a creative and fun way to bond while exploring a new hobby. Engaging in an artistic activity allows both of you to express yourselves, experiment with new techniques, and perhaps even discover hidden talents. Whether you're molding clay into unique shapes or blending colors on a canvas, these classes offer a relaxed environment where you can laugh, learn, and create together.

This shared experience is not only about the art you make but also about the memories you create along the way. Working side by side in a creative space encourages collaboration and communication, strengthening your connection in a fresh and exciting way. Plus, you'll have tangible keepsakes—whether it's a piece of pottery or a painting—that will always remind you of the time spent together, making it a meaningful and lasting gesture.

Don't worry about being perfect—this isn't about creating a masterpiece for a gallery. It's about enjoying the process, finding humor in the imperfections, and valuing the time spent together. Whether your pot looks more like a lump or your painting resembles abstract chaos, the point is to have fun and embrace the creative journey. Let go of any pressure to "get it right" and instead focus on the excitement of trying something new as a team. The moments you share will be far more meaningful than any finished product.

11

Seal Her Day with Gentle Affection

A kiss on the forehead is a gentle and tender gesture that conveys love, protection, and deep affection. Unlike a passionate kiss, a forehead kiss is soft and intimate, symbolizing care and respect. It's a way of saying, "I'm here for you," without needing words. Whether it's before you both head off to work, as a goodnight gesture, or just a spontaneous moment during the day, this simple act can make her feel safe and loved.

This type of kiss can often carry a sense of calm and reassurance, making it especially meaningful in moments when she might be feeling stressed or vulnerable. It's a small but powerful way to show her that you cherish her and are always there to offer comfort and support. The forehead kiss is a quiet expression of your deep connection, reminding her of the unique bond you share.

Now, if your lips are crusted and splitting, don't just leave them like that. Uncrust them! Get some ChapStick, Vaseline, or Carmex, and make sure your lips are ready for action. Trust me, she'll still appreciate the gesture, but she'll definitely appreciate it more if it doesn't feel like her skin is being scuffed.

Unwind, One Soothing Touch at a Time

A couple's massage or spa day is a luxurious way to relax and rejuvenate together. Spending time at a spa allows both of you to unwind and escape the stresses of daily life in a serene and calming environment. Whether it's a soothing massage, a refreshing facial, or a soak in a hot tub, these treatments help to ease tension and promote relaxation, both physically and mentally.

Now, I know some men can feel uncomfortable with the idea of getting a massage—it might seem awkward or not "manly" enough. But let me tell you, it's time to get over that! Massages are not only incredibly relaxing, but they're also great for relieving stress and tension, which everyone—yes, even you—can benefit from. You'll walk out feeling refreshed, more connected to your partner, and probably wondering why you ever hesitated in the first place.

Sharing this pampering experience as a couple enhances your bond as you both emerge feeling refreshed and revitalized. It's a wonderful opportunity to focus on your well-being, connect on a deeper level, and simply enjoy each other's company in a peaceful setting. A spa day is not just about indulgence; it's about taking time to care for yourselves and each other, reinforcing the importance of health, relaxation, and mutual care in your relationship.

13

Spotlight Her Style with Fashionable Compliments

Praising her fashion choices is a simple yet meaningful way to boost her confidence and show that you notice and appreciate her sense of style. Whether she's dressed up for a special occasion or just put together a casual outfit for the day, taking the time to compliment her choices lets her know that her efforts don't go unnoticed. A genuine compliment on her outfit, accessories, or even how she carries herself can make her feel valued and admired.

Now, if you feel like you're lying to her and she has absolutely zero fashion sense, don't worry. Instead of staying silent, find ways to help and encourage her. You can guide her subtly by suggesting styles that you know would look great on her, or even shopping together to explore looks that complement her personality. It's all about helping her feel confident and stylish, without making her feel judged or criticized.

By acknowledging her fashion sense, you're also showing respect for her individuality and the way she expresses herself. It's more than just liking what she wears—it's about appreciating her creativity, confidence, and the thought she puts into presenting herself. This kind of praise can deepen your connection, as she feels seen and appreciated for who she is, both inside and out.

14

Hold Her Close
and Let the World Fade Away

This one is simple, yet so important . . .

A warm, tight hug is one of the most comforting and loving gestures you can share with your significant other. This simple act of physical affection communicates love, support, and a deep sense of connection without the need for words. Whether it's to start the day, after a long time apart, or just because, a strong embrace can make her feel safe and cherished in your arms.

Hugs have a way of melting away stress and reinforcing the bond between you. They can be especially powerful during moments of joy, sorrow, or even everyday life when she needs a reminder that you're there for her. Sharing a heartfelt hug is a universal way of expressing care, love, and the reassurance that she means the world to you.

For those whose significant other didn't grow up hugging or receiving affection, it's important to approach this gesture with patience and understanding. Physical affection may not come naturally to her, and she might initially feel hesitant or unsure how to respond. Start with small, gentle gestures—perhaps a brief touch on the shoulder or a lighter hug—and allow her to grow comfortable with your warmth over time. Respect her boundaries, but let her know that your hugs are a safe space where she can feel loved and supported. In time, she may come to embrace this simple act of connection as something she treasures.

15

Chase the Sunset

Taking her to watch the sunset is a beautifully romantic gesture that allows both of you to pause and appreciate the natural beauty of the world together. Whether you find a quiet beach, a hilltop, or even a favorite spot in your city, watching the sun dip below the horizon creates a serene and intimate atmosphere. The changing colors of the sky, the gentle fading of the daylight, and the shared silence can all contribute to a moment of pure connection.

This simple yet profound experience offers a chance to reflect on your relationship, share your thoughts, or just enjoy the peace of being in each other's presence. The sunset serves as a reminder that sometimes the most meaningful moments are those spent together, appreciating the world around you. It's a time to be present, holding her close as you both take in the beauty of the moment and each other.

16

Lose Yourself in the Stars

Stargazing together is a magical way to connect with each other while marveling at the vastness of the universe. Find a quiet spot away from city lights—perhaps a countryside field, a beach, or even your backyard—and lay down a blanket. As you gaze up at the night sky, the stars provide a stunning backdrop for meaningful conversations, shared dreams, or simply a comfortable silence.

This experience invites both of you to slow down and appreciate the beauty of nature while feeling a sense of wonder and awe. Whether you're identifying constellations, making a wish on a shooting star, or just holding hands under the stars, this peaceful activity fosters a deep sense of intimacy. Stargazing is more than just looking at the sky; it's about finding time to connect, reflect, and enjoy each other's company in the stillness of the night.

For me, there was something so calming about simply relaxing on my cushioned patio bench on my pool deck, looking up at the stars. No complicated plans, no need to travel far—just a comfortable seat, the night sky, and the person I care about by my side. I encourage you to give it a try. Sometimes, the simplest moments of stillness are the most meaningful. It's not about finding the perfect stargazing spot; it's about taking a break from the hustle, soaking in the beauty above, and sharing that quiet magic with her.

17

Spread a Blanket and Make the Moment Yours

A picnic at a scenic spot is a charming way to create a memorable experience together. Choose a location that offers beautiful views—perhaps a lush park, a tranquil lakeside, or a hilltop overlooking the city. The natural surroundings will set the mood, offering a peaceful and relaxed atmosphere where you can enjoy each other's company without the usual distractions. Bring along her favorite snacks, a cozy blanket, and maybe even a bottle of wine to make the experience extra special.

This simple yet thoughtful gesture shows that you value spending quality time with her in a setting that allows for genuine connection. As you share a meal under the open sky, you can talk, laugh, and simply enjoy the moment, creating a lasting memory that both of you will cherish. A picnic allows you to break away from routine and appreciate the beauty of the world around you—and the beauty of your relationship.

To make it even more memorable, think about adding a personal touch. Consider bringing along a playlist of her favorite songs, a few pages from a book or poem she loves, or a small handwritten note to surprise her with. These little details show her how well you know and appreciate her, turning a simple picnic into a truly thoughtful act she won't forget.

18

Engrave Your Love in a Timeless Treasure

Few gestures capture the essence of enduring love like a beautifully engraved gift. Whether it's a piece of jewelry, a watch, or a personalized bracelet, these treasures serve as a lasting reminder of your connection. A simple yet meaningful inscription—her name, a significant date, or a phrase unique to your relationship—transforms an ordinary item into a cherished keepsake. These gifts symbolize not just your affection but the care and intention behind celebrating your journey together.

Personalized gifts hold an unmatched sentimental value. Consider her style and preferences when selecting the perfect item. A sleek watch with an elegant engraving might suit her professional side, while a delicate bracelet with a personal touch could highlight her softer, romantic nature. The effort you put into customizing the piece reflects your awareness of who she is and what she loves, deepening its emotional significance.

Beyond the gift itself, think about the moment of presentation. Surprise her during a quiet dinner at home, hand it to her during a romantic walk, or wrap it beautifully and watch her face light up as she opens it. The act of giving becomes just as meaningful as the item itself, creating a memory tied to the treasure she'll cherish forever. Whether it's for a special occasion or a spontaneous expression of love, the timing and setting elevate the gesture to a moment she'll always remember.

Engraved gifts are timeless because they hold memories within them. Each time she looks at the piece, she'll be reminded of the love, care, and intention that went into it. It's a way to leave a tangible mark on her life, one that speaks volumes without needing words. In a world of fleeting moments, a timeless treasure like this stands as a symbol of the unchanging bond you share.

19

Celebrate Her in Front of Friends or Family

Complimenting or praising her in front of friends or family is a powerful way to show your admiration and respect for her, while also reinforcing her confidence. Publicly acknowledging her strengths, accomplishments, or the qualities you love about her not only makes her feel valued but also shows others how much she means to you. Whether you're praising her intelligence, kindness, or something specific she's done, these words of affirmation can have a lasting impact.

This gesture goes beyond a private compliment; it's about proudly sharing your appreciation for her with those who matter in your lives. It helps to build her self-esteem and strengthens your bond, as she knows that you're proud to be with her and eager to celebrate her in all aspects of your life together. Public praise is a meaningful way to highlight her significance in your life and to let others see the depth of your love and admiration.

You don't have to go overboard or make things awkward to show your admiration. A simple, heartfelt compliment goes a long way without feeling forced or overdone. Avoid exaggerating or trying too hard to impress others—it's about being genuine. Whether it's casually mentioning how amazing she handled a situation or complimenting her on her latest achievement, keep it natural. The goal is to uplift her in a way that feels authentic and effortless, so she knows your praise comes from the heart, not for show.

20

Curl Up and Let the Story Bring You Closer

Cuddling while watching a movie is one of the coziest and most intimate ways to spend time together. Whether you're watching a favorite film, exploring a new series, or enjoying a classic, the act of curling up close on the couch brings a sense of warmth and comfort. As you share the experience of the movie, the physical closeness of cuddling enhances the emotional connection between you.

Now, if cuddling makes her feel like there are two "remotes" on the couch, maybe try something different that allows you to enjoy the moment without instant arousal. Keep it relaxed, and let things unfold naturally. Instant arousal might kill the vibe, but 15 minutes later? That might be just fine.

This simple gesture of affection creates a safe and loving environment where you can both relax and enjoy each other's company. The world outside fades away as you immerse yourselves in the story on screen, with the added comfort of being wrapped in each other's arms. Cuddling during a movie isn't just about the entertainment; it's about creating a space where you can unwind together, feel connected, and savor the closeness you share.

21

Steam Up Your Connection

Here we go! This was one of my favorite things at one point in time. Sharing a bubble bath or shower together is one of the most intimate and soothing ways to connect with your partner. The warm water, steamy atmosphere, and close proximity create a serene environment where you can unwind and enjoy each other's presence without the usual distractions of daily life. Whether it's a candlelit bubble bath with soothing bubbles or a refreshing shower, this shared experience offers a unique blend of physical closeness and emotional tenderness that strengthens your bond.

This moment isn't just about the act of bathing—it's about nurturing your relationship in a space of trust and care. You can take turns washing each other, playfully lathering shampoo, or simply standing under the water together in a comforting embrace. These gestures of touch and attention foster a deeper sense of connection while allowing you both to relax and recharge. It's a private, meaningful experience that transforms an ordinary routine into something truly special.

Now, if the bottom of the shower starts to look like the bottom of a coffee pitcher, just blame it on her this time—and maybe toss in a wink to keep the mood light. Use it as a reminder to freshen things up for next time. After all, these shared moments are about enjoying each other's company and creating cherished memories, even when life gets a little messy.

Exchange Words That Last a Lifetime

Writing love letters to each other is a timeless and romantic way to express your feelings in a deeply personal manner. Taking the time to put your emotions into words allows you to reflect on what your partner means to you and to articulate the depth of your love and appreciation. These letters can capture your most heartfelt thoughts, from cherished memories to dreams for the future, creating a lasting keepsake that your partner can treasure.

Exchanging love letters gives both of you a chance to reconnect on an emotional level, even if you've been together for years. It's a beautiful way to communicate feelings that might not always come up in everyday conversation. The act of writing and receiving these letters can strengthen your bond, reminding both of you of the unique and special connection you share. Whether read immediately or saved for a special moment, love letters are a meaningful gesture that celebrates your relationship.

Now you might be thinking, he already went over this in Chapter 7; however, this approach is different from simply writing her a love letter because it's about mutual exchange—a shared act of vulnerability and emotional connection. Writing letters to each other opens a two-way dialogue, allowing both of you to express your feelings and hear the other's in return. It becomes an intimate ritual, where you both take the time to reflect on your love, creating a deeper level of understanding and appreciation. Unlike a solitary handwritten note, this practice fosters a balanced exchange of emotions, strengthening the bond in a way that feels collaborative and equal.

23

Escape Together and Rediscover Each Other

A weekend getaway is the perfect way to escape the routine of daily life and immerse yourselves in quality time together. Whether you choose a cozy cabin in the mountains, a seaside retreat, or a charming bed and breakfast in a nearby town, a change of scenery offers a chance to relax, explore, and enjoy each other's company without the usual distractions. The excitement of planning and anticipating the trip adds to the joy, making it a shared adventure from start to finish.

This mini-vacation allows you to reconnect on a deeper level, away from the responsibilities and stresses that can sometimes cloud everyday life. Whether you're exploring new places, indulging in local cuisine, or simply lounging in a peaceful setting, a weekend getaway provides the perfect backdrop for creating lasting memories together. It's a rejuvenating experience that can strengthen your bond and leave you both feeling closer and more in tune with each other.

24

Be Her Rock When the Storm Hits

Offering words of encouragement during tough times is a powerful way to support and uplift your partner when she needs it most. Life's challenges can be overwhelming, and knowing that you're there to provide comfort, understanding, and reassurance can make all the difference. Whether she's facing stress at work, dealing with personal issues, or simply having a rough day, your words of encouragement can help her feel seen, valued, and supported.

It's important to be sincere and empathetic in your approach, acknowledging her feelings while reminding her of her strength and resilience. Let her know that you believe in her, that you're proud of how she's handling the situation, and that you're there for her every step of the way. These affirmations not only help her through difficult moments but also deepen your connection by showing that your love and support are unwavering, even in the hardest times.

It's also important to remember that women are naturally more emotional than men, and if your partner tends to be more passionate or dramatic during tough times, it's crucial to find patience in learning how to be supportive. Her emotions may feel overwhelming to you at times, but that's when she needs your steady presence the most. Instead of trying to fix things or dismissing her feelings, focus on being a calm, understanding partner who listens without judgment. By doing so, you create a safe space where she feels validated and loved, no matter how intense her emotions may get.

Run Your Fingers Through Her Hair

Running your fingers through her hair is a gentle, affectionate gesture that can convey love, comfort, and intimacy. This simple act can be incredibly soothing, whether you're lounging together on the couch, lying in bed, or just sharing a quiet moment. The sensation of your fingers softly gliding through her hair can help her relax and feel connected to you on a deeper, more physical level.

This gesture often carries a sense of care and tenderness, showing her that you're attentive to her needs and focused on her well-being. It's a nonverbal way of expressing your affection, making her feel cherished and loved without saying a word. This small but meaningful touch can strengthen your bond, turning an ordinary moment into one of closeness and connection.

In today's world of weaves, bundles, lace fronts, wigs, and expensive hair appointments, it's essential to be mindful of how your woman feels about having her hair played with or messed up. While some women may find it soothing and love the intimacy of your touch, others might be protective of their hair due to the effort and cost that goes into maintaining it. Pay attention to her preferences, and don't assume that running your fingers through her hair is always welcome. Respect her boundaries, and if she's comfortable, this simple act can become a cherished gesture that deepens your connection.

Take Her Hand and Walk Beside Her

Jill Scott has a song that encourages "taking a long walk," and that's great advice, but I'd add just one thing—hold her hand. There's a grounding power in this simple act, creating an unspoken bond that says you're both right there, present with each other. Now, if you're uncomfortable because your palms feel like sandpaper, it's ok: throw some lotion or Vaseline on them. She'll still appreciate the gesture.

Taking a walk together is a simple yet powerful way to connect with your significant other, and holding hands adds an extra layer of intimacy to the experience. As you stroll through your neighborhood, a park, or along a beach, the physical connection of holding hands fosters a sense of closeness and security. It's a gesture that says, "I'm here with you, and I'm here for you," without needing to utter a single word.

Walking hand-in-hand allows you to be present with each other, free from distractions. It's a moment to slow down, share your thoughts, or simply enjoy the silence together. This small act of togetherness can strengthen your bond and remind both of you of the importance of staying connected in the midst of life's hustle and bustle.

27

Melt Her Stress Away, From Head to Toe

Offering a relaxing massage is a thoughtful way to help her unwind and show that you care about her well-being. Whether it's a full-body massage after a long day or simply focusing on her shoulders and neck where she carries tension, this gesture provides both physical relief and emotional comfort. The act of massaging her not only helps to alleviate stress and soreness but also creates an intimate connection between the two of you.

Taking the time to give her a massage demonstrates your willingness to invest in her comfort and happiness. It's a moment where you can both slow down, enjoy each other's company, and let the worries of the day melt away. A relaxing massage isn't just about the physical benefits—it's a way to nurture your relationship by showing her that you're there to support her, both body and soul.

The difference between offering a relaxing massage and giving a gentle shoulder massage lies in the scope and intent of each gesture. A relaxing massage often involves a more deliberate effort to focus on her overall well-being, such as a full-body massage to melt away stress and create a tranquil experience. On the other hand, a gentle shoulder massage is usually more specific and spontaneous, aimed at easing immediate tension in her shoulders and neck. While both are acts of care, a relaxing massage is more immersive and intimate, offering a deeper opportunity to connect emotionally and physically, whereas a shoulder massage is a simpler, quicker way to show affection and attentiveness in the moment.

I took this to the next level by purchasing a really sturdy massage table and spending time watching YouTube videos on massage techniques. I wanted to make sure I wasn't just winging it but actually giving her a thoughtful, skillful experience. Having the right setup not only makes the massage more comfortable for her but also makes the experience feel more intentional and special. It's an investment that pays off in both her relaxation and the quality time we get to share together.

Binge, Bond, and Blanket Up

A movie marathon at home is a cozy and fun way to spend quality time together, allowing you both to unwind and enjoy each other's company in a relaxed setting. Pick a theme—whether it's your favorite film series, a collection of romantic comedies, or a lineup of classic movies—and settle in for a day or night of cinematic enjoyment. Prepare some snacks, dim the lights, and create a comfortable space with plenty of blankets and pillows.

This shared experience is more than just watching movies; it's about creating a warm, inviting atmosphere where you can laugh, cry, and bond over the stories unfolding on the screen. Whether you're revisiting beloved films or discovering new ones together, a movie marathon offers the perfect opportunity to connect, relax, and enjoy each other's presence without the need to leave the comfort of your home.

Now, if your significant other is one of those people who falls asleep during the opening credits, don't take it personally—just consider it part of the experience! You'll be left watching the entire trilogy solo while she snores peacefully next to you, and that's okay. Just make sure to have some snacks on hand for yourself, because when she wakes up halfway through, she's going to ask, "What happened so far?" Embrace it with humor and enjoy the fact that she's still sharing the moment with you, even if she's doing it in dreamland.

29

Deliver Flavor and Fun to Her Doorstep

Gifting her a subscription to a meal kit delivery service is a practical and considerate way to make her life a little easier while also creating opportunities for shared experiences. These services provide all the ingredients and recipes needed to prepare delicious, chef-inspired meals at home, taking the guesswork out of meal planning and grocery shopping. Whether she loves to cook from scratch or prefers the convenience of ready-to-make meals, this subscription can add a touch of variety and enjoyment to your dining routine.

Cooking the meals together can become a fun and engaging activity, allowing you both to try new dishes and improve your culinary skills. It's a great way to spend time together, experiment with different cuisines, and enjoy the satisfaction of creating something delicious as a team. A meal kit subscription not only simplifies your daily routine but also enhances the quality time you spend together in the kitchen.

30

Call Out the Things You Appreciate About Her

Taking the time to share specific things you appreciate about her is a powerful way to strengthen your connection and make her feel truly valued. Instead of general compliments, focus on the unique qualities, actions, or traits that make her special to you. Whether it's her kindness, her sense of humor, her ability to stay calm under pressure, or the way she always knows how to make you smile, these personalized expressions of appreciation show that you're paying attention to who she really is.

By highlighting the little things she might not even realize you notice, you reinforce her confidence and deepen the emotional bond between you. This kind of heartfelt recognition not only makes her feel loved but also encourages a deeper level of communication and understanding in your relationship. It's a reminder that she is seen, cherished, and appreciated for all the wonderful things that make her who she is.

I believe this is an especially great action to take when the two of you aren't in the best place. Sharing specific things you appreciate can serve as a gentle reminder of what drew you to each other in the first place. It helps shift the focus away from negativity and onto the positive qualities that make your relationship special. Not only does it remind you of what you value about her, but it also challenges her to see the good in you and the situation. This practice can help reframe the narrative, creating space for healing, understanding, and a more optimistic outlook.

31

Laugh, Play, and Tickle Her Heart

Engaging in a playful tickle session is an enjoyable way to add fun and spark connection in your relationship. Tickle fights are a simple, spontaneous means of bonding through physical touch and shared amusement, often creating moments of genuine closeness. It's an opportunity to let go of seriousness, embrace your playful side, and relish each other's company in a carefree manner.

While tickling can be an entertaining way to connect, it's important to stay mindful of each other's comfort levels. The goal is to foster moments of delight and affection, so pay attention to her reactions and make sure the experience is enjoyable for both of you. These playful exchanges can break up the monotony of daily life, serving as a reminder of how much fun you can have simply being together.

And be careful—some women may pee or pass gas when tickled too much! The last thing you need is a "cleanup on aisle 3." So, while it's all in good fun, keep it easygoing and know when to ease up before things get out of hand!

32

Make Movie Nights Magical with Favorites and Themed Experiences

Movie nights are a wonderful way to unwind and connect. Curating an evening around her favorite films shows care and attention. Pick a movie she loves—perhaps a romantic comedy that always makes her smile or a classic she's nostalgic about—and set the stage with her favorite snacks, soft blankets, and cozy pillows. The effort you put into creating a comfortable and inviting atmosphere will make her feel valued and appreciated.

To elevate the experience, consider transforming movie night into a themed event. This is your chance to get creative and surprise her with something out of the ordinary. For instance, turn your space into an action-packed Marvel universe marathon, complete with superhero-inspired snacks and decor. Adding playful touches like costumes or matching drinks can make the night feel even more special and memorable.

The planning doesn't have to be elaborate. Start by choosing a theme that reflects her favorite genres or films, and then focus on details that bring the concept to life. A romantic Parisian ambiance for a French film or a nostalgic throwback with retro snacks and music can add layers of fun and meaning. These extra touches show how much you value the time you spend together and how well you know what she loves.

Ultimately, the true magic lies in the connection you build during these moments. Laughing together at the characters' antics, debating plot twists, or simply enjoying each other's company creates memories that last far beyond the credits. Whether it's an intimate evening with her favorite movie or a playful, themed adventure, what matters most is that you're present, making her feel valued and loved.

33

Explore Hidden Gems and New Horizons

Exploring a new city or town together is an exciting way to break from routine and create meaningful experiences. Whether it's a spontaneous day trip to a nearby town or a planned weekend getaway to a city you've both been wanting to visit, discovering new places together can be both adventurous and connecting. Wander through charming streets, visit local attractions, try out new restaurants, and immerse yourselves in the culture and atmosphere of the place.

This shared experience allows you to see the world through each other's eyes, strengthening your connection as you navigate unfamiliar surroundings together. The excitement of exploring new places fosters a sense of curiosity and wonder, reminding you both of the pleasure of discovery and the thrill of new experiences. By stepping out of your comfort zone and into a new environment, you create opportunities for connection, conversation, and a deeper understanding of each other.

This isn't just another weekend getaway—it's about embracing the adventure of discovery together. Exploring a new city or town has its own unique charm, offering fresh sights, unexpected experiences, and opportunities to bond over shared exploration. It's less about the destination and more about the journey you take as a couple, whether it's navigating winding streets, stumbling upon a hidden gem, or laughing at a wrong turn. These moments of discovery and spontaneity bring a different kind of excitement and connection than a traditional getaway, making it all the more memorable.

34

Arrange an Indoor Picnic Basket with Her Favorite Foods

An indoor picnic is a creative and cozy way to enjoy a special meal together without leaving the comfort of home. Set the scene by spreading out a blanket on the living room floor, arranging some cushions for seating, and filling the space with soft lighting or candles to create a warm atmosphere. Prepare a selection of her favorite foods—whether it's finger sandwiches, fresh fruits, cheese and crackers, or even homemade treats—and arrange them beautifully on a platter.

This intimate setting allows you to enjoy the simplicity of a picnic while being sheltered from the elements. The effort of choosing her favorite foods and creating a comfortable, relaxed environment reflects your attention to detail and care for her happiness. An indoor picnic turns an ordinary meal into a memorable experience, giving you both a chance to unwind, chat, and savor each other's company in a unique and personal way.

Send Love and Light: Uplift Her Day, One Text at a Time

Sending supportive and uplifting texts throughout the day is a simple yet impactful way to stay connected and show your partner that she's on your mind, even when you're apart. Whether she's navigating a busy workday, facing challenges, or just going about her routine, receiving a kind message from you can lift her spirits and add positivity to her day. These texts can be anything from a quick "I believe in you" to a more detailed message expressing your love and admiration.

The key is to be genuine and considerate, tailoring your messages to what she might need at that moment. Regularly sending these little reminders of your support reinforces the idea that you're always there for her, no matter what the day brings. This consistent effort to encourage her can deepen your emotional connection, making her feel valued, appreciated, and cherished.

It's important to find balance and not overdo it—too many messages can feel overwhelming or even intrusive, especially if she's busy or dealing with a stressful day. Pay attention to her responses and adjust accordingly, ensuring that your texts are a source of reassurance, not distraction. A well-timed, heartfelt message carries more meaning than a constant stream of texts. By being intentional about when and how often you reach out, you show her that you're in tune with her needs and respectful of her space, which makes your words even more impactful.

36

Gift Her a Build-A-Bear Filled with Love and Personalized Messages

Sometimes, the most meaningful gifts are the ones that combine creativity with personal touches, and a Build-A-Bear customized just for her is a perfect way to do that. You get to design a stuffed animal that reflects her personality and includes personalized messages from you. The experience of creating something unique for her makes this gift truly one of a kind. Add a voice recording, where she can press the paw and hear you say something sweet or funny—it's the kind of surprise that will bring a smile to her face every time she hears it.

What makes this gesture stand out is how it goes beyond just a cute bear. It's about creating a keepsake that holds emotional value, something she can treasure for years. Maybe you add an inside joke or a special memory you both share. The effort you put into making it personal shows that you're willing to invest time into something that speaks directly to her heart.

Again, this is more than just a stuffed animal—it's a way of letting her know that you've thought deeply about her, her preferences, and what would bring her happiness. Whether it's for a special occasion or a "just because" moment, this meaningful gesture will show her just how much you care.

Hold Each Other Close and Dance the Night Away

Holding each other close while dancing is a romantic and intimate way to connect with your partner, allowing you to express your love through movement and touch. Whether it's a slow dance to a favorite song in your living room or a spontaneous twirl in the kitchen, dancing together creates a moment of closeness that words alone can't capture. The act of swaying together, with your arms wrapped around each other, brings a sense of harmony and unity.

This shared experience isn't about perfecting the steps; it's about being present with each other and letting the music guide your emotions. Dancing close allows you to tune out the world and focus solely on the connection between you, fostering a deeper bond. It's a beautiful way to show affection and create memories that you'll both treasure long after the music fades.

I'm not much of a dancer, but one New Year's Eve, in the comfort of my theater room, I found myself swaying to Bruno Mars' 24K Magic album. Normally, I'd be stuck in my head, worrying about my two left feet, but that night, surrounded by familiar walls and with her in my arms, I let go of the self-consciousness. I was completely at ease, and it became an unforgettable memory. It showed me that you don't need a fancy venue or perfect moves—just a willingness to be present and enjoy the moment together.

Make Her Mouth Water with a Delicious Breakfast in Bed

Preparing breakfast in bed is a classic and caring way to pamper your partner and start her day on a high note. Whether it's a weekend surprise or a special occasion, bringing her favorite breakfast items on a tray—complete with a fresh cup of coffee or juice—can make her feel cherished and loved. You can keep it simple with toast and fruit, or go all out with pancakes, eggs, and bacon, depending on what she enjoys most.

The gesture of breakfast in bed is more than just about the meal; it's about creating a moment of relaxation and indulgence where she can savor a leisurely morning without rushing. The effort you put into preparing and serving her breakfast highlights your appreciation for all she does and gives her a chance to unwind and enjoy the comfort of being cared for. This simple act of love can set a positive tone for the rest of the day, making her feel genuinely special.

To take it up a notch, invest in a nice breakfast tray and a quality cloth to elevate the presentation. Learning how to wrap the silverware with a touch of flair adds an extra layer of charm that she'll notice and appreciate. It's the little details—like neatly folded napkins, a small vase with a single flower, or a handwritten note on the tray—that show you've gone the extra mile. These thoughtful touches turn a simple breakfast into a memorable experience, making her feel like she's being treated to a five-star morning right at home.

39

Create Memories at an Amusement Park or Carnival

Visiting an amusement park or carnival together is a thrilling way to break from routine and create lasting memories. The vibrant atmosphere, exciting rides, games, and indulgent treats like cotton candy or funnel cakes bring out the kid in both of you, offering a day filled with excitement and shared delight. Whether you're challenging each other to a game of ring toss, riding a roller coaster, or simply enjoying the sights and sounds, the experience is about letting loose and enjoying time together.

An amusement park or carnival provides countless opportunities to connect, whether it's through shared adrenaline on a ride, winning a prize for her, or holding hands as you stroll through the park. These lively and adventurous experiences can strengthen your bond, reminding you both of the importance of living in the moment and making time to unwind together.

While amusement parks and carnivals are exciting, be mindful of the costs—it's easy to get carried away. Between the ticket prices, overpriced snacks, and games that cost $10 just to win a stuffed animal worth $2, your wallet might feel the thrill ride more than you do. Set a budget beforehand and stick to it, or you might find yourself contemplating whether that giant turkey leg was worth skipping groceries for the week. Remember, the goal is to have fun, not to refinance your car for a day of treats and roller coasters!

. . . But don't complain about the cost either!

40

Drop the Scorecard, Embrace the Partnership

As a former athlete, competition is in my DNA. I thrive on the challenge of pushing limits, testing abilities, and striving for excellence—whether it's on the court, the field, or in life. That drive has shaped who I am, and I carry it with pride. But as much as I love the thrill of competing, I've learned there's a time and place for it. Relationships aren't about dominating or outperforming; they're about connection and balance. Bringing that competitive edge into every interaction can lead to unnecessary tension, shifting the focus from partnership to rivalry.

In love, the goal isn't to "win" but to grow together. That doesn't mean you have to suppress your competitive nature—it just means redirecting it in a way that uplifts rather than divides. Think of your relationship as a team sport. There will be moments to cheer each other on, moments to share the spotlight, and even moments to pass the ball so your partner can shine. Recognizing that your strengths complement hers can transform competition into collaboration, where every victory is shared and celebrated.

Still, I understand the allure of a little friendly rivalry—there's a unique energy in testing each other's limits in a playful way. The key is keeping it easygoing and knowing when to step back. It's okay to challenge her to a game of one-on-one or see who can cook the best steak, but the moment the fun shifts into frustration, it's time to pause. Remember, competition in relationships should always build connection, not walls. A playful game or challenge should end with shared enjoyment and moments you'll both remember fondly, not resentment or unresolved tension.

At the core of it all, love is the ultimate team sport. You can bring your athletic spirit into your relationship, not by keeping score, but by striving to be the best teammate possible. Support her wins, share her struggles, and know when to let competition take a backseat to care. Because in the game of love, the real victory is building a life where both of you feel like you've already won.

41

Speak from the Heart: Admire Her Strengths and Virtues Out Loud

Verbally expressing your admiration for her strengths and virtues is a powerful way to show your appreciation and deepen your emotional connection. Take the time to acknowledge the qualities that make her unique—whether it's her resilience in tough times, her kindness to others, her intelligence, or her unwavering honesty. By openly sharing what you admire about her, you help to reinforce her self-confidence and show that you truly see and value who she is.

These affirmations can be especially meaningful when she's facing challenges or feeling uncertain, as your words can provide comfort and encouragement. Being specific about what you admire shows that you're paying attention to the details that make her special. This type of verbal appreciation not only strengthens your bond but also fosters a positive and supportive atmosphere in your relationship, where both of you feel valued and uplifted.

42

Fresh Sheets, Fresh Start... Make the Bed and Win Her Heart

Taking the time to proactively wash your bed linen and make the bed is a small but impactful way to show care and attentiveness. Nothing beats the feeling of crawling into a fresh, clean bed at the end of a long day, and knowing you made it happen will only add to her appreciation. By doing this without being asked, you're not just handling a chore—you're creating a sanctuary of comfort and cleanliness that both of you can enjoy.

Let's be honest: the state of your bed says a lot about you. If your sheets are musty like a Greyhound bus seat, it's time to take action. And while you're at it, remember to put the pillows back where they belong—not like they've just survived a wrestling match. Proactive bed care isn't just about impressing her; it's about taking pride in your space and creating an environment that invites rest, relaxation, and, let's be real, a better chance of her wanting to spend time there.

And guys, let's talk detergent. No one wants to sniff sheets that smell like gym socks. Use a detergent that leaves a fresh, inviting scent, and throw in a fabric softener for good measure. Bonus points if you use her favorite fragrance—it's a detail that'll earn you major brownie points. Making the bed afterward isn't just the finishing touch; it's your chance to show off those hospital corners (or at least attempt them). It's a small effort that goes a long way in showing her that you care about the space you share.

Take Her Up a Famous Tower for a Romantic View of the City

There's something undeniably romantic about standing atop a famous tower, gazing out at the breathtaking view of a city stretched out beneath you. Taking her to a place like this combines the excitement of adventure with an unforgettable setting for connection. Whether you're in Seattle enjoying the iconic Space Needle, soaking in the panoramic sights from the CN Tower in Toronto, or marveling at the charm of the Hot Springs Mountain Tower in Arkansas, these elevated experiences can take your date—and your relationship—to new heights.

Famous towers offer more than just great views; they create perfect opportunities for shared moments. Imagine pointing out landmarks together, capturing photos that will live in both your memories and your phone's gallery, and having a quiet moment to appreciate not just the view but each other. These lofty settings often feel removed from the busyness of life below, making them ideal for meaningful conversations or simply holding her close while the world seems to slow down around you.

Pro tip: Do your research ahead of time. Some towers offer revolving restaurants, observation decks, or even timed light shows that can make the visit even more magical. Don't forget to check operating hours and plan for clear weather—it's hard to be romantic when all you can see is fog! Whether it's a famous tower nearby or a bucket-list destination, taking her up to see the world from above is a gesture that's sure to leave her feeling on top of the world, literally and figuratively.

44

Explore the Outdoors Together on a Scenic Bike Ride or Hike

Going on a bike ride or hike together is a refreshing way to enjoy each other's company while staying active and exploring the outdoors. Whether you choose a scenic bike trail, a forested hiking path, or a mountain trail with breathtaking views, the experience of moving through nature together fosters a sense of adventure and connection. It's an opportunity to unplug from daily stressors and immerse yourselves in the beauty of the natural world.

This shared activity not only benefits your physical health but also strengthens your emotional bond. As you pedal or walk side by side, there's time for conversation, lighthearted moments, or simply enjoying the peaceful companionship of each other's presence. Whether you're pushing through a challenging incline or coasting down a gentle slope, these moments of shared effort and accomplishment can bring you closer, creating lasting memories of exploration and connection.

Now, if you're the guy who hasn't ridden a bike since middle school or who breaks into a sweat just thinking about bugs, don't worry—you're not alone. Maybe your "bike ride" is more of a wobbly circus act, or your idea of nature is the salad bar at your favorite restaurant. That's okay! The point isn't to become the next Lance Armstrong or Bear Grylls. Just show up, do your best, and embrace the chaos. Who knows? You might actually find yourself enjoying the fresh air…or at least surviving long enough to laugh about it later. And if not, there's always ice cream afterward to make up for it!

45

Give Her a Star and Show Her Your Love is Infinite

Naming a star after her is a romantic and symbolic gesture that expresses your love in a unique and celestial way. By choosing to name a star in her honor, you're giving her a gift that's as timeless and vast as the universe itself. This meaningful act carries profound significance, as it symbolizes that your love for her is as steadfast and enduring as the stars in the sky.

You can do this through various online services, such as the International Star Registry or similar companies, which provide a certificate with the star's name and coordinates. This allows her to look up at the night sky and know that a part of the cosmos is dedicated to her. Naming a star after her is not just a gift; it's a lasting tribute that connects your love to something vast and eternal, reminding her of your affection every time she gazes at the stars.

46

Show Her You Care with a Cozy Cuddle Cushion or Body Pillow

Sometimes, the simplest gifts bring the most comfort, and a cuddle cushion or body pillow is a perfect example of that. Gifting her one of these isn't just about providing her with a cozy accessory; it's about showing that you care about her relaxation and well-being. Whether she loves to curl up with a book, binge-watch her favorite shows, or just get a good night's sleep, a high-quality cuddle cushion or body pillow can make all the difference. It's a meaningful way to give her a hug, even when you're not there.

These pillows come in various shapes and styles, from full-body designs that provide all-over support to cute and quirky cuddle cushions shaped like animals or hearts. Pay attention to her preferences—does she need extra support for her back? Does she have a favorite color or material? Customizing the gift to suit her needs shows that you've put care into making her feel special. Plus, every time she relaxes with it, she'll be reminded of your effort and attention to detail.

And let's face it, guys: sometimes, you might not always be around for every cuddle session. A cuddle cushion or body pillow is a playful way to ensure she stays cozy even when you're not there to wrap your arms around her. But don't worry—you're not being replaced! Think of it as a tag-team partner in the comfort department. Bonus points if you make a joke about it being her "stand-in" for when you're at work or away, keeping the mood lighthearted and fun.

47

Let Her Find Comfort Resting Her Head on Your Shoulder

Inviting her to rest her head on your shoulder is a tender and comforting gesture that conveys safety, trust, and a deep emotional connection. Whether you're sitting together on the couch, lying in bed, or sharing a quiet moment on a park bench, this simple act of affection allows her to feel supported and cherished. It's a way of letting her know that you're there to provide comfort and that she can lean on you, both physically and emotionally.

This small gesture fosters intimacy, creating a peaceful space where she can relax and feel close to you. It's often during these quiet moments that the strength of your relationship is most evident—through the unspoken understanding and shared comfort of being together. Placing her head on your shoulder is more than just a physical act; it's a symbol of your willingness to be her pillar of support, offering a sense of stability and love.

Now, if she has a big head and your shoulder starts to go numb, don't panic—you're not alone in this struggle! Shift subtly, give that arm a quick stretch when she's not looking, and soldier on. Or, better yet, have a plush throw pillow nearby to sneak under her head for support. She'll still get the comfort she needs, and you'll avoid walking around with a lopsided gait the next day. It's all about balance—literally—and making sure she feels loved while you maintain circulation in your arm.

48

Make Time for Each Other by Establishing a Regular Date Night

Life gets busy, and it's easy for weeks to slip by without spending intentional, quality time together. That's why establishing a regular schedule for dates is so important. By setting aside a specific day or time each week or month for a date, you're prioritizing your relationship in a way that feels tangible and heartfelt. It's about creating a shared commitment to nurturing your connection, no matter how hectic your schedules might be.

Having a dedicated date on both of your calendars eliminates the guesswork and excuses. Whether it's dinner at your favorite spot, a casual movie night, or trying a new activity together, knowing that this time is reserved just for the two of you adds a sense of consistency and anticipation to your relationship. Looking forward to these moments gives you both a regular reminder of the importance of your bond.

Think of this as an investment in your relationship. By committing to regular dates, you're building a foundation of connection and shared experiences that strengthen your partnership over time. And while life might occasionally throw a curveball, keeping this commitment shows each other that your relationship is a priority. It doesn't have to be fancy or elaborate every time; what matters most is the consistency and the shared effort to keep the romance alive.

49

Experience Musical Magic by Attending a Live Concert

Attending a live music concert together is an exhilarating way to experience the energy and passion of shared interests while creating lasting memories. Whether it's a favorite band, a symphony, or a local artist, the experience of live music can be both electrifying and intimate, allowing you to connect through the rhythm and emotion of the performance. The atmosphere of a concert—surrounded by the crowd, the lights, and the powerful sound—can make the experience even more unforgettable.

This shared adventure is not just about the music; it's about enjoying a special event together, dancing, singing along, or simply soaking in the moment side by side. The collective excitement and connection of a live performance can deepen your bond, creating a shared memory that you'll both hold dear. Going to a concert together is a perfect way to break from routine, have fun, and celebrate your mutual love for music and each other.

I'll never forget the Coldplay concert I attended at the Rose Bowl. The atmosphere was electric—thousands of glowing wristbands lit up in unison, creating a sea of colors that pulsed to the beat of the music. It wasn't just a concert; it felt like being part of something bigger, a shared moment of pure joy and connection. While I didn't sing along, I fully embraced the energy and vibe of the night. The music, the lights, and the collective excitement of the crowd made it an unforgettable experience, a reminder of how moments like these can bring people closer and create lasting memories.

50

Bonus: Always Try to Find the Good in Her

In any relationship, it's important not to be quick to accuse but to give her the benefit of the doubt. If you truly love her, allow her the opportunity to show that her intentions are pure and of good nature. Trusting in her goodness and being open to understanding her perspective can prevent unnecessary conflict. This doesn't mean turning a blind eye or being naive, but it does mean not being "that guy" who constantly has a problem with everything she says or does.

It's about showing her that you believe in her integrity and that you're willing to listen before jumping to conclusions. Giving her this space to explain herself shows maturity and fosters trust in your relationship. It's a reminder that love involves patience, understanding, and giving each other room to grow without fear of constant criticism.

Choosing to find the good in her also means seeing the beauty in her flaws and imperfections. Everyone has moments where they may not be at their best, but focusing on her positive qualities can shift the dynamics in your relationship. Whether it's her kindness, intelligence, or the unique way she expresses herself, making an effort to see these traits, especially in difficult moments, can deepen your connection and create a more harmonious partnership.

Always trying to find the good in her is a powerful way to nurture love and appreciation in your relationship. While no one is perfect, choosing to focus on her strengths and positive qualities can make a significant difference. Whether it's her kindness, intelligence, or the way she supports others, by actively seeking out what makes her special, you reinforce a sense of value and admiration. This mindset not only boosts her confidence but also strengthens your bond, as she feels truly cherished. Over time, this habit deepens your connection, fostering mutual respect and allowing your relationship to flourish.

Find Peace in Shared Stillness

Meditating together is a calming and deeply connective practice that allows you to share moments of peace and mindfulness. Whether you're experienced in meditation or just starting out, sitting quietly together, focusing on your breath, and being present in the moment can strengthen your bond and promote a sense of unity. Meditation helps to clear the mind, reduce stress, and foster a deeper awareness of each other's presence.

This shared practice can become a regular ritual that enhances your emotional and spiritual connection. By creating a peaceful space where both of you can relax and tune into your inner selves, you open up to a more profound understanding and appreciation of each other. Meditating together is not just about finding personal calm; it's about cultivating harmony in your relationship, providing a shared experience of tranquility and centeredness that can benefit both of you.

52

Turn Your Love into a Masterpiece

Gifting her customized artwork or a painting is a unique and personal way to celebrate your relationship and her individuality. Whether it's an image of a special moment you've shared, a depiction of a place that holds meaning for both of you, or an abstract piece that resonates with her personality, customized art is a meaningful and lasting expression of your love. This type of gift shows that you've put time and effort into creating something truly one-of-a-kind.

Customized artwork or a painting can also serve as a beautiful reminder of your relationship, gracing the walls of your home with a constant symbol of your connection. Every time she looks at it, she'll be reminded of the care you put into creating something so special. This artistic gesture goes beyond material value, offering her something deeply personal that reflects your bond in a creative and enduring way.

53

Dive into Adventure and Keep It Just Between You

Going for a secretive skinny dip together is a playful and adventurous way to connect and create a shared experience filled with excitement and spontaneity. This intimate activity invites you both to step out of your comfort zones and embrace a sense of freedom and closeness that can strengthen your bond. Whether it's under the cover of night at a secluded beach, a hidden lake, or a private pool, the thrill of doing something a little daring together adds to the fun and romance.

The secrecy and spontaneity of a skinny dip can make the experience feel like a special, shared secret between the two of you, deepening your connection through trust and shared excitement. It's a chance to let go of inhibitions and enjoy each other's company in a lighthearted, carefree way, creating memories that are sure to bring smiles and laughter long after the moment has passed.

Now, let me tell you—I don't play about bugs crawling on me or fish nibbling at me in natural bodies of water. If I feel something touch my leg, it's game over, and you'll see me sprinting to dry land like my life depends on it. That's why a private pool or spa is more my speed. I can relax without worrying about being ambushed by nature's little surprises. Call me picky, but I'd rather focus on enjoying the moment than swatting at mosquitoes or dodging fish that think I'm dinner. Sometimes, romance is just better when it's bug-free!

54

Speak Volumes with a Gentle Touch

Stroking her arm or hand affectionately is a tender gesture that communicates love, comfort, and reassurance. This simple yet intimate touch can convey deep emotions without the need for words, making her feel cherished and close to you. Whether you're sitting together on the couch, holding hands in a quiet moment, or even as you fall asleep, gently stroking her arm or hand creates a soothing connection that reinforces your bond.

This act of affection can be especially meaningful during moments when she needs comfort or support. The gentle caress provides a sense of security and warmth, letting her know that you're there for her. Over time, these small gestures of love and care build a strong foundation of trust and intimacy in your relationship, reminding her that your love is always present, even in the simplest of touches.

If this is something new for you, don't be surprised if she looks at you with a mix of curiosity and surprise. She might even raise an eyebrow as if to say, "Who are you, and what have you done with my man?" But don't ruin the moment—look her in the eye, smile, and continue doing what you're doing. That confident, steady affection will melt away any hesitation she has and turn the gesture into something she'll cherish. Sometimes, it's the unexpected little things that leave the biggest impression.

55

Master Something New, Hand in Hand

Learning a new skill together, especially one she's been wanting to try, is a fantastic way to bond and show your support for her interests. Whether it's taking up a new hobby like photography, learning a language, trying out a cooking class, or picking up a musical instrument, diving into something new as a team can be both fun and rewarding. This shared experience allows you to encourage each other, laugh at your mistakes, and celebrate your progress together.

By taking the initiative to explore something she's passionate about, you show that her interests are important to you and that you're willing to step out of your comfort zone to be by her side. Learning together can also open up new dimensions of your relationship, as you discover more about each other's strengths, weaknesses, and how you collaborate. This journey of growth and discovery not only enriches your personal skills but also strengthens the connection you share.

Step Into Rhythm and Romance

Taking a dance class together is a lively and romantic way to connect while learning something new. Whether it's salsa, ballroom, swing, or even a fun hip-hop class, dancing offers a perfect blend of physical activity, creativity, and shared connection. Moving in sync with each other, mastering new steps, and embracing the rhythm of the music can bring you closer as a couple, enhancing your communication and teamwork in an uplifting setting.

Even though I feel like I have two left feet when I dance nowadays, I still give it my best shot. It's not about being perfect or mastering every step; it's about having fun and showing her that I'm willing to step out of my comfort zone for us. Sure, I might stumble or miss a beat, but the laughter and joy we share in those moments make it all worth it. The effort counts more than the technique, and by trying—even when I feel awkward—I'm showing her that she's worth every misstep.

The process of learning to dance together can be filled with laughter, shared challenges, and moments of pride as you master new moves. It's an opportunity to step out of your comfort zone and embrace the experience, no matter your skill level. As you grow more confident on the dance floor, you'll also find that the trust and chemistry between you deepen, making this activity a fun and rewarding way to bond. Dancing together isn't just about the steps—it's about the connection you create through movement and the memories you build along the way.

57

Make Her Feel Like a Movie Star in the Rain

Kissing her passionately in the rain is a timeless, cinematic gesture that can turn an ordinary moment into something magical. There's something undeniably romantic about the spontaneity of sharing a kiss under the rain, with the world around you fading into the background as the droplets fall. The rain adds an element of excitement and unpredictability, making the kiss feel like an adventurous, shared secret between the two of you.

This moment of raw emotion and connection can create a powerful memory that you'll both cherish. Whether it's during a sudden downpour while walking together or a planned embrace in a gentle drizzle, kissing in the rain embodies the essence of living in the moment and embracing the unexpected. It's a way to express your love passionately and unapologetically, making her feel like the leading lady in her very own love story.

Now, if your woman is rocking lashes, wigs, lace fronts, or weaves, and her makeup game is flawless, be mindful of her personality before you go full The Notebook on her. The last thing you want is for her to start melting like a snowman under a heat lamp. A little rain might seem romantic to you, but to her, it could spell disaster. Be proactive—bring an umbrella just in case things don't go as planned. That way, you can still have your cinematic moment while ensuring she doesn't give you the look for forgetting her hair and makeup priorities.

58

Celebrate What Makes Her One of a Kind

Acknowledging and praising her unique skills and talents is a powerful way to show that you value and admire her for who she is. Whether she's an exceptional cook, a creative artist, a skilled problem-solver, or a natural leader, taking the time to recognize and celebrate these qualities can boost her confidence and strengthen your bond. It's important to be specific in your praise, highlighting the things she excels at and expressing genuine admiration for her abilities.

By showing appreciation for what makes her unique, you reinforce her sense of self-worth and make her feel truly seen and valued in the relationship. This kind of recognition not only makes her feel loved but also encourages her to continue pursuing her passions and developing her talents. Praising her skills and talents is a way to celebrate her individuality and remind her that you're proud to be by her side, supporting her in all that she does.

/ 59

Savor the Moment with Every Soft Kiss

Giving her soft, lingering kisses is a tender and intimate way to express your love and deepen your connection. Unlike quick pecks or passionate embraces, these gentle, unhurried kisses communicate a sense of warmth, affection, and presence. Whether you're kissing her on the lips, forehead, or cheek, the slow, lingering nature of these kisses allows you both to savor the moment and fully experience the closeness between you.

These kisses can create a peaceful and loving atmosphere, making her feel cherished and adored. They're perfect for quiet moments together, where you can let the world fade away and focus solely on each other. Soft, lingering kisses are not just about physical touch; they're about conveying your deep emotional bond and making her feel loved in a way that words alone sometimes can't express.

For those who travel often for work, like I do, a soft, passionate kiss is non-negotiable. When I come home, I make it a point to kiss her in a way that says, "I've missed you," and "I'm so blessed and grateful to be back home with you." It's not just about the physical act—it's about showing her that no matter where I've been or how far I've traveled, my heart is always with her. That one lingering kiss can bridge the gap between the time apart and remind her that she's always my anchor, no matter how busy life gets.

Blend Work and Bliss with a Spontaneous Escape

Planning a workcation for her is the perfect way to combine productivity with relaxation in a beautiful setting. Arrange for her to work remotely from a luxurious hotel suite, where she can enjoy peace and quiet away from daily responsibilities. After she finishes her work for the day, she'll be able to check into her suite and unwind in a space tailored just for her. Have her favorite foods and drinks catered and delivered to the room so she can enjoy a stress-free evening.

During her two-day stay, she can take advantage of the hotel's spa, relax by the pool, or indulge in any amenities she enjoys. This solo getaway gives her the opportunity to work in a serene environment while also appreciating much-needed time to herself, free from distractions like kids and household duties. It's a thoughtful way to show that you support her need for balance, productivity, and relaxation.

I recommend doing this at least once a quarter or every six months, depending on your budget, to build consistency. It's not just a one-time gesture; it's about establishing a rhythm of support and care that becomes part of your routine. By planning these workcations regularly, you're creating opportunities for her to recharge and feel valued on an ongoing basis. Plus, it gives her something to look forward to—a break from the grind that helps maintain balance and focus. Think of it as an investment in her well-being and happiness that pays off in a healthier, more connected relationship.

61

Discover Beauty and Meaning Through Art and History

Visiting a local museum or art gallery together is a wonderful way to explore culture, history, and creativity while deepening your connection. Whether you're admiring classic paintings, discovering contemporary art, or delving into exhibits about history or science, this shared experience offers a chance to learn, discuss, and appreciate the world in a new way. Strolling through the galleries, you can take in the beauty, engage in thoughtful conversations, and discover more about each other's tastes and perspectives.

This outing is not just about enjoying the art or exhibits; it's about creating a moment of intellectual and emotional connection. A visit to a museum or gallery can spark inspiration, provoke deep discussions, and even reveal new aspects of each other's personalities. It's a meaningful way to spend time together, enriching both your minds and your relationship in the process.

Piece Together the Memories You Treasure

Creating a personalized puzzle with a special photo is a fun and meaningful way to celebrate your relationship. Choose a meaningful picture—perhaps from a memorable trip, a cherished moment together, or a favorite snapshot of the two of you—and turn it into a puzzle that you can assemble together. As you piece it together, you'll relive the memories captured in the photo, turning the activity into a shared experience filled with connection and smiles.

This personalized puzzle not only serves as a unique and enjoyable pastime but also symbolizes the idea of building something beautiful together, piece by piece. Once completed, the puzzle can be framed as a keepsake, reminding you both of the time spent creating it and the special bond you share. It's a creative and interactive way to show her how much you treasure your shared memories and the life you're building together.

63

Leave Your Love in Her Ears and Heart

Leaving voice memos expressing your love and appreciation is a meaningful way to remind her how much she means to you, even when you're not together. Whether you're apart for the day or just want to surprise her with a sweet gesture, recording a short, sincere message can lift her spirits and make her feel valued. These voice memos can be as simple as telling her you love her, sharing something you admire about her, or recalling a favorite memory you share.

The sound of your voice adds a personal touch that text messages can't quite capture, making your words feel even more intimate and meaningful. She can listen to these messages whenever she needs a boost or just wants to hear your voice, reinforcing your presence in her life even when you're apart. Voice memos are a modern yet deeply personal way to keep the connection strong, showing that your love and appreciation are constant, no matter the distance.

64

Hold Her Close with Your Hands and Eyes

Holding her face gently and gazing into her eyes is a deeply intimate gesture that conveys love, trust, and a profound connection. This simple act of tenderness allows you both to pause and fully immerse yourselves in the moment, expressing your feelings without the need for words. The intensity of eye contact combined with the touch of your hands on her face creates a powerful bond, making her feel seen, valued, and loved.

This gesture is especially meaningful in quiet, private moments where you can focus entirely on each other. Whether it's after a shared laugh, during a tender conversation, or just because, holding her face and looking into her eyes speaks volumes about your affection and commitment. It's a way to communicate the depth of your emotions, reinforcing the unspoken understanding and connection that you share.

Now, if your woman doesn't like her face being touched, proceed with caution—you might catch a side-eye sharper than a chef's knife. For some, the thought of fingers near their perfectly applied makeup or freshly moisturized skin is a major no-go. In these cases, skip the hands and focus on the gaze. Just lock eyes, maybe give a little smirk, and keep your hands firmly at a safe distance. Trust me, she'll appreciate your respect for her boundaries (and her bronzer). Sometimes, intimacy is about adapting to what works for her . . . and avoiding the wrath of smudged eyeliner.

65

Curate the Music That Tells Her Story

Creating a playlist of songs that remind you of her is a meaningful and personal way to express your feelings through music. Whether it's the songs that played during your first dates, tracks with lyrics that reflect your emotions, or tunes that make you think of her smile, each selection demonstrates how much she means to you. This playlist becomes a soundtrack of your relationship, filled with melodies and moments that you both can treasure.

While it's tempting to be goofy by throwing in some tracks like "Pumps & Bumps," "Baby Got Back," or anything by 2 Live Crew, remember to keep the vibe romantic and meaningful. A little humor is great, but you don't want to get too carried away with songs that might not match the mood you're trying to create. Focus on tracks that genuinely remind you of her beauty, strength, and the special moments you've shared. It's all about striking the right balance between fun and heartfelt, so she knows this playlist is truly about her.

Sharing this playlist with her allows you to communicate your love in a unique way, letting the music speak when words might fall short. It's a gift that she can listen to whenever she wants to feel close to you, whether she's having a good day or needs a little comfort. This collection of songs serves as a reminder of your bond and the special moments you've shared, making it a meaningful gesture that resonates long after the music stops playing.

Sweep Her Off Her Feet with a Surprise Night

Planning a surprise date night is a romantic and exciting way to show her how much you care. The element of surprise adds a layer of anticipation and joy, making the evening feel extra special. Whether it's a dinner at her favorite restaurant, a night of stargazing, or a cozy evening at home with a homemade meal and a movie, the key is to tailor the date to her preferences and create an atmosphere where she feels loved and appreciated.

The effort you put into planning the details—choosing the location, setting the mood, and keeping the plans a secret—shows that you're willing to go the extra mile to make her happy. A surprise date night not only breaks the routine but also rekindles the excitement and romance in your relationship. It's a thoughtful gesture that reminds her of your commitment to keeping the spark alive, making it a night to remember.

If you're someone who struggles with planning surprises, don't worry—it's a skill you can develop. I personally recommend starting with a checklist or action list to stay organized. Break the process down into manageable steps, like deciding on a location, arranging logistics, and thinking through the details she'll love. Keep notes on her preferences, such as her favorite foods, music, or activities, so you always have inspiration on hand. If you're worried about forgetting something, set reminders or use apps to help you stay on track. Planning doesn't have to be overwhelming—just take it one step at a time, and before you know it, you'll be pulling off surprises like a pro!

When I plan a surprise, I like to pick places based on stellar Google reviews. It's my go-to move for ensuring the spot delivers a great experience. Whether it's a restaurant, an activity, or a unique venue, those reviews help narrow down the best options. It gives me peace of mind knowing I've done my homework, so I can focus on enjoying the evening with her without worrying about unexpected hiccups. Trust me, those reviews are gold!

67

Write Your Love in Recipes She'll Treasure

Creating a handwritten recipe book filled with her favorite dishes is a personal and meaningful gift that celebrates your shared love of food and the memories you've created together in the kitchen. Whether it's the recipes you've cooked together, family favorites, or dishes that hold special meaning, compiling them into a beautifully crafted book demonstrates your dedication to preserving these moments and the thought you've put into the gesture.

Each recipe can be accompanied by a note about why it's special, tips for perfecting the dish, or a memory associated with it. The handwritten touch adds a layer of intimacy and sentimentality, turning the recipe book into a cherished keepsake. This gift is not just about the food; it's about the love and memories you've infused into every dish, making it a meaningful reminder of your relationship every time she flips through the pages and recreates these favorite meals.

68

Inspire Her with Quotes That Celebrate Her

Sending her quotes that remind you of her and her greatness is a meaningful way to express your admiration and appreciation. Whether it's a line from a book, a lyric from a song, or a powerful quote from a notable figure, these words can encapsulate the qualities you love about her and highlight the strength, beauty, and wisdom she possesses. Each quote serves as a small reminder of how much she inspires you and how much she means to you.

Sharing these quotes with her—whether through text, handwritten notes, or even as a daily or weekly ritual—shows that you're constantly thinking of her and recognizing the impact she has on your life. These quotes can uplift her spirits, boost her confidence, and make her feel truly valued. It's a thoughtful way to celebrate her uniqueness and greatness, letting her know that her presence enriches your life in countless ways.

69

Wrap Yourselves in Warmth and Love

Snuggling under a blanket together is one of the simplest yet most comforting ways to connect with your partner. Whether you're watching a movie, reading a book, or simply enjoying a quiet moment, the warmth of the blanket and the closeness of your bodies create a cozy, intimate atmosphere. This shared physical space fosters a sense of security and love, making you both feel more connected and cherished.

The act of snuggling is not just about the physical warmth; it's about the emotional comfort that comes from being close to someone you love. Wrapped in a blanket together, you can enjoy the serenity of being in each other's presence, letting the outside world fade away. This small but meaningful gesture can deepen your bond, providing a sense of connection and contentment that strengthens your relationship.

Snuggling under a blanket can also be a chance to create playful, lighthearted moments that make the experience even more enjoyable. Maybe you steal a corner of the blanket, leaving her to jokingly demand her share back, or you both chuckle at how tangled up you get trying to find the perfect position. These small, silly interactions bring a sense of fun and spontaneity to an already intimate moment, reminding you both that sometimes the simplest gestures hold the most delight.

70

Send Her to Work with Love in a Lunchbox

Packing a surprise lunch for her workday is a thoughtful way to show you care, even when you're apart. Taking the time to prepare her favorite meal or snacks and tucking them into a lunchbox with a sweet note can brighten her day and make her feel loved. Whether it's a homemade dish or a selection of her favorite treats, the surprise will let her know that you're thinking of her and want to make her day a little easier.

This gesture not only provides her with a delicious meal but also adds a personal touch that can brighten her day during a busy work schedule. The effort you put into planning and packing the lunch demonstrates your attentiveness, reminding her that she's always on your mind. It's a simple yet meaningful way to support her and make her feel valued, even amidst her daily routine.

In addition to preparing or purchasing her favorite meal, elevate the presentation by arranging it neatly and thoughtfully. Use a sleek lunchbox or a decorative container to give it a polished look. Add an extra treat by including a piece of fine chocolate or a gourmet dessert she loves—something that feels like a little indulgence just for her. If you want to take it to the next level, sneak in a small bottle of her favorite sparkling drink or a refreshing beverage in a discreet container. It's those unexpected touches that can turn an ordinary workday into one she'll excitedly share with her coworkers!

71

Be Her Partner in Style and Support

Offering to help her get dressed is a tender and intimate gesture that shows your affection and care in a simple yet meaningful way. Whether it's helping her zip up a dress, choose the perfect accessories, or simply being there to offer a second opinion, your assistance can make the routine of getting dressed feel special. This act of service not only shows your attentiveness but also adds a layer of closeness to your relationship.

Helping her get dressed can also be a fun and playful way to start the day or prepare for a special evening together. It's an opportunity to compliment her, share a moment of connection, and make her feel appreciated and beautiful. This small gesture reinforces the idea that you're a team, supporting each other in all aspects of life, no matter how big or small.

72

Celebrate Your Bond with Coordinated Style

Wearing matching couple's clothing or accessories is a fun and playful way to celebrate your connection and show the world that you're a team. Whether it's coordinating outfits, matching t-shirts with a cute phrase, or accessories like bracelets or hats, this gesture can add a touch of unity and joy to your relationship. It's a lighthearted way to express your bond, showing that you're proud to be together and enjoy sharing little things that bring you closer.

Choosing matching items can be a fun activity in itself, where you can pick out pieces that reflect your personalities or commemorate special moments in your relationship. Wearing these coordinated outfits or accessories can also spark smiles and conversations with others, reinforcing the special connection you share. It's a simple yet meaningful way to celebrate your love and show that you're united in both style and spirit.

Now, let's be clear—you don't want to end up looking like those awkward couples in the 80's JC Penney or Sears photos, rocking matching sweaters and stiff smiles. Think stylish, not cheesy. Skip the full-on identical outfits that scream "twinning overload" and go for subtle coordination, like matching colors or complementary designs. The goal is to look cute and connected, not like you've stepped out of a retro catalog that time forgot. Keep it classy, and let your outfits say, "We're a team," not "We're stuck in a time warp."

73

Celebrate Her Hard Work and Unwavering Dedication

Recognizing and commending her hard work and dedication is a powerful way to show your appreciation for all that she does. Whether she's excelling in her career, managing family responsibilities, or pursuing personal goals, acknowledging her efforts and commitment can boost her confidence and reinforce how much you value her contributions. Take the time to express your admiration for her perseverance, resilience, and the way she handles challenges with grace.

By offering sincere praise, you not only make her feel seen and appreciated but also strengthen the emotional bond between you. Letting her know that you notice her dedication and are proud of her accomplishments fosters a supportive and loving environment where she feels encouraged to continue striving for her best. This recognition is more than just words; it's a reflection of your deep respect and love for her, highlighting the important role she plays in your life and relationship.

Now, if the reality is that you're the one working, taking care of the home, and tending to the kids, it's still important to acknowledge her "hard work and dedication." Even if it seems like her dedication is more focused on doing nothing, at least there's some truth and consistency in that effort, right? While it may be a lighthearted way to look at things, keeping a sense of humor can help maintain harmony. Acknowledging her in this way shows that you're choosing to approach things with understanding, even when the dynamics feel a bit off.

74

Keep Your Connection Close, One Hand at a Time

Holding her hand whenever you can is a simple yet profound way to maintain a physical and emotional connection with your partner. This small gesture of affection speaks volumes, conveying love, support, and a sense of togetherness. Whether you're walking side by side, sitting together at a movie, or just relaxing at home, the touch of your hand in hers can provide comfort and reassurance, reminding her that you're always there for her.

The act of holding hands strengthens your bond by creating moments of intimacy and closeness throughout the day. It's a way to express your love without saying a word, reinforcing your connection in both public and private settings. By making hand-holding a regular part of your relationship, you're nurturing a habit of staying physically connected, which can enhance the overall warmth and affection between you.

75

Bring Her DIY Dream to Life

Completing a DIY project she's been wanting to do is a thoughtful and supportive way to show that you care about her interests and are willing to invest your time and effort into something that matters to her. Whether it's building a piece of furniture, creating home decor, or tackling a craft project, stepping in to help or taking the lead on completing it can bring a sense of accomplishment and joy to both of you.

This gesture demonstrates your commitment to her happiness and your willingness to make her dreams a reality. Working together on the project can also be a fun bonding experience, where you collaborate, learn new skills, and celebrate the results of your hard work. By helping her achieve something she's been passionate about, you're not just completing a task—you're creating a meaningful experience that strengthens your relationship and shows your love in a tangible way.

76

Cheer, Laugh, and Bond in the Stands

Attending a sports game or match together is an exciting way to share in the energy and thrill of live sports while enjoying each other's company. Whether you're cheering for a favorite team, experiencing the excitement of a close game, or simply soaking in the atmosphere of the stadium, this shared experience can create lasting memories. The lively environment, combined with your shared enthusiasm, makes for a fun and dynamic outing.

This experience allows you both to break from the usual routine, engage in lighthearted competition, and bond over a common interest. Whether you're high-fiving after a great play or consoling each other after a loss, the emotions of the game can bring you closer together. Attending a sports event is more than just watching the action—it's about sharing the highs and lows of the experience, celebrating the wins, and simply enjoying the thrill of the moment together.

But what if she's not into sports? No problem—this is your chance to focus on the experience rather than the game itself. Highlight the fun aspects like indulging in stadium snacks, people-watching, or enjoying the electric atmosphere. Make it about the two of you sharing something different, not about turning her into a diehard fan. And if she's completely uninterested, keep it light and playful—she might end up enjoying it more than she expects, especially if she sees how much fun you're having. Just don't spend the whole time trying to explain the rules unless she asks—you're there to connect, not run a sports clinic!

77

Sleep Beside Her, Holding Her Close (Without Wanting Sex)

Sleeping beside her, holding her close without any expectation of sex, is a deeply comforting and intimate way to show your love and commitment. This gesture communicates that your affection goes beyond physical desires, emphasizing the emotional connection and trust you share. Holding her close as you both drift off to sleep offers her a sense of security, warmth, and unconditional love, reinforcing that you're there for her in every way.

Now, if she just so happens to want sex in the moment, by all means, summon the powers of your ancestors and make it count! But the point here is to hold her close without the expectation that it has to lead to anything more. It's about offering comfort and security, letting her feel loved without any pressure. This creates a deeper emotional connection, where physical closeness is a way to nurture intimacy, not just a precursor to sex. She'll appreciate the genuine affection and your ability to be present with her in the moment.

The simplicity of this act—just being there, close to her, with no ulterior motive—can deepen your bond and strengthen the trust between you. It's about creating a space where she feels valued and loved for who she is, not just for what she can offer. This kind of physical closeness is a powerful way to nurture your relationship, showing that your love is rooted in a genuine desire to be close and connected, even in the quietest, most peaceful moments.

78

Brighten Her Day with Blooms of Love

Surprising her with a beautiful bouquet of flowers is a classic and meaningful way to brighten her day and show your affection. Whether it's a bouquet of her favorite blooms, a vibrant arrangement that reflects her personality, or simply a spontaneous selection that caught your eye, this gesture communicates that you're thinking of her and want to make her feel special. The sight and scent of fresh flowers can instantly uplift her mood and bring a touch of nature's charm into her day.

This act of giving flowers, especially when unexpected, is a timeless symbol of love and appreciation. It shows that you're attentive to what she enjoys and willing to go out of your way to make her smile. The effort you put into choosing or arranging the bouquet reflects your care and consideration, turning an ordinary moment into something memorable and heartwarming. It's a simple yet impactful way to express your love, making her feel valued and appreciated.

What makes this even more exciting is that there are companies offering flower subscription services, so you can surprise her with fresh bouquets on a regular basis—maybe monthly. Imagine the delight she'll feel when a new arrangement arrives unexpectedly, brightening her space and reminding her of your affection. These services let you customize the flowers, ensuring she gets her favorite blooms or something new and unique each time. It's a hassle-free way to keep the romance alive, with consistent gestures that show she's always on your mind. Plus, it's like having a little piece of nature delivered right to her door!

79

Walk as the Sun Paints the Sky

Taking a scenic walk during sunset or sunrise is a romantic way to spend quality time together, embracing the beauty of nature while strengthening your bond. The quiet, peaceful atmosphere of these times of day creates the perfect backdrop for meaningful conversations or simply enjoying each other's presence in silence. Whether it's the golden hues of a sunset or the soft light of a new day, these moments can feel magical, offering a sense of calm and connection.

Walking together as the sun rises or sets allows you to share in the tranquility of the moment, appreciating the world around you and the relationship you've built. It's an opportunity to pause and reflect on life's beauty, both in nature and in your partnership. This simple yet profound experience can leave both of you feeling refreshed, closer, and more in tune with each other, making it a cherished memory you'll both carry with you.

Capture Your Love in a Jar of Memories

Creating a memory jar filled with notes of cherished moments is a heartfelt way to celebrate the special experiences you've shared together. Each note can capture a memory—whether it's a simple day spent together, a milestone in your relationship, or a small but meaningful gesture that made you both smile. Over time, this jar becomes a treasure trove of your relationship's highlights, offering a tangible reminder of the love and happiness you've built together.

This gift is more than just a collection of memories; it's a symbol of the journey you've shared and the many ways you've grown together. Whenever she wants to reminisce or needs a reminder of your love, she can pull out a note and relive that special moment. The memory jar is a unique and personal way to express your appreciation for all the little things that make your relationship so meaningful, reinforcing the bond you share in a deeply sentimental way.

Put Your Heart into Words She'll Treasure

Writing a poem to express your feelings for her is a deeply personal and romantic way to convey the depth of your love and admiration. A poem allows you to capture your emotions in a creative and meaningful way, turning your thoughts and feelings into beautiful verses that she can treasure. Whether it's a simple rhyme or a more elaborate composition, the effort and sincerity behind your words will speak volumes about how much she means to you.

Your poem doesn't have to be perfect; it just needs to come from the heart. You can reflect on the qualities you adore in her, the memories you've shared, or the dreams you have for your future together. By putting your feelings into words, you're giving her a piece of yourself that she can hold onto, a reminder of your love that she can revisit whenever she wishes. This intimate gesture is a timeless expression of affection, making her feel cherished in a way that only words can.

For an even more romantic touch, consider reading the poem to her in an intimate setting before presenting it to her. Whether it's by candlelight at home, during a quiet moment in the park, or somewhere meaningful to your relationship, this creates a deeply personal moment she'll never forget. Your voice will bring the words to life, adding an emotional layer to your heartfelt expression. The act of reading it aloud shows vulnerability and confidence, turning the gesture into an unforgettable declaration of your love.

82

Leave Mirror and Fridge Notes That Lift Her Spirits Daily

Placing uplifting messages on the bathroom mirror or fridge is a simple yet powerful way to brighten her day and remind her of your love and support. Whether it's an encouraging quote, a sweet note, or a few words expressing your appreciation, these messages can provide a boost of positivity when she least expects it. The bathroom mirror and fridge are places she's likely to visit first thing in the morning or throughout the day, making them perfect spots for little surprises that can set a positive tone.

These notes can be as creative or straightforward as you like—written on sticky notes, cards, or even with erasable markers. The key is to make them personal and genuine, reflecting your emotions and the encouragement you want to share. This simple yet meaningful act demonstrates that she's on your mind and that you want to brighten her day, reinforcing the idea that she is treasured and appreciated every single day.

83

Sweeten Her Day with a Delicate Treat

Surprising her with her favorite candy or ice cream is a sweet and simple way to show that you're thinking of her. This kind gesture can brighten her day, whether it's a spontaneous treat after a long day or just because you know it's something she enjoys. By remembering and indulging her favorite sweet, you show your attentiveness to her preferences and your desire to add a little extra happiness to her life.

The act of picking up her favorite candy or ice cream shows that you pay attention to the small things that make her happy. It's a lighthearted way to say, "I care about you," and can turn an ordinary moment into something special. Sharing a sweet treat together also creates a moment of connection, where you can enjoy each other's company and savor the simple pleasures in life.

If you want to turn it up a notch, check out high-end grocery stores that carry gourmet ice cream brands you won't typically find in your local supermarket. These premium brands don't skimp on flavor pieces—think rich ribbons of caramel, chunks of brownies, or swirls of real fruit compote. Picking up a pint (or two) of these indulgent treats shows that you're going the extra mile to make her feel special. It's not just about satisfying her sweet tooth; it's about creating an elevated experience that lets her know she deserves the very best.

84

Turn Everyday Outings into Playful Romance

Flirting with her when you're out in public is a playful and affectionate way to keep the spark alive in your relationship. Whether it's a teasing comment, a knowing glance, or a light touch on the arm, these small gestures can make her feel special and remind her of the chemistry that drew you together in the first place. Public flirting adds an element of excitement and fun to your interactions, showing that your attraction to her is as strong as ever.

This kind of lighthearted affection in public also demonstrates your pride and happiness in being with her, letting her—and everyone else—know how much she means to you. It reinforces the connection between you, turning everyday outings into moments of romance and joy. By flirting with her, you keep the romance alive and ensure that she always feels desired, appreciated, and loved.

If you flirted with her to get her, why not flirt with her to keep her? A playful wink, a cheeky compliment, or a subtle touch can reignite the same butterflies you both felt in the beginning. It's a fun way to show her that even after all this time, you still see her as the captivating woman who caught your eye. Plus, when you flirt in public, it adds a little thrill to the moment—it's like sharing an inside joke or a secret just between the two of you. It keeps the connection fresh, exciting, and full of life.

85

Craft a Coupon Book Full of Love and Fun

Creating a coupon book filled with various favors or activities is a fun and creative way to offer personalized gestures of love and care. Each coupon can be redeemed for something special, like a homemade dinner, a relaxing foot massage, a day free of chores, or even a spontaneous adventure of her choice. The possibilities are endless, and the best part is that the coupons can be customized to her preferences and your unique relationship.

This gift allows her to choose when and how to enjoy the favors, making it an ongoing reminder of your commitment to her happiness. It's a creative way to show that you're willing to go the extra mile to make her feel loved and appreciated. Whether she redeems them all at once or saves them for when she needs a little pick-me-up, the coupon book is a delightful and interactive way to keep the romance and fun alive in your relationship.

Nowadays, most people have printers and access to editing software—even on their phones—so creating a coupon book shouldn't be too difficult. Use a simple template or design it from scratch to make it feel personal and unique. Add creative touches like colorful borders, playful fonts, or even little inside jokes that make the coupons extra special. If you're feeling crafty, you can handwrite them on fancy paper or cardstock for a more intimate touch. The key is to put thought into each coupon, ensuring they reflect her favorite activities and the little things she loves most about being with you.

86

Show You've Still Got It by Carrying Her to Bed

Carrying her to bed is a sweet and romantic gesture that showcases your affection and care. Whether she's fallen asleep on the couch after a long day, or you just want to surprise her with a playful act of chivalry, lifting her into your arms and carrying her to bed creates a moment of closeness and tenderness. This simple act can make her feel cherished and protected, reinforcing the bond between you.

It's a gesture that goes beyond the physical—carrying her to bed shows that you're attentive to her needs and willing to go out of your way to make her feel comfortable and loved. It's a small, intimate moment that can turn into a cherished memory, reminding her of how much she means to you. This act of care and affection is a beautiful way to end the day, ensuring she feels valued and adored as she drifts off to sleep.

Now, if for some reason you find yourself attempting the impossible and struggling to lift her, it might be a sign to get back in the weight room! After all, many women appreciate a physically strong man. While the gesture is about tenderness and care, being able to carry her with ease certainly adds to the romance. So, if you're feeling a little out of shape, take it as motivation to build your strength—not just for her, but for yourself too. It's a win-win that'll leave you both feeling more confident.

87

Display Your Love Through Digital Memories

Gifting her a digital photo frame preloaded with photos is a meaningful and modern way to celebrate your shared memories. By carefully selecting and uploading a collection of cherished photos—whether they capture special moments, everyday smiles, or milestones in your relationship—you create a personalized and dynamic display of your love story. Every time she looks at the frame, she'll be reminded of the wonderful journey you've experienced together.

This gift allows her to relive your favorite memories with just a glance, bringing warmth and joy to any room. The digital photo frame can be updated with new photos, making it a dynamic keepsake that grows with your relationship. It's a perfect way to keep your connection front and center in her life, celebrating your shared experiences and the love that continues to flourish over time.

88

Honor Every Achievement She Earns

Showing pride in her accomplishments, whether big or small, is a powerful way to uplift and support her. By celebrating her achievements—whether it's a major career milestone, completing a challenging project, or simply handling a tough day with grace—you demonstrate your appreciation for her hard work, resilience, and dedication. Let her know that you recognize and value all she does, and that her efforts do not go unnoticed.

Publicly praising her accomplishments, sharing in her excitement, or surprising her with a small token of recognition can boost her confidence and reinforce her self-worth. This kind of encouragement demonstrates that you are genuinely invested in her success and happiness. By consistently celebrating her victories, you build a foundation of mutual respect and admiration that deepens your relationship and makes her feel appreciated and treasured every day.

89

Share the Beliefs That Shape Your Heart

Opening up about your strongest beliefs is a meaningful way to deepen your connection and build a foundation of trust and understanding in your relationship. Sharing your core values, principles, and what drives you in life allows her to see a deeper, more vulnerable side of you. Whether it's your beliefs about love, faith, family, or personal integrity, discussing these topics fosters mutual respect and insight into each other's worldviews.

This level of openness can lead to important conversations about how your beliefs align or differ, helping you both to navigate your relationship with greater clarity and empathy. It also shows that you trust her with your innermost thoughts and that you value her opinion and perspective. By sharing what matters most to you, you create a space for honest dialogue and strengthen the emotional bond that ties you together.

While this is something that should ideally happen early in the relationship, it's important to remember that both of you grow and evolve over time. Your beliefs may shift as you experience life together, and revisiting these conversations ensures you stay connected as individuals and as a couple. Being mindful of this evolution allows your relationship to adapt and thrive, even as your perspectives change. These ongoing discussions not only strengthen your bond but also provide a framework for navigating challenges and celebrating milestones together with mutual understanding.

90

Transform Chaos into Calm Together with Care

Helping her organize or declutter a space is a practical and caring way to support her and show that you're invested in her well-being. Whether it's tackling a messy closet, organizing a home office, or decluttering a shared living area, your assistance can make a potentially overwhelming task more manageable and even enjoyable. This gesture demonstrates your willingness to be there for her, not just in the fun moments, but also in the everyday tasks that contribute to a more peaceful and organized life.

Working together to create a tidy and functional space can bring a sense of accomplishment and relief, making the environment more pleasant and stress-free. It's also an opportunity to bond over a shared goal, turning what might seem like a chore into a rewarding experience. Your support in helping her organize or declutter shows that you're committed to creating a harmonious home and that you care about making her life a little easier.

If your significant other struggles with letting go of things and could give the folks on Hoarders a run for their money, tread lightly. Start with small, manageable areas, and focus on creating wins that don't feel overwhelming. Instead of insisting on drastic changes, approach the task with patience and understanding. Offer to help sort items into categories like "keep," "donate," and "maybe." Be mindful that what seems like clutter to you may hold sentimental value for her, so let her take the lead on what stays and what goes. And if all else fails, frame it as a way to make space for future treasures—sometimes the promise of new possibilities is the best motivator!

Explore Unique Eats and Moments

Trying out a new restaurant or food truck together is an adventurous and enjoyable way to explore new flavors and create shared memories. Whether it's a trendy eatery in your neighborhood, a highly recommended food truck, or a hidden gem you've both been curious about, discovering new culinary experiences adds excitement and novelty to your routine. It's a fun way to break away from the usual spots and try something different, whether it's a new cuisine, an innovative dish, or a unique dining atmosphere.

This shared culinary adventure allows you to bond over your mutual love for food, engage in lively conversations about your experiences, and perhaps find a new favorite place to return to. It's not just about the food; it's about the experience of exploring together, enjoying each other's company, and making the outing a special occasion. Trying out new restaurants or food trucks adds a sense of adventure to your relationship, making everyday moments feel fresh and exciting.

Master the Art of Truly Listening

This is definitely a tough one for some. Practicing the art of truly listening to her is one of the most powerful ways to show your love and respect. When she speaks, give her your full attention—put away distractions, make eye contact, and focus on what she's saying. Listening deeply means not just hearing her words, but also understanding her emotions, concerns, and needs. By doing so, you show her that her thoughts and feelings matter to you, fostering a deeper emotional connection.

Active listening involves asking meaningful questions, reflecting on what she's shared, and responding with empathy. This approach helps to build trust and ensures that she feels heard and understood. In moments of happiness or challenge, your willingness to listen without judgment or interruption can offer her the reassurance and support she needs. Practicing true listening deepens your connection, fostering a relationship rooted in mutual respect and open communication.

I personally like to follow the 80/20 rule: listen 80% of the time and speak 20%. Even when what she's saying doesn't quite make sense to you, or might not be completely factual, practice patience. Give yourself the opportunity to fully process what she's sharing before jumping to conclusions. Sometimes, just giving her more space to express herself leads to clarity or a new perspective you hadn't considered. And, remember, you won't always make perfect sense either. It's important to have patience with yourself, too—sometimes you need space to gather your own thoughts. By listening with an open mind, you show her that her voice matters, and that can deepen your connection.

Heal and Strengthen Through True Forgiveness

Forgiving her and asking for her forgiveness are essential steps in maintaining a healthy and loving relationship. No relationship is without its challenges, and sometimes hurtful words or actions can create tension or misunderstandings. Offering genuine forgiveness when she has wronged you demonstrates your commitment to the relationship and your willingness to move forward without holding onto resentment. It's an act of love that heals wounds and rebuilds trust.

Equally important is the ability to recognize when you've hurt her and to sincerely ask for her forgiveness, especially for where you've fallen short. Admitting your mistakes, acknowledging your shortcomings, and expressing remorse show that you value her feelings and the strength of your bond. This mutual practice of forgiveness fosters a compassionate and understanding environment where both of you can grow together. It strengthens your connection by ensuring that love, rather than anger or pride, guides your relationship, allowing both of you to find peace and continue building a future together.

For me, the forgiving part was never as tough as the forgetting. I used to keep a mental inventory of things done to me—sometimes, I still do—but it's not healthy. Holding onto those grudges only adds unnecessary stress to your life and your relationship. Trust me, I've preached this to myself for years: learn to let it go. Carrying that baggage only weighs you down, and in the end, true forgiveness is about freeing yourself from the past, not just brushing things under the rug. Letting go allows you to move forward with a clearer mind and a lighter heart.

94

Secretly Take Note of Her Clothing and Shoe Styles and Sizes

Secretly taking note of her clothing and shoe styles and sizes is a considerate way to show that you pay attention to the details that make her unique. By quietly observing what she enjoys wearing—her favorite colors, patterns, cuts, and brands—you can surprise her with gifts that reflect her personal style. Knowing her sizes allows you to select items that will fit perfectly, making the gesture even more special.

This attentiveness demonstrates that you care about her preferences and want to make her feel special. It also comes in handy when you want to plan a surprise, whether it's a new outfit, a pair of shoes she's been eyeing, or something as simple as a cozy sweater. By understanding her style and size, you can confidently pick out something she'll love, showing that you're attuned to her tastes and eager to bring her joy.

This is also about actively—but silently—paying attention to what she's bringing home and how her preferences evolve. Be mindful that her sizes may change over time, and that's perfectly normal. Keeping up with these changes without making a big deal out of it shows sensitivity and thoughtfulness. It's not just about memorizing a number on a tag—it's about understanding her needs and making her feel seen and appreciated, no matter how her wardrobe or body may shift. Plus, this quiet observation makes your surprises feel even more personal and well-timed.

95

Offer to Be Her Fitness Partner for Life

Offering to be her workout buddy is a supportive and motivating way to strengthen your relationship while prioritizing health and fitness together. Whether she enjoys running, yoga, weightlifting, or trying new fitness classes, joining her in these activities shows that you're committed to her well-being and eager to share in her interests. Exercising together can be a fun and rewarding way to bond, push each other toward your goals, and celebrate your progress as a team.

Being her workout partner means more than just showing up at the gym—it's about encouraging her, setting challenges, and offering support when the going gets tough. It's a way to show that you're in this together, helping each other stay accountable and motivated. The shared experience of working out can bring you closer, fostering a sense of camaraderie and teamwork that extends beyond the gym and into your everyday lives.

Now…be smart about how you bring this up. You know your woman better than anyone, and the last thing you want is for her to think you're subtly suggesting she's gained weight or that her back has gotten too big. That could set off alarm bells and create unnecessary tension. Instead, frame it as a way to spend quality time together and support each other's health goals. Approach it with enthusiasm for fitness, not as a critique of her appearance. By being thoughtful and encouraging, you can motivate each other and strengthen your bond without misunderstandings.

96

Give Her Space to Breathe and Reset

Giving her the space she needs to reset is a loving and understanding way to support her well-being. Life can be overwhelming, and everyone needs time to recharge and find balance. By recognizing when she needs a break—whether it's some quiet time alone, a day to herself, or even a solo getaway—you show that you respect her needs and want what's best for her. This space allows her to refresh her mind and spirit, returning to the relationship feeling more centered and at peace.

Granting her this time without pressure or judgment demonstrates your trust in her and your commitment to her happiness. It also reinforces the idea that you're supportive of her self-care, understanding that a healthy relationship sometimes requires time apart to nurture individual well-being. By giving her the room to breathe and reset, you contribute to a stronger, more balanced partnership where both of you can thrive.

97

Learn, Laugh, and Create Delicious Memories Together

Taking cooking or baking classes together is a flavorful and interactive way to bond while learning something new. Whether you're both beginners in the kitchen or aiming to enhance your culinary expertise, these classes offer an enjoyable opportunity to collaborate, try out new recipes, and craft delicious dishes or treats. The experience of preparing food together can be filled with humor, creativity, and, of course, the satisfaction of savoring the results of your efforts.

These classes allow you to explore different cuisines, discover new ingredients, and develop techniques that you can bring back to your own kitchen. Beyond the practical skills, the experience fosters communication, cooperation, and a shared sense of accomplishment. Whether you're crafting the perfect soufflé, mastering the art of homemade pasta, or decorating a batch of cupcakes, cooking or baking classes are a wonderful way to create lasting memories and strengthen your relationship through the love of food.

Massage Her Feet After a Long, Rough Day

Massaging her feet after a rough day is a thoughtful and caring way to help her unwind and show that you're attentive to her needs. After a long day on her feet, a gentle foot massage can provide immense relief, easing away tension and stress. This simple but intimate gesture demonstrates your love and concern for her well-being, offering her a moment of relaxation and comfort.

As you massage her feet, you're not only helping her physically but also creating a space where she can feel cared for and cherished. The act of taking the time to soothe her tired feet shows that you notice the little things and are willing to go the extra mile to make her feel better. It's a small but meaningful way to support her, turning an ordinary evening into a special moment of connection and love.

Now, if her feet look like she's been busting bricks in a martial arts exhibition, you might want to wrap up that massage and book her an appointment with a heavy-duty expert—someone with Craftsman or Milwaukee-level equipment! Just kidding, of course, but seriously, do your best to give her feet a much-needed break. Even if they've seen better days, your care and effort will go a long way in making her feel pampered and appreciated. It's about showing her that you're willing to help her unwind, no matter what.

Offer to Gently Wash and Pamper Her Body

Offering to wash her body is an intimate and tender gesture that goes beyond physical care to express deep affection and love. Whether it's in the shower or a relaxing bath, this act of service allows you to care for her in a gentle, nurturing way. By washing her body, you're not just attending to her physical needs but also creating a moment of trust, closeness, and connection that deepens your bond.

This gesture can be both soothing and sensual, especially if she enjoys using exfoliating scrubs or other skincare products. There's nothing quite like a thorough back scrub during a shower or bath, providing her with a luxurious experience that leaves her feeling refreshed and rejuvenated. It's a way to show that you're fully present, attentive to her needs, and eager to offer your love in a way that makes her feel cherished and valued. Washing her body can turn an everyday routine into a special moment of connection, making her feel pampered and deeply cared for.

It's important to be mindful and appreciate a woman's body during this intimate act. While guys might wash themselves with the intensity of scrubbing a dirty skillet, this is not the time for that approach. Take your cues from her—learn how she likes to be scrubbed, whether it's a gentle touch with a loofah or a soothing massage with a body wash. This is an opportunity to slow down, show her that you value every part of her, and treat her with the care she deserves. By being attentive to her preferences, you turn what could be routine into a deeply personal and loving gesture.

100

Bonus: Pour Into Her Spiritually, Take Her to a Religious Service

Taking her to a religious service is a meaningful way to share your faith and deepen your spiritual connection as a couple. Whether it's a regular service, a special holiday celebration, or an uplifting community event, attending a service together allows you to grow closer not just emotionally but also spiritually. This shared experience can strengthen your bond by aligning your values, beliefs, and hopes for the future.

Being together in a place of worship provides a sense of peace and unity, offering an opportunity to reflect on your relationship in the context of a higher purpose. It's a time to pray together, support each other in your spiritual journeys, and connect with a community that shares your faith. Taking her to a religious service demonstrates your commitment to nurturing your relationship on all levels, including the spiritual, and reinforces the importance of faith in your lives together.

Be mindful of her comfort zone when inviting her to a service, especially if it's new for her. I learned this the hard way when I took her to a "high-spirited" church, and she spent the entire service looking around like she was about to be robbed or taken out by the woman next to her who was waving her hands with fervor. While your intentions may be good, it's important to choose a setting where she can feel comfortable and engaged rather than overwhelmed. If she's new to this kind of experience, start with a gentler introduction and let her ease into the spiritual journey at her own pace.

For those who may not follow a religious tradition, finding ways to nurture your spiritual or emotional connection can still be a meaningful experience. You might consider engaging in activities that promote mindfulness, reflection, or shared values, such as meditation, nature walks, or attending community events that foster a sense of unity and belonging. The goal is to find a way to connect on a deeper level, whether it's through a shared sense of purpose, mutual respect, or the pursuit of personal growth.

Whether or not religion plays a role in your lives, taking time to engage in activities that align with both your values and hers can strengthen your bond. Consider participating in a community service project, attending an event that supports a cause you both care about, or simply spending time together reflecting on your hopes and dreams for the future. These moments of connection can deepen your relationship and help you grow together as a couple, creating a sense of shared meaning and purpose without the need for religious practices.

101

Sow a Seed into Her Business Idea

Sowing a seed into her business idea is a powerful way to show your belief in her dreams and ambitions. Whether it's offering financial support, helping with initial startup costs, or contributing your skills and expertise, your investment in her business venture demonstrates your commitment to her success. This act of faith in her abilities and vision can provide the encouragement and resources she needs to take the next step toward making her idea a reality.

Supporting her entrepreneurial goals goes beyond financial assistance—it's about showing that you're her partner in every sense, willing to stand by her as she pursues her passions. By sowing this seed, you're not only helping her grow her business but also strengthening your relationship through shared goals and mutual support. Your belief in her potential can inspire her to reach new heights, knowing that you're there to cheer her on and contribute to her journey.

I've seen firsthand the amazing things that can happen from planting a seed like this. I noticed she was working on an old, busted-up laptop for another company and decided to surprise her with a brand-new one, complete with a note about how great she is and how she could use her talents to start something for herself. At the same time, I made sure to hold down the fort, giving her the stability and space she needed to push forward and make her business a reality. That simple gesture helped supercharge her success by removing financial barriers and letting her focus on her passion. Supporting her in every way possible, both emotionally and practically, made all the difference.

102

Explore the Wonders of Nature Side by Side

Visiting a zoo or aquarium together is a delightful way to spend the day, surrounded by the wonders of nature and the excitement of discovering new animals or marine life. Whether you're admiring majestic lions, playful otters, or colorful tropical fish, this shared experience offers plenty of opportunities for fun, learning, and connection. Exploring the exhibits side by side allows you to enjoy the beauty of the natural world while creating new memories together.

A trip to the zoo or aquarium is not just about the animals—it's about the joy of exploring something new with each other, engaging in lighthearted conversation, and maybe even finding a favorite animal to revisit. The relaxed pace of the day gives you time to bond, enjoy each other's company, and appreciate the simple pleasures of spending time together. It's a perfect outing for couples who love nature, animals, and the chance to create lasting memories in a vibrant and educational setting.

103

Light Up Your Love with DIY Candles

Using a DIY candle-making kit together is a creative and cozy way to bond while crafting something beautiful and fragrant for your home. Whether you're both new to candle-making or already have some experience, this activity allows you to collaborate on designing candles with your favorite scents, colors, and shapes. The process of melting wax, adding fragrances, and pouring it into molds can be both fun and relaxing, giving you time to chat, laugh, and enjoy each other's company.

Creating candles together also adds a personal touch to your living space, with each candle representing a memory of the time spent together crafting it. Once your candles are made, you can light them during a romantic dinner, a cozy evening at home, or simply to add warmth to any room. This DIY project is not just about the final product—it's about the experience of working together, learning something new, and making something that you can both enjoy long after the candles are lit.

104

Tell Her Exactly How Much She Means to You

Taking the time to openly share how much she means to you is one of the most powerful ways to strengthen your relationship and make her feel truly valued. Whether it's through a heartfelt conversation, a written letter, or even a simple but sincere text message, expressing your love and appreciation for her can deepen your emotional connection and reaffirm your commitment. Let her know the specific qualities you admire, the ways she enriches your life, and how grateful you are to have her by your side.

This kind of open and honest communication can have a profound impact, reminding her of her worth and the special place she holds in your heart. It's important to be genuine and specific, highlighting the little things as well as the big ones that make your relationship unique. By sharing your feelings with her, you not only make her feel loved but also create a foundation of trust and understanding that can carry you through any challenges that may arise.

This can't be something you go to only during adversity or whenever you're in the doghouse. Sharing how much she means to you should be a regular practice, not a last-minute strategy to smooth things over. Make it a point to express your appreciation in the good times, too—when things are running smoothly, and there's no particular reason to do it other than because you truly feel it. This consistency reinforces the strength of your bond, showing her that your love and gratitude are constants in your relationship, not just damage control.

105

Let Go of Unrealistic Expectations About Her

One of the most meaningful ways to nurture your relationship is to release unrealistic expectations you may have placed on her. It's natural to want your partner to be their best self, but expecting perfection or holding her to an idealized standard can lead to unnecessary stress and tension. She's human, with strengths, flaws, and complexities, just like you. Accepting her as she is allows her to feel loved and valued for her true self, not for how well she fits into a mold.

Unrealistic expectations can create pressure, making her feel like she's constantly falling short, even when she's giving her all. Whether it's expecting her to always be cheerful, have endless energy, or meet every need without faltering, it's important to recognize that life doesn't work that way. Instead of focusing on what she's not, appreciate what she is—someone who loves you, tries her best, and shares her journey with you.

By letting go of these expectations, you create a space where both of you can thrive as individuals and as a couple. Celebrate her efforts, even when things aren't perfect, and show gratitude for the ways she adds value to your life. The freedom from judgment fosters trust, compassion, and an environment where love can flourish authentically. When you focus on acceptance instead of perfection, you strengthen your relationship in ways that last a lifetime.

106

Teach Her Skills You're Passionate About

Offering to teach her something you're skilled at is a wonderful way to share your passions and expertise while strengthening your bond. Whether it's playing a musical instrument, cooking a favorite dish, fixing things around the house, or mastering a sport, teaching her something you excel at creates an opportunity for you both to connect on a deeper level. It's a chance to share a part of yourself, letting her into your world and showing her what you love.

This experience can be both fun and rewarding as you guide her through the learning process, offering patience, encouragement, and praise. It's also a way to demonstrate your support and investment in her growth, showing that you're eager to share your knowledge and help her develop new skills. Teaching her something you're good at not only brings you closer but also creates lasting memories of teamwork, focus, and shared achievement.

107

Take Her Out for a Game of Mini-Golf

Taking her out for a game of mini-golf is a fun and lighthearted way to spend time together while enjoying some friendly competition. Mini-golf's cheerful atmosphere provides the perfect backdrop for humor, playful banter, and connection as you navigate the whimsical courses. Whether you're striving for a hole-in-one or simply enjoying the experience, the relaxed setting allows you to bond without the formality of other activities.

This outing is about more than just the game—it's an opportunity to enjoy each other's company in a carefree setting. You can share playful banter, cheer each other on, and maybe even discover a new shared hobby. Mini-golf offers a break from the usual routine, providing a memorable experience that combines fun, connection, and a bit of adventure. It's a simple yet meaningful way to create new memories together.

108

Guard Her Heart with Every Thoughtful Action

Protecting her heart means being mindful of the trust she's placed in you and ensuring that her emotional well-being is safeguarded, even when she's not around. Your actions, words, and decisions should reflect the same care and respect as if she were standing right beside you. This means establishing and maintaining boundaries with others, especially when it comes to friendships with women. It's not just about avoiding wrongdoing—it's about being proactive in making her feel secure and prioritized in your life.

A key part of this is ensuring she knows your female friends and feels comfortable with those relationships. Transparency builds trust, and introducing her to the women in your life shows that you have nothing to hide. At the same time, it's essential to be honest with yourself about the nature of those friendships. Make sure they are genuine, platonic connections—not "potentials" or bench players waiting for an opportunity. If there's even a hint of ambiguity, it's time to reevaluate and make sure your priorities align with protecting her heart.

Guarding her heart is about honoring your commitment, both in her presence and in her absence. It means avoiding situations or behaviors that could lead to misunderstandings or harm the trust you've built. By ensuring your boundaries are clear and your intentions are pure, you not only protect her heart but also reinforce the foundation of respect and love that keeps your relationship strong. When she knows her heart is safe with you, it deepens the connection and strengthens the bond you share.

109

Surprise Her with Luxurious, Popular Perfumes

Surprising her with a popular perfume is a meaningful way to show that you care about her preferences and want to make her feel special. A carefully chosen fragrance can be a deeply personal gift, one that complements her style and adds to her confidence. Whether it's a classic scent she's always adored or a trendy new perfume that's caught her attention, the effort you put into selecting the perfect fragrance reflects your attentiveness to her tastes and desires.

Perfume has the power to evoke emotions and create lasting memories, making it a gift she can enjoy daily. Each time she wears the perfume you selected, she'll be reminded of the care and affection behind your gesture. This simple yet luxurious act of love enhances her routine, reinforcing how much she means to you and how well you understand her preferences.

I personally like stores like Neiman Marcus and other high-end retailers for this kind of gift. Not only do they carry some of the most coveted fragrances, but the staff can guide you on what's popular and even suggest complementary pairings. Whether it's layering scents or matching the perfume to her style, these experts make the selection process easy and enjoyable. Plus, shopping in such an upscale environment adds to the experience, making the gift feel even more luxurious and special.

Embark on a Horseback Adventure Together

Going horseback riding together is a unique and adventurous way to connect while enjoying the beauty of nature. Whether you're both experienced riders or trying it for the first time, this activity offers an opportunity to bond over a shared experience that can be both exhilarating and serene. Riding through scenic trails, feeling the rhythm of the horse beneath you, and taking in the surrounding landscape can create a memorable and peaceful outing.

Horseback riding encourages teamwork and trust, both with your horse and each other. It's a chance to step away from the usual routine, embrace the outdoors, and maybe even learn something new about each other in the process. The combination of physical activity, natural beauty, and the simple joy of being together makes horseback riding a wonderful way to deepen your connection and create lasting memories.

III

Gift a Gourmet Food Subscription She'll Love

Gifting her a subscription to a food service is a practical and considerate way to bring convenience and variety to her life. Whether it's a meal kit delivery service, a subscription for gourmet snacks, or even a wine or coffee club, this gift offers her the opportunity to explore new flavors and enjoy delicious treats without the effort of planning or shopping. It's a gift that keeps on giving, adding enjoyment and simplicity to her routine with each delivery.

A food service subscription can also be an opportunity for both of you to explore new cuisines and enjoy meals together, turning dinner time into a fun and creative experience. Whether she's a foodie who loves discovering new dishes or someone who appreciates the convenience of having meals planned out, this gift shows that you care about her tastes and want to make her day-to-day life a little easier and more enjoyable.

112

Celebrate Every Milestone with Praise and Love

Marking her milestones with celebrations and praise is a meaningful way to honor her achievements and show your support. Whether she's reached a personal goal, achieved a professional milestone, or completed a long-term project, taking the time to acknowledge her success reinforces how proud you are of her hard work and dedication. Celebrating these moments, whether with a special dinner, a heartfelt note, or a small gathering of loved ones, makes her feel valued and appreciated.

Your praise and recognition can boost her confidence and motivation, letting her know that her efforts are seen and cherished. By making a point to celebrate her milestones, you show that you're invested in her journey and that you're eager to share in the joy of her accomplishments. This kind of encouragement strengthens your bond, creating a relationship where mutual respect and admiration thrive.

You can also put these milestones on your calendar as an annual tradition to celebrate her achievements. Whether it's the anniversary of her promotion, the launch of her business, or the day she completed a significant goal, making it a recurring event shows that you honor her accomplishments consistently. It's a sincere way to say, "I see you, and I celebrate all that you've done." This habit not only keeps her motivated but also creates cherished moments of recognition that you both can look forward to year after year.

113

Deepen Intimacy Using a Feather and Blindfold

Using a blindfold and feather to heighten intimacy is a playful and sensual way to explore deeper levels of connection and trust in your relationship. When one partner is blindfolded, the removal of sight amplifies other senses, making every touch, sound, and sensation more intense and engaging. A feather adds a tantalizing element to this experience, with its soft, delicate touch creating a heightened awareness and anticipation.

Gently running a feather along her skin while she's blindfolded can create a range of sensations, from soothing to thrilling, depending on how and where it's used. This combination encourages open communication, as the blindfolded partner relies on the other to guide the experience, deepening the trust between you. The feather's light touch enhances the focus on sensation, turning your intimate moments into an exploration of pleasure and connection, where every touch is felt more deeply and cherished.

If you do it right, especially after a few drinks, you might just unleash her inner beast, and she'll transform into She-Hulk—but don't worry, that's a good thing! The blindfold and feather combo, paired with a little liquid courage, can amplify sensations and reactions in ways you won't see coming. If she starts grabbing at you or flips the script entirely, congratulations—you've officially awakened her alter ego. Just hang on and enjoy the ride, because once she's in the zone, there's no turning back!

Take Charge of an Unforgettable Date Night

Taking charge of planning a special date night is a considerate way to show your love and initiative, creating an evening that she can fully enjoy without any stress or effort on her part. Whether it's a romantic dinner at a favorite restaurant, a cozy night in with her favorite movie and homemade meal, or an adventurous outing trying something new, your thoughtful preparation will make her feel valued and cared for.

By handling all the details—from choosing the venue or activity to arranging any necessary reservations or preparations—you give her the gift of being able to relax and simply enjoy the moment. This gesture shows that you're attentive to her preferences and eager to create a memorable experience that's all about celebrating your relationship. Planning a special date night not only strengthens your bond but also reinforces your commitment to keeping the romance alive.

Remember, the goal here is to take initiative, so resist the urge to involve her in the planning like you normally might. It's tempting to fall back on having her take over, but this is your opportunity to step up. If there's something you're unsure about—whether it's picking the right restaurant or setting the mood—educate yourself, put in the effort, and make it happen. Planning a date night isn't rocket science, and you'll score major points just by showing her you can handle it. Trust yourself and just do it!

115

Unwind Together at a Beach or Lake

Visiting a nearby beach or lake together is a refreshing way to escape the everyday routine and enjoy the beauty of nature. Whether you're lounging on the sand, taking a leisurely swim, or simply strolling along the shoreline, the tranquil environment provides the perfect backdrop for relaxation and connection. The sound of the waves, the feel of the sand or water, and the open sky create a peaceful atmosphere where you can unwind and share meaningful moments.

A trip to the beach or lake offers countless opportunities for bonding, whether you're building sandcastles, enjoying a picnic, or watching the sunset together. It's a chance to leave behind the stress of daily life and focus on each other, creating lasting memories in a serene and beautiful setting. This kind of outing not only strengthens your connection but also allows you to appreciate the simple pleasures of being together in the great outdoors.

116

Prepare a Romantic, Blissful Bubble Bath

Giving her a romantic bubble bath is a luxurious and intimate way to pamper her and create a relaxing atmosphere where she can unwind and feel cherished. Start by preparing the bath with a special bubble bath liquid that she loves—something with a soothing scent like lavender, vanilla, or jasmine. For an extra touch of indulgence, consider adding a bath bomb that fizzes and releases nourishing oils and captivating aromas into the water.

To elevate the ambiance, scatter rose petals across the water's surface, creating a beautiful and romantic visual effect. Arrange candles around the bathroom to provide a soft, warm glow, enhancing the tranquility of the setting. You can also play some relaxing music in the background, whether it's her favorite soft tunes, classical music, or calming nature sounds, to help her fully relax and escape into the moment.

As she enjoys the bath, you can offer a glass of wine, champagne, or herbal tea to complement the experience. This thoughtful and carefully prepared bubble bath not only gives her a chance to de-stress but also shows your deep affection and attention to detail. It's a gesture that allows her to feel truly pampered and loved, turning an ordinary evening into a memorable and intimate experience.

117

Whisper Sweet Words While Kissing Her Neck

Gently kissing her neck and whispering that you love her is an intimate and romantic gesture that can instantly make her feel adored and cherished. The neck is a sensitive and delicate area, and a soft kiss there can evoke powerful emotions, creating a moment of closeness and affection. This tender act not only expresses your love physically but also deepens your emotional connection by showing her that you care about her deeply.

Whispering "I love you" as you kiss her neck adds an extra layer of warmth and sincerity to the moment. The combination of your touch and your words can create a powerful experience that she'll remember fondly. This gesture can be shared during a quiet moment, before bed, or simply when you want to remind her of your deep feelings. It's a simple yet profound way to reinforce your bond and make her feel truly special and loved.

118

Curate a Delectable Cheese and Charcuterie Board

Creating a nut, cheese, and charcuterie board is a delightful way to enjoy a relaxing and intimate evening together. Start by selecting a variety of cheeses—soft brie, sharp cheddar, tangy blue cheese, or creamy goat cheese. Complement these with an assortment of cured meats like prosciutto, salami, and chorizo, and add a selection of nuts such as almonds, walnuts, or pecans for a satisfying crunch. Include some fresh or dried fruits, olives, and perhaps a touch of honey or fig jam to balance the flavors.

To make the experience even more special, hang out on the porch or under a gazebo, where you can enjoy the fresh air and the serene atmosphere. The setting provides a perfect backdrop for unwinding and engaging in meaningful conversation. Pair your charcuterie board with a complementary wine, such as a crisp white, a bold red, or even a sparkling rosé, depending on your preferences and the flavors of your board.

As you sip wine and savor the carefully chosen selections, take the time to connect, share stories, and simply enjoy each other's company. This thoughtful and cozy setup turns an ordinary evening into a memorable, intimate experience, allowing you both to relax and appreciate the moment together.

119

Plan a Fun, Immersive Themed Dinner Night at Home

Planning a themed dinner night at home is a creative and enjoyable way to break from routine and add a bit of adventure to your dining experience. Choose a theme that excites both of you, whether it's a specific cuisine like Italian, Mexican, Japanese, or soulful Southern cuisine, known for its rich, comforting flavors. For a Soul Food night, think fried chicken, collard greens, mac and cheese, cornbread, and sweet potato pie.

To set the mood, decorate your dining area to match the theme. For an Italian night, drape a red-and-white checkered tablecloth, light candles, and play some classic Italian music in the background. For a Soul Food night, consider using earthy tones, warm lighting, and some classic Motown or jazz tunes to create an inviting atmosphere. Dressing up according to the theme can add an extra layer of fun and immersion to the evening.

During the meal, you can incorporate themed activities or games that align with the evening's vibe, such as wine or cocktail pairings, trivia, or even a movie that fits the theme. This themed dinner night isn't just about the food; it's about creating an immersive experience that allows you both to enjoy something new and exciting together, all within the comfort of your own home. It's a thoughtful way to show your love and creativity, making the evening both special and memorable.

120

Build a Blanket Fort for Cozy Connection

Building a tent and having a cozy night in is a playful and nostalgic way to reconnect and enjoy each other's company in a fun, relaxed setting. Start by gathering blankets, pillows, and sheets to create your tent, draping them over furniture to make a snug, private space. Add plenty of cushions and soft blankets inside to create a comfortable nest where you can both relax.

Once your tent is ready, bring in some snacks, your favorite drinks, and perhaps a laptop or tablet for streaming movies or shows. You can also play games, read aloud to each other, or simply talk while snuggled up in your makeshift hideaway. To add to the atmosphere, consider using string lights or battery-operated candles to give the fort a warm, inviting glow.

This cozy night in offers a break from the usual routine, allowing you to escape into your own little world where it's just the two of you. It's a chance to unwind, share smiles, and enjoy the simple pleasure of being close. Building a tent together is a reminder that you don't need anything fancy to create special moments—just a bit of creativity, a lot of love, and the happiness of being together.

121

Share Your Heart Through Timeless Love Poems or Literature

Gifting her a book of love poems or romantic literature is a timeless and meaningful way to express your feelings and share in the beauty of words. Choose a collection of classic love poems, contemporary works, or a novel that resonates with the themes of love and romance. Whether it's the passionate verses of Pablo Neruda, the heartfelt sonnets of Shakespeare, or a beloved romantic novel, this gift shows that you appreciate the power of words to convey deep emotions.

You can personalize the experience by writing a heartfelt inscription on the inside cover, explaining why you chose this particular book for her or highlighting your favorite passage. You might also select a book that holds special meaning in your relationship—perhaps one that you've mentioned before, or a story that reflects your journey together.

This gift isn't just about the literature itself; it's about the thought and care you've put into selecting something that speaks to the bond you share. Reading these poems or stories together can spark meaningful conversations, evoke shared emotions, and deepen your connection. It's a gift that can be revisited time and again, each reading bringing new layers of understanding and appreciation.

122

Experience the Thrill of Racing Go-Karts Together

Spending hours together racing go-karts is a thrilling and playful way to bond and inject some adrenaline-fueled fun into your relationship. Whether you're both competitive or just looking to enjoy the ride, go-karting offers the perfect blend of excitement and laughter. As you zoom around the track, you can challenge each other to friendly races, share tips on improving your speed, and celebrate each other's victories.

Go-karting allows you to break away from the ordinary, adding a sense of adventure to your time together. The fast-paced nature of the activity brings out your playful sides, letting you enjoy the moment without any distractions. After racing, you can reflect on the experience, perhaps over some snacks or drinks at the venue, and relive the fun moments from the track.

This outing isn't just about the thrill of the race—it's about creating shared memories, enjoying each other's company in a high-energy environment, and simply having a blast together. It's a great way to connect, laugh, and embrace a little bit of friendly competition.

123

Sit Down and Uncover Family Histories to Deepen Connection

Sitting down to talk about each other's family history is a meaningful way to deepen your understanding of one another and strengthen your bond. Sharing stories about your families—their origins, traditions, triumphs, and challenges—allows you to connect on a deeper level, providing insights into the values and experiences that have shaped each of you. This conversation can uncover shared heritage, reveal unique cultural aspects, and help you both appreciate the diverse backgrounds that you bring into your relationship.

Discussing family history also opens up opportunities to explore your roots and reflect on how your upbringing influences who you are today. It can be a time to share fond memories, honor the legacies of loved ones, and even laugh about quirky family anecdotes. By learning more about each other's family histories, you build a stronger emotional foundation, fostering a sense of unity and mutual respect.

This dialogue not only enriches your connection but also creates a sense of belonging, as you both become more familiar with the stories and traditions that are important to one another. It's a beautiful way to honor your pasts while looking forward to the future you're building together.

124

Make Yourself as Presentable as the Day You Met Her (...or Better)

Making yourself as presentable as the day you met her—or even better—is a considerate way to rekindle the excitement and admiration that marked the beginning of your relationship. Taking the time to groom yourself, dress up nicely, and pay attention to the details shows that you still care deeply about impressing her and keeping the romance alive. Additionally, maintaining your physical fitness and attractiveness is important not only for your own well-being but also as a sign of respect for her and your relationship. It demonstrates that you value her enough to keep yourself in good shape and continue being the person she was initially drawn to.

This act of getting dressed up and staying in shape isn't just about appearance; it's about creating an opportunity to revisit the feelings of those early days when everything felt fresh and exciting. Whether you're planning a special date night or just want to surprise her, presenting yourself at your best can reignite that initial spark, making her feel valued and loved all over again. It's a simple yet powerful way to show that your love for her continues to grow and that you're committed to maintaining the qualities that first attracted her.

It's easy to fall into the trap of getting comfortable and letting yourself go, but you should love yourself enough to present yourself as a top-shelf offering—regardless of your income, socio-economic status, or culture. My grandma once told me, "Every time she sees you, make her feel it." She said this to me during a low point in my life when I wasn't bringing my A-game. That stuck with me because, at the end of the day, only you control how well you present yourself. So, level up! When you look your best, it reflects self-respect and shows her that you're still putting in the effort, just like you did in the beginning.

125

Explore Historical Sites for a Day

Taking a day trip to explore nearby historical sites is a wonderful way to combine adventure, learning, and quality time together. Visiting these sites allows you to delve into the rich history of your surroundings, discovering stories, architecture, and artifacts that connect you to the past. Whether it's an old battlefield, a historic home, or a local museum, these excursions provide an opportunity to share in the experience of learning something new and deepening your appreciation for the world around you.

This kind of outing also fosters meaningful conversation as you explore and discuss what you've learned, creating memories rooted in both education and connection. The change of scenery, coupled with the sense of discovery, can refresh your relationship and bring you closer as you experience something out of the ordinary. It's a day spent not only in each other's company but also in enriching your minds and hearts with the stories that shaped your area's history.

126

Feeling Nostalgic? Play Old Video Game Consoles Together

Feeling nostalgic? Dust off those old video game consoles and enjoy a fun, retro gaming session together. Whether it's the classic Mario Kart, Street Fighter, or Sonic the Hedgehog, playing these old-school games can transport you both back to simpler times, filled with carefree fun and laughter. It's a perfect way to relive cherished memories or introduce each other to favorite games from your past.

This activity not only taps into the joy of nostalgia but also offers a relaxed, playful environment where you can compete, collaborate, and simply enjoy each other's company. The shared experience of playing these games, with their pixelated graphics and iconic soundtracks, can spark conversations about childhood memories and favorite pastimes, strengthening your bond through shared joy and friendly competition.

Find out what she played growing up—it might be something you've never tried before. Whether she was a Tetris queen, a Tekken champion, or spent hours rescuing Princess Peach, revisiting those games shows you're interested in her childhood favorites. Plus, it's a great way to let her shine if she's still got those skills. If she didn't game much, introduce her to your old favorites and share why you loved them. Either way, it's about creating a fun, nostalgic moment that brings you both closer together.

Celebrate Her Journey of Growth and Transformation

Acknowledging her personal growth and positive changes is a powerful way to show your support and appreciation for the efforts she's made to better herself. Whether she's been working on her career, mental health, physical fitness, or emotional well-being, recognizing her progress demonstrates that you see and value her hard work. This kind of encouragement not only boosts her confidence but also strengthens your relationship by reinforcing that you're paying attention and that you truly care about her journey.

When you acknowledge her growth, be specific about the changes you've noticed and why they impress or inspire you. This shows that your praise is genuine and thoughtful, deepening the emotional connection between you. Celebrating her achievements, big or small, reinforces that you're proud of the person she's becoming and that you're committed to supporting her as she continues to evolve. This validation can be incredibly meaningful, helping her feel loved and appreciated for who she is today and who she's striving to be.

128

Make a Practice of Holding Her Hand Across the Table at Dinner

Holding her hand across the table at dinner is a simple yet powerful gesture that expresses love, affection, and connection. Whether you're dining out at a fancy restaurant or sharing a meal at home, reaching out to hold her hand shows that you're fully present and engaged in the moment. This act of tenderness can make her feel cherished and close to you, even in the midst of everyday routines.

This small gesture reinforces the bond between you, creating a moment of intimacy in an otherwise ordinary setting. It's a way of saying, "I'm here with you," without needing words, and it can turn a regular dinner into a special experience. Holding hands across the table adds warmth and affection to your meal, reminding her that your connection is always at the forefront, no matter where you are or what you're doing.

129

That Messy Vehicle of Hers... Wash It!

Washing her vehicle for her is a thoughtful and practical gesture that shows you care about the little things in her life. Taking the time to clean her car—inside and out—demonstrates your willingness to go out of your way to make her day a little easier and brighter. Whether it's giving the exterior a good scrub, vacuuming the interior, or even adding a nice air freshener, this simple act of service can leave her feeling appreciated and cared for.

This gesture not only helps keep her vehicle looking great, but it also relieves her of a task she might not have the time or energy to tackle. By doing this for her, you show that you're attentive to her needs and willing to support her in practical ways. It's a small, yet meaningful, way to express your love and commitment, reminding her that you're always there to help, even with the everyday tasks.

Now, I've known some women who absolutely thrive in clutter—if it's not cluttered, they just don't feel right. So, if your woman's car looks like the set of Sanford and Son, don't get frustrated or intimidated. Just take it one step at a time, tackling the mess little by little. It may feel like you're trying to eat an elephant, but with patience, you'll get there someday. The key is to keep your cool and approach it with a sense of humor and care. She'll appreciate the effort, even if the progress is slow!

Don't Just Watch... Create a Bond... Fold Towels Together

Folding towels together may seem like a mundane task, but it's an opportunity to turn an everyday chore into a moment of connection. Instead of sitting back and watching her do the laundry, join in and help out. By folding towels or any other household tasks side by side, you show that you're a partner in all aspects of life, even the small, everyday duties. This simple act of teamwork can lighten her load and make the chore more enjoyable.

Working together on something as routine as folding towels also gives you a chance to chat, share a laugh, and simply enjoy each other's company. It's a reminder that even the most ordinary activities can be meaningful when done together. By participating in the little tasks, you reinforce the idea that you're a team, and that every moment—whether grand or simple—matters in your relationship.

131

Savor Romance at a Scenic Winery

Taking her to a nice winery is a romantic and sophisticated way to spend quality time together while enjoying the beauty of nature and the pleasure of fine wine. Whether you're exploring a local vineyard or traveling to a renowned wine region, the experience offers a relaxing and intimate setting to connect and unwind. Stroll through the vineyard, take in the picturesque views, and learn about the wine-making process as you sample different varieties of wine together.

A visit to a winery is not just about tasting wine—it's about savoring the moment, enjoying the ambiance, and creating lasting memories with each other. Pair your wine tasting with a delicious meal or a picnic on the grounds to make the day even more special. This outing provides a perfect backdrop for deep conversation, laughter, and shared appreciation of the finer things in life, all while strengthening your bond through a shared, enjoyable experience.

I personally invested in an unforgettable experience by planning a wine tour via the Napa Valley Wine Train, and it was worth every moment. The two-and-a-half-hour train ride through the stunning Napa Valley aboard a fully restored Pullman rail car created an immersive journey like no other. The tasting menu, featuring seven courses served as an amuse-bouche and three duo plates, elevated the entire experience into a luxurious adventure. If you're looking to truly impress, consider options like this, where every detail is designed to create a sophisticated and romantic outing she'll treasure forever.

Reassure Her of Your Trust and Faith in Her

Reassuring her of your trust and faith in her is a crucial way to strengthen your relationship and provide emotional security. Trust is the foundation of any strong partnership, and letting her know that you believe in her abilities, decisions, and integrity can deepen your connection. Whether she's facing a challenging situation or just needs a reminder, expressing your unwavering support and confidence in her can uplift her spirits and reinforce her self-esteem.

This reassurance doesn't have to be grand; it can be as simple as a heartfelt conversation, a supportive message, or even a gesture that shows you're by her side no matter what. By consistently affirming your trust and faith in her, you create a safe space where she feels valued and understood. This strengthens your bond, as she knows that she can rely on you not just in good times but also when she needs encouragement and belief in her capabilities.

Be Her Hero When She's Under the Weather

When she's feeling under the weather, stepping up to care for her is one of the most loving and compassionate ways to show your devotion. Being her support system during sickness means more than just asking how she's feeling—it's about actively helping her recover. Ensure she stays hydrated with water, teas, or electrolyte drinks, and if she's missing any medications, supplements, or other remedies, take the initiative to go out and purchase what's needed. Your attentiveness not only eases her physical discomfort but also reassures her emotionally, letting her know she's cared for and cherished.

Take it a step further by preparing comforting foods to aid her recovery, like homemade soups or broths that nourish her body and lift her spirits. Cooking from scratch demonstrates your effort and love, especially when you focus on ingredients that promote healing, like fresh vegetables, herbs, and lean proteins. I remember making chicken noodle soup from scratch for my partner once, but I went a little overboard with the cayenne pepper. She ended up sweating and blowing her nose like crazy, but she laughed through it and, most importantly, got better. Sometimes, it's the imperfect, heartfelt gestures that mean the most.

Don't sit around waiting for her to get up and care for herself, as this is not the time to be passive. Avoid asking questions like "What do you want me to do?" or acting disinterested—it's not the time for selfishness or thoughtlessness. Instead, take the lead by anticipating her needs and being proactive. Small actions, like bringing her a cozy blanket, making sure her phone charger is within reach, or even just checking in regularly, can make a huge difference. Your presence and engagement show her that she's not in this alone and that you're genuinely invested in her comfort and recovery.

When you care for her during moments of vulnerability, you're showing her that you're there for her no matter what. From fluffing her pillows to ensuring she gets enough rest, your actions reflect the depth of your commitment. Being present, thoughtful, and proactive turns a challenging time into an opportunity to strengthen your bond and remind her of the love and security she has in you. In those moments, it's not just about her getting better—it's about the comfort of knowing she can count on you, always.

134

Plan a Surprise Outing to Her Favorite Makeup Store

Planning a surprise outing to her favorite makeup store is a spontaneous way to show that you pay attention to her interests and enjoy making her happy. Whether she's a makeup enthusiast or simply enjoys trying out new products, taking her to a store she loves will make her feel special and appreciated. The element of surprise adds excitement to the outing, turning a regular shopping trip into a memorable experience.

During the visit, encourage her to explore, try on different products, and pick out a few items she's been wanting. Your presence and support make the experience even more enjoyable, showing that you're invested in what makes her happy. This outing isn't just about the makeup; it's about sharing in something she loves, making her feel understood and valued, and creating a fun, spontaneous memory together.

Now, I must forewarn you…when I did this, I left with a receipt longer than one from CVS—sheesh! Between the palettes, lipsticks, and skincare products she "just had to have," the shopping spree felt like an endurance event. But seeing the smile on her face made it all worth it. If you're brave enough to embark on this journey, set a budget or prepare yourself for the whirlwind of swatches, testers, and beauty jargon. It's not just a shopping trip—it's an adventure that shows her you're willing to dive into her world, even if it comes with sticker shock!

135

Explore Sweet Heaven Together with Chocolate Tasting

Going chocolate tasting together is a delightful and indulgent way to spend time with each other, exploring the rich and varied world of chocolates. Whether at a local chocolatier, a specialty shop, or a chocolate festival, tasting different types of chocolates allows you to discover new flavors and appreciate the craftsmanship behind each piece. From dark and decadent to creamy and sweet, there's a chocolate to suit every palate, making this outing a sensory adventure.

As you sample different varieties, take the time to discuss your favorites, compare notes, and maybe even learn about the origins and techniques behind the chocolates. This shared experience not only satisfies your sweet tooth but also brings you closer as you enjoy something luxurious and fun together. It's a perfect way to break from the ordinary and create a memory that's as sweet as the chocolates you're tasting.

136

Make Her Chocolate or Her Favorite Flavor Covered Strawberries

Making her chocolate-covered strawberries, or strawberries coated in her favorite flavor, is a sweet and romantic gesture that's sure to delight her. This simple yet thoughtful treat combines the lusciousness of fresh strawberries with the richness of chocolate or another favorite coating, creating a delicious and visually appealing dessert. Whether you dip them in dark, milk, or white chocolate, or get creative with flavors like caramel, matcha, or coconut, the effort you put into preparing these treats shows your love and attention to detail.

The process of making these treats can be just as enjoyable as the final result. Carefully select the ripest strawberries, melt the chocolate to the perfect consistency, and maybe even add some decorative touches like drizzles, nuts, or sprinkles. Present them on a beautiful plate or tray, and surprise her with this indulgent homemade dessert. Not only will she appreciate the effort and care you put into making something special just for her, but she'll also savor every bite, knowing it was made with love.

If you're not naturally gifted in the kitchen, don't worry—this is a low-pressure way to impress her. My first attempt at making chocolate-covered strawberries wasn't exactly Instagram-worthy, but by my second and third tries, I got the hang of it. Each batch looked better than the last, and the effort didn't go unnoticed. Even if your first round isn't perfect, she'll appreciate the love behind it. Plus, improving with each attempt shows your dedication, which makes the gesture even sweeter.

137

Encourage Her with Belief in Her Limitless Potential

Communicating your belief in her capabilities and potential, especially beyond the success she's already achieved, is a powerful way to uplift and encourage her. While it's important to celebrate her accomplishments, it's equally vital to let her know that you see even greater possibilities in her future. By expressing your faith in her ability to reach new heights, you inspire her to continue growing and pursuing her dreams with confidence.

This kind of support goes beyond mere praise—it's about acknowledging her strengths and affirming that you believe she can achieve even more. Let her know that you see qualities in her that may not yet be fully realized, and that you're excited to witness her journey as she continues to evolve. This reassurance not only boosts her self-esteem but also strengthens your bond, showing that you're committed to supporting her every step of the way, no matter what challenges or opportunities lie ahead.

138

Offer to Wash, Treat, and Brush/Comb Her Hair

Offering to wash, treat, and brush or comb her hair is a deeply caring and intimate gesture that shows your dedication to her comfort and well-being. Hair care can be a relaxing and soothing experience, and by taking the time to help her with it, you demonstrate your willingness to nurture her in a personal and tender way. Whether it's a simple wash and condition or a full treatment with masks and oils, your attention to her needs can make her feel cherished and pampered.

This act of care goes beyond the physical aspect—it's an opportunity to connect emotionally as well. As you gently massage her scalp, apply treatments, and brush or comb through her hair, you create a peaceful and intimate atmosphere where she can relax and feel completely at ease. The gentle touch and focused attention on her well-being can strengthen your bond, making her feel loved and valued in a way that words alone might not convey.

Before I wrap up this chapter, let me tell you—if you can master parting her hair at the scalp and get really good at applying a hot oil treatment, especially if your woman is a woman of color, good sir, you are winning. Treating her hair properly can be an intimate and rewarding experience, and trust me, it feels almost as satisfying to her as using a Q-tip in your ear! Taking the time to care for her hair not only shows your attention to detail but also creates a deep sense of connection and appreciation for her beauty and comfort.

139

Surprise Her with a Late-Night Cocktail or Mocktail

Surprising her with a late-night cocktail or mocktail is an indulgent way to end the day on a high note. Whether she prefers a classic cocktail like a martini or mojito, or a refreshing, non-alcoholic mocktail, preparing a drink that suits her taste shows that you're attentive to her preferences and eager to make her feel special. The effort you put into crafting the perfect drink, whether it's mixing ingredients, garnishing with fresh fruit, or adding a creative twist, adds a personal touch that she'll appreciate.

Serving this late-night treat in a cozy setting, perhaps with some soft music playing in the background or a candlelit atmosphere, can turn an ordinary evening into a memorable, intimate experience. It's a simple yet meaningful gesture that allows you both to unwind together, share a quiet moment, and enjoy the connection that comes from thoughtful surprises. Whether you're celebrating a special occasion or just savoring the end of a busy day, a well-prepared cocktail or mocktail is a delightful way to show your love and care.

140

Attend a Book Reading or Poetry Slam

Attending a book reading or poetry slam together is a unique and enriching way to connect over a shared love of literature and the arts. These events offer a chance to experience the power of words in a live setting, whether you're listening to an author discuss their latest work or watching poets perform their pieces with passion and emotion. The atmosphere is often charged with creativity, making it an inspiring and thought-provoking outing.

Sharing this experience can lead to deep conversations and a greater appreciation for each other's perspectives. Whether you both enjoy discussing the themes of the works presented or simply soaking in the ambiance, attending a literary event together can strengthen your bond through a mutual love of storytelling and expression. It's a meaningful way to spend time together, expanding your horizons and creating memories that go beyond the ordinary.

Even if this isn't your usual thing, keep an open mind to the experience. You might be surprised by how much you enjoy the raw emotion of a poetry slam or the insights shared by an author. Even if the material doesn't resonate with you, your willingness to be there and share the moment speaks volumes. It's about connecting with her interests and showing her that you're game to explore new things together. Who knows—you might walk away with a newfound appreciation for the art—or at the very least, an interesting story to laugh about later.

141

Design a Custom Map of Your Love Story Locations

Creating a customized map that highlights the special places you've visited together is a heartfelt way to celebrate the journey you've shared as a couple. This personalized map can showcase the locations of your first date, memorable trips, significant milestones, and other places that hold meaning for both of you. Marking these spots on a beautifully designed map not only serves as a visual representation of your shared experiences but also as a unique piece of art to display in your home.

This gesture allows you to revisit those treasured memories each time you look at the map, sparking conversations about the adventures you've had and the bond you've built along the way. It's a creative way to honor your relationship and the many places that have shaped your story. Whether you add notes, photos, or dates to each location, this customized map will be a lasting reminder of the journey you're on together.

142

Be Specific in Your Compliments About Her Actions or Qualities

Being specific in your compliments about her actions or qualities is a powerful way to make her feel truly seen and appreciated. Instead of general praise, focus on the particular traits or behaviors that you admire—whether it's her kindness in helping others, her resilience in tough situations, or her creativity in solving problems. By pinpointing what you love about her, you show that you're paying close attention and that you genuinely value who she is.

These specific compliments carry more significance because they reflect your deep understanding and appreciation of her unique qualities. They not only elevate her confidence but also enhance the emotional bond between you, as she feels seen and valued for the things that set her apart. Whether you're acknowledging how she handled a challenging task or expressing admiration for her kind actions, being precise in your praise ensures that she knows exactly what makes her extraordinary in your eyes.

143

Strike a Pose: Try Yoga Together

Offering to try yoga with her is a wonderful way to support her interests and spend quality time together in a healthy, relaxing activity. Yoga promotes physical well-being, mental clarity, and emotional balance, making it a perfect practice to share with a partner. Whether she's a seasoned yogi or just starting out, joining her on the mat shows that you're eager to connect through a practice that she enjoys and values.

Practicing yoga together can strengthen your bond as you work on poses, breathing exercises, and mindfulness techniques side by side. It's an opportunity to encourage each other, share in the challenges and successes, and enjoy the calming benefits of yoga. This shared experience can deepen your connection and introduce a new way of relaxing and staying fit together, enhancing both your relationship and your individual well-being.

Be patient with yourself, especially if you're 40+. When I tried yoga, every movement I made sounded like bubble wrap, and getting up from the mat was like listening to Optimus Prime transform. But here's the thing—she'll appreciate the effort, even if your downward dog looks more like a struggling turtle. Yoga isn't about perfection; it's about being present and sharing the experience. Laugh at yourself, embrace the challenge, and remember, the point is to connect with her, not to nail every pose.

144

Create a Recurring Calendar of Event Dates Important to Her

Creating a recurring calendar of event dates that are important to her is a considerate way to show that you value the meaningful moments in her life. Whether it's her birthday, anniversaries, significant milestones, or even smaller events like her favorite annual festival or a personal achievement, setting reminders for these dates ensures that you never miss an opportunity to celebrate what's important to her. This gesture reflects your dedication to being attentive and recognizing the occasions that matter most to her.

By taking the initiative to remember and plan for these important dates, you show that you're attentive to her needs and desires. It also allows you to prepare in advance, whether it's planning a surprise, organizing a celebration, or simply sending a heartfelt message. This ongoing attention to detail strengthens your relationship, as it reinforces that you're always thinking of her and ready to make each special moment count.

145

Ride the Rails on a Scenic Train Adventure

Taking a scenic train ride or tour together is a romantic and leisurely way to explore beautiful landscapes while enjoying each other's company. Whether it's a short journey through picturesque countryside, a historic railway tour, or an extended trip through mountains or along a coastline, the experience offers a unique perspective on the world around you. The gentle rhythm of the train, coupled with stunning views, creates a serene atmosphere perfect for relaxation and conversation.

This kind of outing allows you both to unplug from the hustle and bustle of everyday life and immerse yourselves in the journey. As you watch the scenery unfold outside your window, you can share stories, reflect on your adventures, or simply enjoy the quiet moments together. A scenic train ride not only provides a memorable travel experience but also offers a wonderful opportunity to strengthen your bond in a tranquil and beautiful setting.

I mentioned this in the chapter about visiting a winery, but it's worth repeating: a scenic train ride can elevate any outing into something truly unforgettable. When I planned a wine tour via the Napa Valley Wine Train, the combination of stunning landscapes, a luxurious ride, and curated experiences made it more than just transportation—it was an adventure in itself. Whether your train ride includes dining, historical insights, or just breathtaking views, the key is choosing an experience that resonates with both of you. These moments of shared discovery and relaxation will stay with you long after the train reaches its destination.

146

Soar, Swing, or Zip? Time for Adventure Date Thrills

Planning an adventure experience like a hot air balloon ride, zip-lining, or another thrilling activity is a fantastic way to create unforgettable memories together. These kinds of experiences offer a mix of excitement and wonder, pushing you both out of your comfort zones and into exhilarating new environments. Whether you're soaring above the landscape in a hot air balloon, feeling the rush of zip-lining through the treetops, or trying something equally adventurous, these shared moments of thrill and exploration can deepen your bond.

Engaging in adventure activities together also reinforces teamwork and trust, as you support each other through the experience. The adrenaline and sense of accomplishment from completing these activities can bring you closer, creating a shared sense of achievement and adventure. These experiences are not just about the thrill; they're about connecting on a deeper level, facing challenges together, and celebrating the joy of life and love in the most exhilarating ways possible.

Know your limits. I tried zip-lining in Mexico, and let me tell you, my long legs got whipped by every tree, shrub, and blade of grass—I looked like I had just lost a fight with the jungle. As for hot air balloons, I've convinced myself that I'll need a sedative just to step into the basket, but one day, I'm going to do it. The point is to embrace the adventure, even if it's not perfect. Whether you're laughing through the nerves or celebrating your bravery, the experience will be unforgettable—for better or for hilarious.

147

Get Her Locked and Loaded on the Gun Range

Taking her to a gun range is an exciting and empowering activity that allows you both to learn a new skill or practice one together. Whether she's already familiar with firearms or it's her first time, visiting a gun range offers a unique experience that combines focus, discipline, and a bit of adrenaline. It's a chance to challenge each other's accuracy, enjoy some friendly competition, and build confidence in a controlled, safe environment.

The experience can also be a bonding opportunity, as you guide each other through the techniques and celebrate your improvements. Whether you're shooting targets, discussing safety protocols, or simply enjoying the experience, visiting a gun range together creates a shared memory that's both thrilling and educational. It's a different kind of date that offers excitement and the opportunity to learn and grow together.

Now, if she turns the gun sideways and starts shooting like she's in a scene from Set It Off, you might want to keep an eye on her from now on!

148

Set Sail by Renting a Boat for a Day

Renting a boat for a day is a fantastic way to enjoy a peaceful and adventurous outing on the water together. Whether you're cruising along a serene lake, exploring a coastal bay, or sailing down a river, the experience offers a perfect blend of relaxation and exploration. You can take in the beautiful views, enjoy the gentle sway of the boat, and spend quality time together away from the hustle and bustle of daily life.

This outing provides opportunities for various activities, such as swimming, fishing, or simply sunbathing on the deck. Pack a picnic to enjoy on board, or dock at a scenic spot for a meal with a view. Renting a boat allows you both to unwind, reconnect with nature, and share in the adventure of navigating the open water. It's a day of freedom and tranquility, where the two of you can create lasting memories in a serene and picturesque setting.

If your budget allows for it, a luxury boat rental can elevate the experience with plush seating, gourmet catering, or even a private captain to handle the navigation. This creates a stress-free, indulgent outing that's hard to beat. Whether you go big or keep it simple, the key is tailoring the experience to your preferences and making the most of your time together on the water.

149

Snuggle Under the Stars in a Hammock Hideaway

Snuggling up in a hammock together is a cozy and intimate way to relax and enjoy each other's company. Whether you're in your backyard, at a park, or on a camping trip, a hammock provides a perfect spot for the two of you to unwind, sway gently, and simply be close. The enclosed space of the hammock creates a sense of privacy and comfort, making it easy to share quiet moments, have a heartfelt conversation, or simply enjoy the peace of being together.

As you lay side by side, you can enjoy the warmth of the sun, the cool breeze, or the shade of the trees, letting the hammock cradle you both in a serene and tranquil environment. It's a wonderful way to slow down, disconnect from the outside world, and focus on each other. Whether you're reading, napping, or just enjoying the moment, snuggling in a hammock brings you closer, turning an ordinary day into a special memory.

I did this one evening on a beachfront property in Aruba, and it was beyond refreshing—she absolutely loved it. The gentle sway of the hammock, the sound of the waves, and the warm Caribbean breeze made the moment unforgettable. There's something magical about finding a beautiful spot to simply relax and soak in each other's presence. If you ever have the chance to try this in a tropical setting, don't hesitate—it's a memory you'll both cherish forever.

150

Bonus: Surprise Her with Her Dream Pet

Surprising her with a pet she's always wanted is a really out of the park, heartwarming gesture that shows you've paid attention to her desires. To add an element of fun and suspense, consider bringing her home a stuffed animal version of the pet first, placing it inside a toy cage or a box. Let her think this is the surprise, building up her anticipation. Once the moment has settled, reveal the actual pet she's been dreaming of. Since most pets come in store-provided containers, you should be able to hide the real animal for a few minutes to maximize the surprise.

This creative approach to gifting a pet makes the experience even more memorable. It shows not only that you listened to what she wanted but also that you took the time to turn the moment into something fun and playful. Just ensure you're ready for the responsibility that comes with the new addition to your home!

151

Are You Two Goal Getters? Be Her Accountability Partner

Offering to be her accountability partner for a goal she's working on is a supportive and encouraging way to show your commitment to her success and well-being. Whether she's striving to achieve a fitness milestone, advance in her career, or develop a new habit, having you by her side as an accountability partner can make a significant difference. Your involvement demonstrates that you're invested in her journey and willing to provide the motivation, encouragement, and support she needs to stay on track.

As her accountability partner, you can help her set realistic goals, check in regularly on her progress, and celebrate her achievements along the way. This partnership not only strengthens your bond but also builds a deeper sense of trust and collaboration in your relationship. By being there to cheer her on, offer constructive feedback, and hold her accountable to her commitments, you reinforce that you're a team, dedicated to helping each other grow and succeed.

152

Give Her S'more Love with Cozy Bonfire Nights

Having a bonfire and making s'mores together is a fun and nostalgic way to enjoy a cozy evening outdoors. Whether you're in your backyard, at a campsite, or by the beach, gathering around a crackling fire creates a warm and inviting atmosphere perfect for relaxation and conversation. The simple pleasure of roasting marshmallows over the fire, melting chocolate, and sandwiching them between graham crackers brings out the joy of shared childhood memories while creating new ones together.

As the flames flicker and the night sky unfolds above, you can enjoy the sweet treats and the comfort of each other's company. The experience of sitting by the fire, toasting s'mores, and perhaps even sharing stories or listening to music, offers a perfect blend of relaxation and connection. A bonfire night with s'mores is more than just a delicious treat—it's an opportunity to slow down, savor the moment, and enjoy the magic of a simple, yet memorable, evening together.

If she's not big on marshmallows, don't let that stop you. Get creative with alternatives! Try roasting fruit like pineapple or strawberries, or substitute the marshmallows with peanut butter, Nutella, or even caramelized bananas. You can also turn the experience into a gourmet adventure by offering fancy chocolate varieties or flavored crackers to customize the treat. The goal is to enjoy the warmth of the fire and the sweetness of the moment together, marshmallows or not. Who knows—you might just discover a new favorite bonfire tradition!

Share Love with Forehead Kisses That Warms Her Heart

Giving her a tender forehead kiss in passing is a simple yet profoundly affectionate gesture that conveys love, care, and reassurance. A gentle kiss on the forehead, whether as you're leaving for the day or just moving from one room to another, shows that you're thinking of her and cherishing her presence in your life. It's a subtle way to express your feelings, offering comfort and warmth in a moment that might otherwise go unnoticed.

This small act of love can strengthen your emotional bond, making her feel valued and secure. It's a reminder of your affection that requires no words, only the sincerity of your touch. A forehead kiss in passing is more than just a kiss—it's a tender, intimate moment that says, "I'm here for you," and "You matter to me," creating a lasting impact in the simplicity of daily life.

154

DIY and Personalize a Personal Craft with Her Name

Creating a DIY gift or craft with her name on it is a personal and thoughtful way to show your love and creativity. Whether it's a handmade piece of jewelry, a custom-painted sign, or a personalized photo frame, adding her name to the item makes it uniquely hers. The time and effort you put into crafting something special just for her speaks volumes about your affection and attention to detail.

This kind of gift goes beyond material value—it's a reflection of the care and attention you've put into honoring her uniqueness. As she sees her name beautifully incorporated into the gift, she'll be reminded of your love and the effort you put into making her feel special. Whether it's a small token or an elaborate project, a DIY gift with her name on it is a keepsake she'll cherish, knowing it was made with love and intention.

Many of us are handy in the garage or with woodworking tools, so it shouldn't be difficult to get creative in your own way. Whether you're carving her name into a piece of reclaimed wood, crafting a custom jewelry box, or even laser-engraving something unique, use your skills to make it personal. For those less experienced, don't overthink it—simple projects like painting her name on a canvas or customizing a mug can be just as meaningful. The key is showing her you put thought and effort into creating something one-of-a-kind that celebrates her.

155

Explore Culture and Cuisine at a Festival Together

Attending a cultural festival or fair together is an exciting way to immerse yourselves in a vibrant atmosphere filled with music, art, food, and traditions from different cultures. Whether it's a local street fair, an international food festival, or a celebration of a specific heritage, these events offer a chance to explore new experiences and learn more about the world around you. The lively environment, with its colorful displays and diverse performances, creates an opportunity for you both to enjoy something out of the ordinary.

As you walk through the festival, sampling different foods, watching performances, or participating in cultural activities, you'll create shared memories while broadening your horizons. This outing not only deepens your connection but also allows you to appreciate the richness and diversity of different cultures together. It's a fun and meaningful way to spend time, fostering curiosity and joy as you discover new tastes, sounds, and traditions side by side.

156

Passport to Romance Anyone? Surprise Her with a Trip Abroad

Surprising her with an international trip is an extraordinary way to show your love and create unforgettable memories together. Planning a getaway to a destination she's always dreamed of visiting—or even a place that's completely new to both of you—demonstrates your commitment to making her dreams come true. The excitement of exploring a different country, culture, and environment can be a thrilling adventure that brings you closer as a couple.

From the moment you reveal the surprise to the day you set foot in a new land, the journey will be filled with anticipation, discovery, and shared experiences. Whether you're strolling through ancient cities, lounging on a tropical beach, or savoring local cuisine, the memories you create on this trip will be ones you'll cherish forever. An international trip is more than just a vacation; it's an opportunity to step out of your comfort zones together, explore the world, and deepen your bond in a truly special way.

To make the trip that much more memorable, I recommend investing in business class flights and booking a 5-star hotel in your destination country. The added comfort of spacious seats, exceptional service, and luxury accommodations can elevate the entire experience, turning a great trip into an unforgettable one. It's a gesture that shows her she deserves the very best, making the adventure not just about the destination but also about the journey you take together in style and comfort.

If you have financial constraints, don't worry—there are plenty of flight and hotel deal websites that can help you plan an amazing trip on a budget. Platforms like Skyscanner, Kayak, or Hopper can help you find affordable flights, while websites like Booking.com or Airbnb offer discounted accommodations. You may not end up in your dream destination, but there are plenty of beautiful and exciting locations abroad that will still create a magical and memorable experience for both of you.

157

Boost Her Confidence by Celebrating Her Resilience

Recognizing and praising her resilience in tough situations is a powerful way to show your admiration and support for her strength. Life often throws challenges our way, and the way she handles adversity, stays strong, and continues to push forward deserves acknowledgment. By expressing your appreciation for her resilience, you validate her efforts and remind her that you see and respect the inner strength she brings to difficult circumstances.

When you praise her resilience, be specific about what you admire—whether it's her ability to stay calm under pressure, her determination to keep going despite setbacks, or the grace with which she navigates tough times. This recognition not only boosts her confidence but also reinforces the emotional bond between you, showing that you're there for her through thick and thin. Celebrating her strength in challenging moments deepens your connection and helps her feel supported and valued in the relationship.

158

Purchase Her Preferred Feminine Products

Taking the initiative to purchase her preferred feminine products is an emotionally aware gesture to show that you care about her comfort and well-being. This simple act demonstrates your attentiveness to her needs and your willingness to support her in all aspects of her life. By being mindful of the specific products she prefers—whether it's a particular brand, type, or size—you show that you've paid attention and are ready to help without hesitation.

This gesture, though small, can mean a lot to her, as it reflects your understanding and empathy. It shows that you're not only aware of the practicalities of her life but also respectful and supportive of her needs, even in areas that might be considered private or sensitive. By doing this, you reinforce your role as a caring and dependable partner, willing to step in and make her life a little easier whenever possible.

I've never understood why some men make such a big deal out of this. I've seen guys at Walmart creeping through the tampon aisle like they're sneaking around to buy illegal substances! There's no reason to feel awkward—it's a normal part of life, and helping her out by grabbing what she needs shows that you care about her comfort and well-being. Being confident and mature about it speaks volumes, and trust me, she'll appreciate the effort without a second thought.

159

Preventive Maintenance, Sir... Her Snacks Matter

Surprising her with her favorite snack is a sweet and simple way to show that you're thinking of her and know what brings her joy. Whether it's a bag of her favorite chips, a special chocolate bar, or a beloved fruit, taking the time to pick up her go-to treat is an act that can brighten her day. The element of surprise adds an extra layer of delight, especially when she's least expecting it.

This small act of kindness shows that you're attuned to her likes and preferences, reinforcing the connection between you. It's a reminder that love often resides in the little things—those everyday moments of care and consideration that make her feel valued and appreciated. Whether she's having a tough day or just in need of a pick-me-up, a surprise snack can instantly lift her spirits and remind her how much you care.

160

It's a Berry Sweet Idea to Go Fruit Picking Together

Going fruit picking at a local orchard is a fun and refreshing way to spend time together outdoors, enjoying the beauty of nature and the simple pleasure of harvesting fresh fruit. Whether it's apples in the fall, strawberries in the spring, or peaches in the summer, visiting an orchard offers a chance to experience the joy of picking your own produce straight from the source. The activity is not only enjoyable but also provides an opportunity to connect with each other in a peaceful and idyllic setting.

As you walk through the orchard, filling your baskets with ripe, juicy fruit, you can chat, laugh, and enjoy the fresh air. The experience allows you to slow down, savor the moment, and appreciate the abundance of nature. Once you've collected your haul, you can look forward to enjoying the fruits of your labor together, whether by baking a pie, making preserves, or simply sharing a fresh, healthy snack. Fruit picking is a delightful way to create lasting memories while engaging in a wholesome and rewarding activity.

161

Order Her a Journal to Document Shared Experiences

Gifting her a custom engraved journal to document your shared experiences is a thoughtful and sentimental way to celebrate your journey together. This personalized journal, with her name, initials, or a meaningful quote engraved on the cover, becomes a treasured keepsake where she can record the special moments, adventures, and memories you create as a couple. It's a beautiful way to encourage her to reflect on your relationship and to cherish the milestones you've reached together.

This journal can serve as a space for her to jot down thoughts after a memorable date, recount a shared trip, or simply express her feelings about your relationship. Over time, it will become a rich collection of memories, filled with the story of your love and growth as a couple. The custom engraving adds a personal touch, making the journal uniquely hers and showing that you've put thought into creating a meaningful gift that she can use to capture the essence of your life together.

To make the journal even more personal, I recommend writing a heartfelt journal entry for her to fold up and place inside the book as a memoir. Express your thoughts on a cherished moment you've shared or express your hopes for the future of your relationship. This added touch makes the journal not just a gift, but also an intimate reminder of how much she means to you. It's something she'll treasure every time she opens it, turning it into a source of comfort and inspiration.

Turn the Page by Sharing a Best-Selling Book

Sharing a best-selling book with her is a unique way to connect over literature and introduce her to a story or topic that has captivated readers worldwide. Whether it's a novel that's topping the charts, a gripping memoir, or a thought-provoking non-fiction work, choosing a book that aligns with her interests—or one you think she'd enjoy—demonstrates your attentiveness to her tastes and your desire to share meaningful experiences.

You can enhance the gesture by discussing the book together after she's read it, exchanging thoughts and perspectives on the story, characters, or ideas presented. This shared literary experience can deepen your connection, sparking insightful conversations and perhaps even inspiring new interests. Whether it becomes a new favorite for her or simply a pleasant read, sharing a best-selling book is a way to bond over the power of a great story.

163

Secure Smiles with Stolen Kisses Throughout the Day

Playfully stealing kisses throughout the day is a simple yet powerful way to keep the spark alive in your relationship. These quick, spontaneous gestures of affection—like a kiss on her forehead while she's cooking or a peck on her cheek as you pass by—are small reminders of your love that can brighten her day. Each stolen kiss adds a moment of closeness and warmth, even in the middle of busy routines, reminding her that she's always on your mind.

This playful habit also brings an element of fun to your relationship. A kiss in the middle of a conversation or a gentle surprise kiss while she's focused on something else can make her laugh and lighten the mood. It's a way of saying, "I love you" without words, creating shared moments of happiness that deepen your connection. These little surprises inject excitement and affection into everyday life, proving that romance doesn't need to be grand to be meaningful.

Over time, these stolen kisses become a language of their own—a way of staying connected throughout the day. Whether you're at home, out running errands, or in the middle of a busy schedule, these small acts of affection show her that she's loved and appreciated in every moment. It's about finding an added measure of peace in the ordinary and turning those fleeting opportunities into lasting memories that make your relationship uniquely yours.

164

See Her Heart in Action: Volunteer for Her Passion

Volunteering together for a cause she cares about is a meaningful way to support her passions while making a positive impact on your community. Whether it's working at a local food bank, participating in a charity run, or helping out at an animal shelter, joining her in giving back not only strengthens your bond but also shows that you're invested in the things that matter most to her.

This shared experience allows you to connect on a deeper level as you work side by side to contribute to a cause that holds significance for her. It's an opportunity to see her in a different light, witnessing her compassion and dedication firsthand. Volunteering together not only enriches your relationship but also leaves you both with a sense of fulfillment, knowing that you've contributed to something meaningful together.

165

Create a Themed Dress-Up Night for Two

Having a themed costume night is a playful way to inject creativity and excitement into your relationship. Picking a theme—whether it's classic 1920s flapper style, superheroes, or characters from your favorite movie—lets you both step out of your usual roles and into something fun and unexpected. Dressing up together isn't just about the costumes; it's about sharing the anticipation and excitement of creating a unique experience that's all your own.

To make the evening even more special, pair your costumes with activities that match the theme. Watch a movie or show that fits your chosen look, play themed games, or cook a meal that ties into your costumes. If you're feeling adventurous, you can even host a small costume night with friends and turn it into a lighthearted contest. The key is making the night immersive and enjoyable, celebrating your shared creativity and sense of humor.

The process of planning and dressing up together can be just as enjoyable as the event itself. From brainstorming ideas to putting on the finishing touches, you'll share laughs and create memories long before the night begins. A themed costume night is more than just dressing up—it's a way to break the routine, bond over something playful, and bring a little whimsy into your relationship.

166

Hobby Love: Curate a Personalized Gift Box

Creating a gift box full of items for her hobby or interest is a personalized way to show that you care about what makes her happy. Whether she's passionate about painting, gardening, cooking, or a specific type of craft, curating a collection of items that align with her interests demonstrates your attentiveness and support for her passions. Each item in the box should be chosen with care, reflecting her tastes and helping her dive deeper into the activities she loves.

This gift box could include practical tools, supplies, books, or even small luxuries that enhance her hobby experience. For example, if she loves painting, you might include high-quality brushes, a sketchpad, and a set of paints. If she's into gardening, consider adding seeds, gloves, and a charming plant pot. The thought and effort you put into assembling this gift will show her that you appreciate her unique interests and are eager to encourage her creativity. It's a gesture that not only supports her hobbies but also strengthens your connection through a shared appreciation of what brings her happiness.

167

Spark Meaningful Conversations by Diving into Her Dreams

Having meaningful conversations about her dreams and ambitions shows her that you're truly invested in her happiness and growth. By taking the time to ask about her goals—whether they involve her career, personal development, or a creative passion—you demonstrate that her aspirations matter to you. It's a way of saying, "I see you, and I care about what excites and motivates you." These talks aren't just about gathering information; they're about building a deeper understanding of what drives her.

It's important to ensure your interest and listen with pure intent, care, and investment into what's important to her. Ask open-ended questions, encourage her to elaborate, and show genuine curiosity about her answers. Let her know you're not just hearing her words but truly understanding the meaning behind them. By creating a safe space where she feels comfortable sharing her dreams, you reinforce your role as her partner and biggest supporter.

These conversations go beyond words—they empower her to pursue her goals with confidence, knowing she has someone in her corner who believes in her. Whether it's brainstorming solutions, cheering her on, or simply being there to listen, your involvement reinforces the idea that her dreams are just as important to you as they are to her. These moments of connection remind her that she's not alone on her journey and that you're excited to help her make those dreams a reality.

168

'Seas' the Day by Surprising Her with a Beach Trip

Taking her on a surprise trip to a beach is a romantic and refreshing way to escape the routine and enjoy each other's company in a serene, natural setting. Whether it's a secluded local beach or a well-known coastal spot, the sound of the waves, the feel of the sand between your toes, and the fresh sea breeze create the perfect environment for relaxation and connection. The element of surprise adds an extra layer of excitement, making the outing even more special.

You can spend the day lounging on the sand, swimming, collecting seashells, or simply taking a peaceful walk along the shoreline. Pack a picnic to enjoy by the water or treat her to a meal at a beachfront café. This surprise beach trip offers an opportunity to unwind and appreciate the beauty of nature together, creating memories that will last long after the sun sets. It's a romantic gesture that shows how much you value your time together and your desire to create joyful experiences.

169

Be Her Proactive Fixer-Upper Hero... Her "Maintenance" Man

Taking care of household maintenance or repairs without being asked is a simple yet impactful way to show your love and reliability as a partner. Whether it's tightening a loose cabinet hinge, fixing a squeaky door, or tackling a bigger project like repairing a leaky faucet, handling these tasks unprompted demonstrates your attentiveness and initiative. It's not just about maintaining a functional home—it's about showing that you care enough to step up and take responsibility for the shared space you both value.

This proactive approach also relieves her of the mental load of keeping track of every household task. By addressing repairs or maintenance before they become an issue, you create a more harmonious environment where she feels supported and appreciated. It's a practical way of saying, "I've got us covered," and it reassures her that you're a dependable partner who's willing to share the workload.

Beyond practicality, these small acts of service can deepen your connection. It's not just about fixing what's broken; it's about contributing to a home that's comfortable, safe, and filled with love. Even something as simple as replacing a burned-out lightbulb can send the message that you're invested in making life easier and better for both of you. Your actions reflect your commitment, making your home a reflection of the care you put into your relationship.

170

Climb Higher in Your Relationship with Indoor Rock Climbing

Trying indoor rock climbing or bouldering together is an exciting way to add adventure and physical challenge to your relationship. Whether you're both new to climbing or have some experience, this activity offers a great opportunity to test your limits, build trust, and support each other as you tackle the walls. Indoor climbing gyms provide a controlled environment where you can safely learn the techniques, build strength, and overcome obstacles together.

This shared experience fosters teamwork and communication, as you encourage each other to push through challenges and celebrate each other's successes. The physicality of the activity, combined with the mental focus required to navigate the routes, creates a fun and engaging way to bond. Plus, the sense of accomplishment you'll both feel after completing a climb will add to the excitement and satisfaction of having conquered something new together. It's a thrilling way to connect, stay fit, and create lasting memories.

Be prepared for some hilarious moments—especially if you're anything like me, gripping the wall like a cat stuck on a screen door while desperately trying not to look down. And let's not forget the unflattering harness situation, which does wonders for your self-esteem. But hey, the laughs are part of the fun! Whether you're conquering the wall or sliding down like a reluctant spider, you'll have plenty of stories to share—and probably a newfound respect for each other's upper body strength.

171

Pamper Her with a Bath Bomb and Essential Spa Kit

Creating a spa kit with bath bombs, essential oils, and other pampering items is thinking outside the box in a way that helps her relax and indulge in some well-deserved self-care. A personalized spa kit can include her favorite bath bombs, soothing essential oils like lavender or eucalyptus, luxurious body lotions, scented candles, and even a plush bathrobe or soft towels. This curated collection of relaxation essentials allows her to transform an ordinary bath into a rejuvenating spa experience at home.

Presenting her with this spa kit shows that you care about her well-being and want to encourage her to take time for herself. It's a gift that promotes relaxation, stress relief, and self-care, allowing her to unwind and recharge whenever she needs it. Whether she uses the kit for a quiet evening alone or you join her for a shared pampering session, this thoughtful gesture will make her feel cherished and cared for.

172

Celebrate Her Continuous Support and Understanding

Thanking her for her continuous support and understanding is one of the most meaningful ways to strengthen your relationship. Her patience, empathy, and unwavering encouragement likely play a huge role in helping you navigate life's challenges and celebrate its successes. Whether it's her ability to listen when you need advice, her willingness to compromise, or simply her comforting presence, expressing your gratitude shows her how much you value everything she brings to your partnership.

Take the time to make your thank you intentional. It could be a heartfelt conversation where you highlight specific instances where her support meant the world to you, a thoughtfully written note that she can keep and revisit, or even a surprise gift that reflects her impact on your life. The key is to make her feel seen and appreciated for the steady, ongoing care she provides, even when it's behind the scenes.

Gratitude isn't just a one-time thing—it's a habit that keeps love and connection alive. Thanking her regularly for her understanding and support reminds her that you don't take her efforts for granted. It's not about grand gestures, but about letting her know that her constant presence is noticed and cherished. These moments of acknowledgment strengthen your bond and ensure she knows just how much she means to you.

173

Surprise Her with a Visit to a Popular Nail Salon

Surprising her with a visit to a popular nail salon is a solid way to make her feel pampered and appreciated. You almost can't go wrong with this one. Whether she's into intricate nail designs, a classic manicure, or a soothing pedicure, this gesture gives her the opportunity to unwind and indulge in some well-deserved self-care. Choosing a salon known for its quality ensures she'll have a luxurious experience, and the element of surprise turns an ordinary day into something truly memorable.

This isn't just about the nails—it's about showing her that you notice and value the little things that make her happy. You could make it even more special by upgrading her service or choosing a package that includes a massage or other spa treatments. Better yet, if you're feeling bold, join her for a couples' pedicure. Even if it's not your thing, the effort and shared experience will make her feel even more cherished.

If she's a nail salon regular, surprising her with a visit to a trendy or highly-rated spot she hasn't tried yet can make it feel extra special. Throw in a latte or her favorite snack on the way there, and you've just turned a routine beauty appointment into a relaxing and thoughtful outing. It's a simple but impactful way to remind her that her happiness and well-being are always a priority to you.

174

Play On: Plan a Couple's Game Night with Her Favorite Games

Planning a couple's game night with her favorite games is a fun and interactive way to spend quality time together, blending a bit of friendly competition with plenty of laughter and connection. Whether she enjoys classic board games, card games, or even video games, curating an evening filled with her favorites shows that you're attentive to what she loves and eager to share in her enjoyment.

Setting the scene with cozy seating, snacks, and perhaps some soft background music can make the night feel even more special. As you play together, you can bond over shared victories, lighthearted teasing, and the joy of simply spending time in each other's company. A couple's game night is not just about the games—it's about creating a playful and relaxed atmosphere where you can unwind and connect on a deeper level, all while having a great time.

If she's got extrovert tendencies, you might want to consider inviting another mature couple to join in on the fun. There's something special about spending time with like-minded, mature couples who share similar values. It not only adds another layer of enjoyment to the evening, but it can also strengthen your relationship by surrounding yourselves with positive, supportive influences. Plus, a little friendly competition never hurts, and it's a great way to bond and create lasting memories together.

175

Not a Nail Tech? You Are Today... Give Her a Pedicure

Offering to give her a pedicure is a creative action suited to pamper her and show your love—even if you've never done it before. With countless tutorials online, learning the basics is easier than ever, and the effort you put into it will speak volumes. Soak her feet in warm water, gently massage them, and, if she trusts you with polish, apply her favorite color. The care and attention you show in this small but intimate gesture will make her feel cherished and appreciated.

To elevate the experience, create a spa-like atmosphere in your home. Set the mood with soft lighting, soothing music, and maybe even a few candles. Gather all the essentials: a foot soak, nail clippers, a file, polish, a foot scrub, and some lotion for a relaxing massage. Even if your technique isn't perfect, the ambiance and thoughtfulness will make the experience memorable and meaningful for both of you.

If the idea of applying polish feels intimidating, don't stress—focus on the pampering. The massage alone can make her day, especially if she's been on her feet or dealing with a busy schedule. The key is your effort and attention, not perfection. And who knows? You might discover a hidden talent—or at the very least, earn a few laughs while creating a sweet memory together.

176

Sip Love Daily by Gifting Her a Custom Mug

Gifting her a personalized mug or tumbler is a heartfelt way to add a touch of sentiment to her daily routine. Whether she enjoys coffee, tea, or staying hydrated on the go, a customized mug or tumbler with her name, a favorite quote, or a special design will remind her of your affection each time she uses it. This practical yet personal gift shows that you've put care into creating something truly unique for her.

You can tailor the design to reflect her personality, favorite colors, or even a shared memory. Every time she takes a sip from her personalized drinkware, she'll think of you and the effort you put into making her feel special. It's a small gesture that can brighten her day, adding a bit of warmth and love to her morning coffee or afternoon tea, and it serves as a daily reminder of your bond.

177

Provide a Safe Space for Her to Share Her Fears

Creating a safe space for her to share her fears is one of the most meaningful ways to show your love and support. Life's challenges can be overwhelming, and having a partner who listens without judgment and offers comfort can make all the difference. By providing a calm, open, and non-judgmental environment, you allow her to express her worries and anxieties freely, knowing that she will be met with understanding and compassion.

This act of listening goes beyond just hearing her words—it involves empathizing with her emotions and offering reassurance that she's not alone. Whether she's dealing with work stress, personal challenges, or deeper insecurities, your willingness to be there for her, without trying to fix everything, strengthens your emotional bond. This safe space helps her feel supported, valued, and loved, reinforcing that your relationship is a sanctuary where she can always find solace and understanding.

Listening with pure intent is key to creating this safe space. It's not about waiting for your turn to speak or listening for the sake of obligation—it's about truly hearing her with the goal of understanding and being her safe haven. Approach the conversation with empathy, patience, and curiosity, focusing on her words and emotions rather than formulating a response. When you listen to learn, rather than to fix or defend, you show her that her feelings matter and that she can trust you with her vulnerability. This level of attentiveness fosters deeper intimacy and ensures she always feels secure in opening up to you.

Hands on the Wheel, and Hers in Yours

Holding hands while driving or traveling is a simple yet intimate way to maintain a connection during your journeys together. Whether you're on a road trip, commuting, or simply driving around town, reaching over to hold her hand brings comfort, warmth, and a sense of closeness. This small gesture shows that you're present and attentive, even in the midst of everyday activities.

The act of holding hands while traveling reinforces your bond and creates a sense of security and affection. It's a quiet reminder that, no matter where you're going, you're in it together. This gesture turns an ordinary drive into a moment of connection, making the time spent on the road more meaningful and intimate. It's a way to show your love through the little things, making her feel cherished and valued every step of the way.

On another note, while holding hands during a drive can be a beautiful and intimate gesture, it's essential to remember the importance of safety on the road. In some countries, the UK for example, police are likely to stop you if they notice you taking your hands off the wheel for prolonged periods, as it can be seen as a distraction. This is a crucial point to keep in mind, as driving with both hands on the wheel is essential for maintaining full control of the vehicle and ensuring the safety of everyone in the car. If you want to hold her hand while driving, just be safe in doing so as proceeds from this book will not be used to pay your fines.

179

Escape Close to Home with a Nearby Staycation

Planning a staycation at a nearby hotel or Airbnb is a great opportunity to enjoy a getaway without the hassle of long-distance travel. Whether it's a luxurious hotel in your city, a cozy cabin in the countryside, or a chic Airbnb in a neighboring town, this mini-vacation offers the perfect blend of relaxation and exploration. You can unwind in a new environment, enjoy amenities like a pool, spa, or room service, and take a break from the usual routine.

This staycation allows you to focus on each other without the distractions of daily life. You can explore local attractions, dine at nearby restaurants, or simply enjoy the comfort of your temporary home away from home. It's a thoughtful way to surprise her with a change of scenery and quality time together, creating the feel of a vacation with all the convenience of staying close to home.

Unlike a workcation, which blends productivity with relaxation, a staycation is entirely about unwinding and reconnecting. There's no need to check emails, meet deadlines, or juggle work responsibilities—it's all about stepping away from the grind and indulging in leisure. A staycation provides the opportunity to fully disconnect and prioritize enjoying each other's company without the pressure of balancing work. It's a genuine retreat, meant to recharge your relationship and remind you both of the pleasure in simply being together.

180

Purchase Cooking Utensils with Heartfelt Messages

Purchasing cooking utensils with engraved messages is a heartfelt way to bring a personal touch to her everyday kitchen activities. Whether it's wooden spoons, spatulas, or cutting boards, having a meaningful message, her name, or an inside joke engraved on these items turns them into cherished keepsakes. Each time she uses them, she'll be reminded of your love and thoughtfulness, making even routine cooking tasks feel special.

This gesture is particularly meaningful if she enjoys cooking or baking, as it combines her passion with a personal touch. You can choose messages that reflect your relationship, offer words of encouragement, or simply make her smile. These personalized utensils are not just tools—they're a daily reminder of your connection and the care you put into making her feel appreciated.

181

Share A Cozy Dream Together and Bond Forever

Sharing a cozy nap together is a simple yet deeply intimate way to connect and recharge with each other. Whether you cuddle up on the couch, snuggle under the blankets in bed, or even relax in a hammock, napping together allows you to enjoy a peaceful moment of closeness. The act of resting side by side, feeling each other's warmth, and drifting off to sleep creates a sense of security and comfort that strengthens your bond.

A shared nap can be a gentle escape from the stresses of daily life, providing a moment of quiet where you can simply be present with one another. It's a small but meaningful gesture that shows you value spending time together, even in the most restful and relaxed way. Whether it's a quick afternoon snooze or a longer weekend nap, this shared experience can leave you both feeling refreshed and more connected.

182

Stay Aligned with Love by Booking Her a Chiropractor

Booking an appointment for her to visit a chiropractor is a thoughtful way to show you care about her health and well-being. Whether she's been dealing with back pain, tension from stress, or just everyday discomfort, a chiropractic session can provide relief and help her feel more aligned and refreshed. Taking the initiative to set up the appointment demonstrates your attentiveness and willingness to support her physical health.

To make the experience extra special, do some research to find a highly rated chiropractor in your area—preferably one with a warm and welcoming atmosphere. Share with her why you thought this would be beneficial, emphasizing your desire to see her feeling her best. If she's new to chiropractic care, reassure her by explaining the benefits, such as improved posture, reduced pain, and greater overall comfort.

This gesture isn't just about addressing physical issues; it's also about giving her the time and space to focus on self-care. Helping her prioritize her health by arranging something as considerate as a chiropractic session shows how much you value her well-being. It's a small but impactful way to support her in feeling strong, refreshed, and ready to take on whatever life brings her way.

183

Crack the Code with Escape Room Adventures Together

Visiting an escape room together is a thrilling way to test your teamwork, communication, and problem-solving skills. These immersive challenges transport you into scenarios where you must work together to solve puzzles, uncover hidden clues, and beat the clock to "escape." The adrenaline rush of racing against time adds excitement, while the unique themes—ranging from solving a murder mystery to defusing a bomb—make each experience unforgettable.

This is an ideal activity for couples who love a challenge and enjoy thinking on their feet. It encourages collaboration and creativity as you combine your strengths to navigate the puzzles. Whether you crack the code in record time or laugh your way through with trial and error, the experience fosters a sense of camaraderie and teamwork. Even the moments of frustration can bring you closer as you learn to support each other under pressure.

I personally enjoy escape rooms and believe they're perfect for those who are analytical or thrive on solving complex problems. They provide an opportunity to step into a different world and immerse yourselves in something completely out of the ordinary. For couples who love mental challenges and intellectual stimulation, this is more than just a date—it's a dynamic bonding experience that leaves you feeling accomplished and closer than ever.

184

Gently Remind and Encourage Her to Prioritize Self Care

Men don't do this enough, but reminding and encouraging her to take care of herself is one of the simplest yet most meaningful ways to show your love. Life's demands can be overwhelming, and women often put others first, leaving little time for their own needs. A gentle reminder to slow down, take a breath, or focus on her well-being is an act of care that helps her feel seen and valued. Whether it's encouraging her to sleep in, take a walk, or treat herself to something she loves, your support can lighten her load and brighten her day.

This isn't about telling her what she should do but offering heartfelt suggestions. Maybe you notice she's been working too hard and could use a spa day, or you remind her how much she enjoys painting and nudge her to pick up the brush again. It's about being attentive and understanding her needs even when she doesn't voice them. Your encouragement sends the message that her happiness and health are as important to you as they should be to her.

Sometimes the most loving thing you can do is help her recognize her worth and remind her to prioritize herself. Whether it's bringing her a cup of tea and suggesting she takes a moment to relax, or insisting she schedules that overdue check-up, your actions show that you're invested in her well-being. It's not just about her physical health but her mental and emotional balance, too. Helping her take care of herself strengthens your bond and ensures she feels loved, appreciated, and supported every day.

185

Invest in Yourself Through Counseling

Being willing to refine yourself where you're weaker is one of the greatest gifts you can give to your relationship. While you may excel in many areas, acknowledging where you struggle and seeking guidance through counseling is a powerful way to grow. It's not about admitting failure; it's about embracing the opportunity to better yourself and, in turn, your relationship. Counseling offers a professional perspective that can help you navigate challenges, identify blind spots, and develop tools to strengthen your emotional intelligence and communication skills.

By investing in counseling, you're not just helping yourself—you're catering to her by becoming a more refined and self-aware partner. A relationship thrives when both individuals are committed to growth, and counseling is a tangible step toward that commitment. Whether it's learning to manage stress, improving conflict resolution, or addressing deeper insecurities, the changes you make will ripple outward, positively impacting your connection with her and others around you.

Taking this step also sets a powerful example. It shows her that you value the relationship enough to put in the effort to improve. This isn't just about fixing problems; it's about building a stronger foundation for the future. When she sees your willingness to invest in self-improvement, it reassures her that you're serious about nurturing your partnership and creating a healthier, happier dynamic.

There's nothing wrong with going to counseling—it's not a sign of weakness but of wisdom. All you have to do is remove ego and pride, understanding that continual education and self-improvement make us better individuals and partners. Seeking guidance from a professional is no different than learning a skill or upgrading your tools—it's an investment in becoming the best version of yourself. By being open to this process, you demonstrate strength, humility, and a deep commitment to personal and relational growth.

186

Pack a Surprise Snack Bag for a Day Out

Packing a surprise snack bag for a day out is a considerate way to show that you're tuned into her preferences and eager to make her day better. Whether you're heading out for a hike, a road trip, or a day of exploring, having a bag filled with her favorite snacks ready to go adds a personal touch to your plans. Including a mix of sweet and savory treats, along with a special drink or two, reflects the thought you've put into making the day enjoyable for her.

This act is about more than just providing snacks; it's about being attentive to her needs and showing that you've planned ahead to make things easier and more enjoyable. By considering her preferences, you create a moment that focuses on her comfort and happiness, ensuring she feels cared for throughout the outing. It's a simple yet effective way to demonstrate your care in a tangible way.

The element of surprise adds an extra layer of delight, as she discovers the effort you've put into preparing something just for her. This small but impactful gesture turns an ordinary day into something memorable. Beyond keeping her energized, it shows that in even the smallest details, you're always thinking about how to make her life a little brighter.

It's Written in the Stars: Plan a Date Night at a Planetarium

Going to a planetarium or observatory together is a unique and awe-inspiring way to connect while exploring the wonders of the universe. Whether you're gazing at the stars through powerful telescopes, learning about distant galaxies, or enjoying a captivating show under the dome of a planetarium, this experience offers a chance to share a sense of wonder and curiosity about the cosmos.

This outing is not just about the spectacle of the stars; it's also about the conversations that follow, as you reflect on the vastness of the universe and your place within it. The serene and contemplative environment of a planetarium or observatory can deepen your connection, as you both marvel at the beauty and mystery of the night sky. It's a memorable and educational experience that brings a touch of magic to your time together.

Some popular locations to consider include the Griffith Observatory in Los Angeles, known for its stunning views and interactive exhibits, and the Hayden Planetarium in New York City, which features state-of-the-art shows narrated by renowned scientists. For those seeking a hands-on experience, the Lowell Observatory in Flagstaff, Arizona, offers telescope viewing under some of the clearest skies in the country. No matter where you go, these destinations provide an unforgettable journey into the stars, making it a perfect outing for curious and adventurous couples.

Give Her Sweet Dreams: Gift Comfort with New Bedding

Gifting her a memory foam mattress topper or a new bedding set is a caring way to improve her comfort and overall well-being, especially if your current mattress or bedding has seen better days. A memory foam topper can rejuvenate your bed, turning it into a cozy and supportive retreat that helps her rest more soundly and wake up feeling refreshed. If you opt for a bedding set, choose one made from soft, high-quality materials and a design that matches her style, adding a sense of elegance and coziness to her space.

This gift is more than just practical—it's a way to show you value her rest and relaxation. By upgrading your shared sleep environment, you're addressing wear and tear while enhancing her daily comfort. Whether she enjoys the sensation of sinking into a soft, inviting bed or appreciates the look of fresh, beautifully coordinated bedding, this gesture highlights your dedication to creating a comfortable and welcoming space for her.

189

Give Her Grace During Challenging Moments

Giving her grace during challenging moments is one of the most impactful ways to demonstrate love and emotional maturity in your relationship. It's inevitable that conflicts will arise, and emotions will run high, but how you choose to handle these moments can either deepen your connection or create unnecessary damage. Resolving not to yell, fight, or match her tone—even when things get heated—is a decision to lead with patience and respect. This doesn't mean suppressing your feelings but rather choosing to respond in a way that fosters growth for both of you.

As men, it can be especially challenging to tolerate aggressive energy, as we're often conditioned to avoid or confront it directly, particularly with other men. When a woman expresses frustration or anger in a heightened way, it's natural to feel the same instinct to fight back or shut down. However, recognizing that this is not about "winning" the moment but about understanding her emotions allows you to rise above the situation. Walking away when the conversation becomes flagrant or disrespectful is not a sign of weakness; it's an act of maturity. By giving the space for things to cool down, you create an opportunity for more meaningful and productive communication later.

This approach caters to her being as a woman because it acknowledges her emotional depth without diminishing it. Women often need to feel heard, even when their delivery may not be ideal. By showing restraint and maintaining your composure, you model the kind of calm and respect that allows her to reflect on her own tone and approach. It's not about enabling harmful behavior but demonstrating the grace you would want if the roles were reversed. This act of grace provides her with the security to express herself while giving her the chance to grow emotionally.

Ultimately, giving her grace during challenging moments is an investment in the long-term health of your relationship. It shows her that you value peace and mutual respect over fleeting pride or reactive emotions. This approach fosters an environment where both partners can feel safe, understood, and committed to personal growth. As you handle conflicts with patience and love, you create a foundation of trust and maturity that strengthens your bond and inspires both of you to become better versions of yourselves.

190

Plan a Sunrise Romance with a Morning Coffee or Breakfast Date

Planning a surprise morning coffee or breakfast date is a pleasant action that starts the day with love and connection. Whether you arrange a cozy breakfast at home, complete with her favorite coffee and a delicious meal, or take her to a charming café she loves, this gesture shows that you're thinking of her from the moment you wake up.

The spontaneity of a surprise breakfast date adds excitement and warmth to your morning, turning an ordinary routine into a special occasion. It's a great way to enjoy each other's company in a relaxed setting, creating a positive tone for the rest of the day. Whether it's a weekday treat before work or a leisurely weekend morning, this gesture will make her feel cherished and appreciated from the start of the day.

191

Seeing Is Believing: Help Her Create a Vision Board

Helping her create a vision board for her dreams and goals is a supportive and inspiring way to show your commitment to her aspirations. A vision board is a powerful tool that visually represents her ambitions, serving as a daily reminder of what she wants to achieve. By sitting down together to select images, words, and symbols that reflect her goals—whether personal, professional, or spiritual—you show that you're invested in her future.

This activity is not just about crafting a board; it's about engaging in meaningful conversation about her dreams and how you can support her in reaching them. As you work together, you'll deepen your understanding of what drives her and how you can be a partner in her journey. The finished vision board will be a tangible expression of her goals, created with your encouragement and love, serving as a motivating and uplifting presence in her life.

192

Have Dinner on the Move with a Progressive Dining Delight

Having a progressive dinner where you try different courses at various restaurants is a fun and adventurous way to explore new dining experiences together. Start with appetizers at one spot, move on to the main course at another, and finish with dessert at a final location. This approach turns an ordinary dinner into an exciting culinary journey, allowing you to sample a variety of flavors and atmospheres throughout the evening.

This type of dining experience not only introduces you both to new places but also keeps the night dynamic and full of surprises. As you travel between locations, you can share your thoughts on each course, discuss your favorites, and enjoy the thrill of discovering new restaurants. A progressive dinner adds a sense of adventure and spontaneity to your date night, making it a memorable and unique way to spend time together.

Just be prepared for the logistics—you might feel like food critics on a mission or contestants on a scavenger hunt for the perfect meal. If one place takes forever with the breadsticks or the waiter accidentally drops your dessert, laugh it off and keep the fun rolling. After all, the night's about the adventure, not perfection. And hey, if the portions are tiny, at least you won't feel guilty ordering that extra dessert at the final stop—you've earned it!

193

Picture Perfect Nostalgia with a Polaroid Camera and Film

Gifting her a Polaroid camera with film is a nostalgic and creative way to help her capture and cherish moments in a tangible form. Unlike digital photos that often get lost in the shuffle, Polaroid pictures offer the instant gratification of holding a memory in your hand moments after it happens. Whether she's capturing everyday moments or special occasions, a Polaroid camera allows her to create a physical collection of memories that she can display, share, or keep as personal mementos.

This gift is not just about the camera—it's about encouraging her to document and celebrate the beauty of life's fleeting moments. You can make it even more special by starting the collection with a few photos of the two of you, adding a personal touch that sets the tone for the memories she'll create. The Polaroid camera is a fun and thoughtful way to blend creativity with nostalgia, giving her a way to treasure the present in a way that feels both retro and timeless.

194

Time Travel Together, Recalling and Reliving Special Moments

Recalling and reliving special moments you've shared together is a heartfelt way to celebrate your relationship and reflect on the journey you've taken as a couple. Whether it's reminiscing about the first time you met, laughing about a funny mishap during a vacation, or cherishing the memory of a romantic surprise, these shared reflections reinforce the bond you've built over time. Talking about these moments brings them back to life, reminding you both of how far you've come and the love that continues to grow between you.

To make it even more meaningful, try recreating some of those cherished memories. Surprise her by taking her back to the spot where you had your first date, cooking a meal that reminds her of a special trip, or watching a movie you both loved at the beginning of your relationship. These simple gestures don't just honor the past—they breathe new life into old memories, letting you relive the intimate connection you felt in those moments.

Sometimes, recalling these memories can lead to hilarious or touching discoveries. Like the time you thought you were suave on your first date but spilled water all over the table—or when she insisted you take just one more photo during a trip, and now that picture is framed in your home. These stories become treasures, and retelling them reinforces the joy and authenticity of your relationship.

195

Create Love by Candlelight: A Romantic Dinner at Home

Surprising her with a candlelit dinner at home is a romantic way to turn an ordinary evening into something unforgettable. Whether you're celebrating a special occasion or just want to show your love, preparing her favorite meal and creating an intimate atmosphere with candles and soft music sets the perfect tone. It's a simple yet powerful gesture that shows her how much you care.

Plan the evening with attention to detail—select a carefully curated menu, set the table beautifully, and consider adding a bottle of her favorite wine or some fresh flowers. The effort you put into this dinner says so much, demonstrating that you're committed to making her feel valued and cared for. It's not about perfection; it's about creating an atmosphere where she can unwind and feel truly special.

The cozy ambiance of a candlelit dinner at home allows for meaningful conversation and uninterrupted time together. Sharing a meal in such a setting fosters connection and makes the evening feel magical. It's a beautiful way to celebrate your relationship and create lasting memories in the comfort of your own home.

196

Bond Over a Thoughtful Scavenger Hunt at Home

Organizing a personalized scavenger hunt at home is a fun and creative way to surprise her with an engaging and thoughtful experience. You can design a series of clues that lead her to different spots around the house, each revealing a small gift, a sweet note, or a memory you've shared. The final destination could be something special, like a beautifully set table for dinner, a cozy setup for a movie night, or even a gift you've prepared just for her.

This scavenger hunt combines elements of surprise, adventure, and romance, making it a creative way to express your love. The care you put into designing clues that reflect your relationship will make the experience even more memorable. It's an engaging and playful way to spend time together, and the personal touch behind each clue will remind her of the strength of your bond.

197

Discover Local Gems and Nearby Landmarks Together

Visiting a nearby landmark or tourist attraction is a wonderful way to explore your local area and create new memories together. Whether it's a historical site, a famous monument, a beautiful park, or a quirky museum, taking the time to experience something new in your own city or town can be both fun and enriching. It's an opportunity to break out of your routine and discover hidden gems or popular spots you've never visited before.

This outing allows you to be tourists in your own area, offering a fresh perspective on the place you call home. As you explore, you can learn more about the history, culture, and unique features of your surroundings, all while enjoying each other's company. The experience of discovering something new together can spark interesting conversations and bring you closer, making it a meaningful and memorable date that combines adventure with local charm.

198

Buy Her a Surprise Outfit and Plan a Romantic Friday Date

Surprise her by buying a beautiful outfit, complete with a dinner dress, stylish heels, and accessories, and plan a romantic Friday dinner to kick off the weekend. After a long week of work, kids, and responsibilities, this thoughtful gesture will give her a much-needed break and a glamorous start to the weekend. Carefully select a dress that reflects her style and personality, paired with heels that make her feel confident and accessories that add the perfect finishing touch.

Arrange the dinner at a special restaurant or create an elegant dining experience at home, setting the scene with soft lighting, candles, and her favorite music. Present her with the outfit and encourage her to take her time getting ready, knowing that you've taken care of all the details. This surprise not only shows your appreciation for everything she does but also gives her a moment to feel pampered and cherished. It's a romantic way to express your love, making her feel special and turning an ordinary Friday night into an unforgettable evening.

One mistake I made when I was younger was thinking everything had to be name brand or high-end. The truth is, it's all about knowing your significant other and understanding what she likes, not just slapping a designer label on it. Know your financial limits and work within them—there are plenty of ways to find a stylish outfit without breaking the bank. Whether it's picking something from her favorite local boutique or finding a hidden gem online, it's the thought and effort that count, not the price tag.

199

Embrace Moments That Matter: Show Gratitude for Togetherness

Expressing gratitude for the time you spend together is a meaningful way to strengthen your bond and remind her how much you value your relationship. Whether it's a simple "thank you" for a fun day out, a heartfelt message after a quiet evening at home, or a note expressing how much you appreciate her presence in your life, acknowledging the moments you share shows that you don't take them for granted.

This practice of showing gratitude can deepen your connection by highlighting the importance of even the smallest interactions. It encourages both of you to focus on the positives in your relationship and reinforces the idea that your time together is cherished and meaningful. By regularly expressing your appreciation, you create an atmosphere of mutual respect and love, making your relationship stronger and more fulfilling.

Bonus:
Speak with Integrity About Her, Both in Private and Public

How you speak about your partner when she's not present reveals as much about your character as it does about the state of your relationship. While occasional consultations with trusted, wise counsel are necessary to seek guidance on challenges, consistently speaking ill of her to others is not only damaging but also a sign of deeper issues that demand attention.

When you choose to highlight her flaws or air grievances without acknowledging her strengths, you not only diminish her in the eyes of others but also erode the foundation of respect and trust in your relationship. It creates a narrative that might feel one-sided and unfair, leaving her without the opportunity to represent herself.

Consider the men who consistently speak ill of their partners or blame them for everything that goes wrong. One man I know rarely has a kind word to say about his wife, turning every conversation into a list of her perceived faults while absolving himself of any responsibility. Another struggles to maintain relationships, yet each failed connection becomes another tale of how he was wronged, as if every woman he's been with is conspiring against him. These patterns are not only distasteful but also reflective of a lack of self-awareness and accountability. When a man cannot take responsibility for his role in the relationship, he undermines both his partner's dignity and his own ability to grow and foster healthy connections.

Instead, focus on balance. If you feel the need to share challenges, ensure it is done with someone who will guide you toward resolution—not someone who will fuel negativity. Just as important, remember to voice her positive qualities. Recognize her kindness, intelligence, humor, or resilience in conversations. Show others that your partner is someone you admire and respect, even during hard times.

When accountability is missing, and negative words become the norm, it's often a sign of avoidance. Ask yourself: Are these repeated complaints masking an unwillingness to address your role in the dynamic? Are you unfairly shifting blame to her instead of owning your part? Being accountable for your actions and words is essential in building a strong, respectful relationship.

Make it a priority to be her champion, not her critic. The energy you bring into conversations about her should uplift and affirm her worth. If challenges exist, address them directly with her rather than creating a public narrative that isolates and belittles her. Speaking with integrity about her—whether in her presence or absence—ensures that your words align with the respect and love she deserves.

Take a Romantic Late-Night Stroll Under the Stars

Taking a late-night walk together is a peaceful and intimate way to unwind and connect at the end of the day. The quiet of the night, the soft glow of streetlights, and the cooler air create a serene atmosphere perfect for relaxed conversation or simply enjoying each other's company in silence. Choose a well-lit, safe area for your walk, such as a nearby park, a quiet neighborhood, or a city promenade, ensuring that you can fully enjoy the experience without any concerns.

This late-night stroll offers a chance to slow down, reflect on the day, and share your thoughts in a calm, unhurried environment. It's a simple yet meaningful way to bond, as the stillness of the night allows you to focus entirely on each other. Whether you're discussing your dreams, reminiscing about shared memories, or just walking hand in hand, a late-night walk can turn an ordinary evening into a special, intimate moment that brings you closer.

202

Plan a Scenic Day Trip with Spontaneous Adventure

Planning a surprise day trip to a nearby town or scenic spot is a wonderful way to break the routine and enjoy a spontaneous adventure together. Choose a destination within a short drive, such as a charming small town, a picturesque park, a hiking trail, or a beautiful lake. The element of surprise adds excitement, turning an ordinary day into a special getaway.

Pack some snacks or plan to explore local eateries, visit quaint shops, or simply take in the natural beauty of the area. This day trip gives you both a chance to relax, explore, and create new memories together, all while enjoying each other's company in a fresh setting. It's a thoughtful and fun way to show her that you're always thinking of ways to make your time together special and memorable.

203

Ride Love's Wave by Renting Jet Skis for Two

Taking a day to rent jet skis at a lake or marina is an exhilarating way to shake up your routine and enjoy the outdoors together. Whether you're seasoned pros or hopping on for the first time, the excitement of speeding across the water and feeling the cool spray of the waves is unmatched. It's an adventure that combines the freedom of exploration with the thrill of water sports, offering an unforgettable experience for both of you.

This outing isn't just about the adrenaline—it's also about creating moments of connection. Laughing as you figure out the controls, playfully racing each other, or stopping in the middle of the water to take in the views makes the day as romantic as it is adventurous. After the ride, you can relax by the shoreline, enjoy a picnic, or simply soak up the sun while reliving the best moments of your time on the water.

For couples looking for something a little different, jet skiing is the perfect mix of fun and spontaneity. It lets you break free from the ordinary, test your adventurous sides, and create memories you'll laugh about for years to come—especially if one of you accidentally takes an unexpected splash!

204

Reassure Her She's the One, Your Forever Choice

Reminding her that she's the only woman you want in your life is a powerful affirmation of your love and commitment. In a world full of distractions, making it clear that she holds a unique and irreplaceable place in your heart can bring her a deep sense of security and confidence in your relationship. Whether through words, actions, or both, letting her know that she's the one you choose, every day, reassures her of your unwavering devotion.

You can express this sentiment in various ways—a heartfelt conversation, a loving note, or simply taking a moment during your day to look into her eyes and tell her how much she means to you. This reaffirmation strengthens your bond and reminds her that your love is exclusive and enduring. It's a simple yet profound way to show her that, in your life, she is and always will be the only woman you desire and cherish.

If she is doing her best for you, she should never have to question her place in your life. Your consistent words and actions should leave no room for doubt. It's about ensuring she feels valued, respected, and seen for all the effort she pours into the relationship. Letting her know that her love and care are reciprocated creates a foundation of trust and appreciation that eliminates insecurity, allowing her to thrive in the confidence of being your chosen partner.

205

Share Inspiring Quotes and Words of Love That Lift Her Up

Sharing quotes that inspire and celebrate her worth is a considerate way to remind her of her value and inner strength. Whether she's navigating challenges or could use a little encouragement, finding and sharing impactful quotes can lift her spirits and reinforce how much she matters to you. These quotes can focus on themes like confidence, perseverance, empowerment, or anything that aligns with her journey and character.

You can share these quotes in a variety of ways—sending them as texts throughout the day, writing them on sticky notes and leaving them around the house, or even creating a personalized quote book filled with words that reflect her worth. This small but impactful gesture shows that you're always thinking of her and that you see and appreciate her for who she is. It's a beautiful way to support her emotionally and remind her of her inherent value.

206

Create Playful Fun with a Pillow Fight Royale

Engaging in playful wrestling or a friendly pillow fight is a charming way to bring fun and spontaneity into your relationship. Whether it's tossing pillows across the bed or playfully grappling for the "last word" on the living room floor, these lighthearted moments are a perfect way to tap into your inner child and let loose. It's not about winning but about sharing giggles and enjoying each other's playful side.

These activities are also a great way to unwind and shake off the stress of the day. A playful pillow fight can become an instant mood booster, helping you both relax and bond in the process. The physical interaction fosters intimacy and connection, while the laughter you share reinforces the joy and fun of simply being together. These moments of silliness can be a welcome break from routine, reminding you both to prioritize fun and togetherness.

And let's be real—this is your chance to show off your Matrix-style moves as you dodge pillows in slow motion or channel your inner wrestler (within reason, of course). Just make sure to avoid the fragile decor and, if you're going to bring the drama, commit fully—who doesn't love a "mock victory pose" after the fluff settles? It's all in good fun and guarantees a memory you'll both laugh about later.

Mom's Day Off: Get the Kids to Treat Her Like a Queen

Organizing a day where the kids cater to her is a beautiful way to show appreciation for everything she does as a mother. It's not just about giving her a break—it's about involving the children in expressing love and gratitude. Whether they bring her breakfast in bed, tidy up around the house, or create handmade cards and crafts, this thoughtful gesture turns the spotlight on her and celebrates all that she gives to the family.

This experience also teaches children an important life lesson: the value of appreciation and gratitude. It's a chance for them to recognize her efforts and understand that saying "thank you" isn't reserved for Mother's Day or special occasions. Encouraging them to actively participate fosters a sense of empathy and helps them build a habit of showing love through actions, not just words.

The happiness she'll feel seeing her kids take the lead in making her day special is priceless. Whether it's a child's slightly lopsided pancake or a warm hug, these moments become cherished memories. By creating this tradition, you're not only expressing love for her but also teaching your children to grow into considerate, caring individuals who understand the value of showing appreciation for the people who brighten their lives every day.

Feed Her Spirit by Bonding, Reading Together from a Spiritual Source

Reading to her from your source of spiritual guidance is a deeply meaningful way to nurture both your connection and your shared spiritual journey. Whether you're reading passages from religious texts, uplifting literature, or meditative writings, this act invites reflection, comfort, and inspiration into your relationship. It's an opportunity to explore your beliefs together, creating a sense of unity that transcends the everyday and touches the soul.

Choose readings that resonate with your shared values or ones that offer wisdom, encouragement, or peace. Whether it's a verse that speaks to perseverance during challenging times or a passage celebrating love and gratitude, the words become a foundation for deeper conversations. This shared practice fosters understanding and opens the door to discussing how your spiritual beliefs shape your life as individuals and as a couple.

This gesture is also about creating a moment of quiet intimacy. Sitting together, sharing words that inspire and uplift, shows her that your connection isn't limited to physical or emotional realms—it extends into the spiritual. By engaging in this practice, you demonstrate your commitment to growing together in all aspects of life, making your bond richer and more fulfilling.

209

Pockets Full of Love: Hide Sweet Notes for Her to Find

Leaving love notes in her pockets for her to find later is a sweet and unexpected way to remind her of your affection throughout the day. These small, handwritten notes can be tucked into the pockets of her coat, jeans, or even her handbag, offering little surprises that brighten her day when she least expects it. Whether the notes contain loving messages, compliments, or inside jokes, they serve as tangible reminders of your love and thoughtfulness.

The joy of discovering these hidden notes adds an element of surprise and warmth to her daily routine. Each note becomes a moment of connection, even when you're apart, making her feel cherished and appreciated. This simple yet powerful gesture shows that you're always thinking of her, turning ordinary moments into opportunities for love and affection.

Buy Her a Special Necklace... But Make It Fun

Surprising her with a special necklace can be made even more memorable by adding a playful twist to the presentation. Start by purchasing a beautiful necklace that you know she'll love. Then, place the necklace in its case and hide it at the bottom of a brown paper bag. Fill the bag with balled-up paper or gift bag filler to conceal the case.

Next, stop by a gas station and pick up a candy necklace—the kind you might find in a novelty section. Place the candy necklace on top of the filler, along with a lighthearted note that says something like, "I know you love sweet things, so here's a little something to brighten your day." When she opens the bag, she'll initially find the candy necklace and may chuckle at the playful gift. But as she digs deeper into the bag, she'll discover the real surprise: the beautiful necklace hidden at the bottom.

This fun and imaginative approach adds an element of surprise to the gift-giving experience, making the moment unforgettable. It's a playful way to show your care and attention, leaving her with a smile and a new piece of jewelry to treasure.

Dream Out Loud by Discussing and Building a Vision Together

Taking the time to discuss and build a shared vision for your future together is a powerful way to align your goals, dreams, and values as a couple. This process involves open and honest conversations about where you both see yourselves in the coming years—whether it's related to your careers, family, lifestyle, or personal growth. By identifying common goals and aspirations, you create a roadmap for your relationship that reflects both of your desires and ambitions.

This activity is not just about planning but also about deepening your connection by understanding each other's hopes and dreams. You can create a physical vision board that represents your shared future, or simply have regular conversations to check in on your progress and adjust your plans as needed. This collaborative approach fosters a sense of unity and partnership, ensuring that you're both moving forward in a direction that supports your relationship and individual growth. It's a way to dream together and actively work towards a future that excites and fulfills both of you.

Create "Treasures of Us" with a Relationship Time Capsule

Creating a time capsule of your relationship is a meaningful way to preserve memories and look forward to the future together. Gather items that represent important moments, milestones, or shared experiences in your relationship—these could include letters, photos, small mementos from trips, or even notes about your hopes and dreams for the future. Place these items in a box or container, and choose a date in the future when you'll open it together.

This activity not only allows you to reflect on the journey you've shared so far but also gives you something special to look forward to. As you select items for the time capsule, you'll have the chance to relive some of your favorite memories and discuss what's important to you both. Sealing the time capsule together symbolizes your commitment to your shared future, making it a cherished keepsake that you can revisit in years to come.

213

Be Her Safe Ride Home After a Girls' Night Out

There's something deeply comforting about knowing you can rely on someone at the end of a night out, and offering to pick her up after a girls' night is a small but impactful way to show you care. Whether she's had a few drinks, feels tired, or simply doesn't want the hassle of finding a ride, your presence can be a relief. This gesture isn't just practical—it communicates that her well-being is always a priority to you.

Girls' nights are her time to unwind and enjoy herself with friends, and your offer to pick her up ensures she can fully relax without worrying about logistics. It's not about feeding your insecurities, snooping, hovering, or intruding on her fun; instead, it's about providing peace of mind. Knowing that she has someone she trusts to bring her home safely adds an extra layer of security and comfort to her night.

This act of awareness and protection is especially meaningful in situations where she might feel vulnerable. Late-night rideshare services or taxis can sometimes be unpredictable, and walking alone at night isn't always safe. By offering to be her safe ride home, you eliminate those concerns, allowing her to focus on enjoying her evening with friends.

It's not just about driving her home—it's about being dependable, no matter the hour. Maybe she texts you midway through the night asking for a pick-up, or perhaps you proactively let her know you'll be waiting when the night winds down. Either way, your willingness to show up reinforces that you're someone she can count on. Even better, add an extra touch—grab her a bottle of water or her favorite snack for the ride home. These small details make the gesture even more thoughtful, reminding her that you care about her comfort as much as her safety.

214

Show Affection in Action by Making Your Love Publicly Known

Showing affection in public is a simple yet powerful way to express your love and pride in your relationship. Whether it's holding hands while walking, giving her a quick kiss, or wrapping your arm around her in a crowded place, these small gestures of affection demonstrate that you're not afraid to show the world how much she means to you. A public display of affection (PDA) can vary from subtle touches to more obvious signs of love, depending on what makes both of you feel comfortable.

However, it's essential to be mindful of your surroundings and the cultural norms of the place you're in. In some countries or regions, PDAs might not be permitted or socially acceptable, so it's important to respect local customs and regulations. When in a place where a PDA is appropriate, these gestures can turn ordinary experiences into moments of connection and intimacy, reminding her that your love is constant and unwavering, no matter where you are.

215

Draw a Personal Masterpiece of Something Meaningful

Drawing something meaningful for her is a deeply personal way to express your love and creativity. Whether you're an experienced artist or just enjoy doodling, the effort you put into creating a piece of art specifically for her speaks volumes. It could be a portrait of her, a sketch that represents a special memory you've shared, or even an abstract piece that symbolizes your feelings for her.

The meaning behind the drawing is what makes it special. It shows that you've taken the time to create something unique and heartfelt, just for her. Presenting her with this drawing not only gives her a beautiful piece of art to cherish but also demonstrates the depth of your connection. It's a gift that goes beyond words, capturing your feelings in a way that's both creative and intimate.

216

Bake a Special Dessert or Sweet Treat for Her from Scratch

Baking a special dessert for her from scratch is a sincere way to show how much you care. Whether it's a gooey chocolate cake, soft-baked cookies, or a tangy lemon tart, creating something with your own two hands reflects your effort and care. It's not just about the dessert itself but the intention and love you put into the process, making it a memorable gesture that she's sure to value.

The beauty of baking from scratch lies in the personal touch. You're not just following a recipe—you're tailoring it to her tastes and preferences. Maybe you'll sprinkle extra chocolate chips in the batter because she loves them or use a specific fruit that brings back fond memories. The homemade nature of the dessert sets it apart from anything store-bought, turning a simple treat into a heartfelt symbol of your dedication.

When the baking is done, serving the dessert is an opportunity to create a cozy, memorable moment together. Whether you enjoy it over coffee, after dinner, or even with a glass of wine, sharing the dessert transforms the act of baking into a shared experience of sweetness and connection. And even if your first attempt isn't Pinterest-perfect, she'll love the effort and the thought behind it—because love always tastes better.

217

Share Love from Above Together on a Helicopter Tour

Taking a scenic helicopter tour is an exhilarating way to experience breathtaking views and create unforgettable memories together. Whether it's soaring over a city skyline, flying above stunning landscapes, or getting a bird's-eye view of famous landmarks, a helicopter tour offers a unique perspective that's both thrilling and awe-inspiring. This adventure allows you to see the world from a completely different angle, making it a once-in-a-lifetime experience.

The excitement of the helicopter ride, combined with the beauty of the scenery below, creates a shared experience that you'll both cherish. It's a perfect way to celebrate a special occasion, add some adventure to your relationship, or simply enjoy an extraordinary date. After the tour, you'll have plenty to talk about and memories that will last long after the helicopter has landed.

218

Show Pride in Your Relationship and Her Role in It

Showing pride in your relationship and her role within it is a meaningful way to honor her and celebrate the love you share. It's about letting her know, through words and actions, that you value her deeply and are grateful for everything she brings to your partnership. Whether it's the way she supports you, her unique qualities, or the strength she brings to your shared journey, acknowledging these contributions reinforces her significance in your life and makes her feel truly appreciated.

There are countless ways to express this pride. Talk about her accomplishments and the impact she has on your life when speaking with friends and family. Share a heartfelt social media post that celebrates your love story and highlights what makes her special. Even in private moments, take the time to remind her of how proud you are to have her by your side. These gestures show that you see her as an integral part of your life and that you're not afraid to let the world know.

Celebrating her and your relationship is also about creating a sense of security and confidence in your partnership. When she sees how proud you are of her, it strengthens the bond you share and reassures her that her efforts and presence are deeply valued. It's not just about grand gestures—it's the everyday affirmations, the public acknowledgment, and the private gratitude that together create a foundation of mutual respect, love, and admiration.

219

Make It Picture Perfect by Framing Love in a Surprise Photoshoot

A surprise photoshoot is a creative and caring way to celebrate your love and create lasting memories. Whether it's a session designed to highlight her individuality or one that captures your connection as a couple, the effort you put into planning this surprise will show her just how much you appreciate the moments you share. It's more than just taking pictures—it's about creating an unforgettable experience filled with joy, affection, and a touch of romance.

If the shoot is just for her, make it all about honoring who she is. Choose a photographer who knows how to make her feel confident and comfortable, and consider what she loves most—perhaps a stunning outdoor setting, a cozy studio, or a location with personal significance. Let her know that this is her moment to shine, and add special touches like a bouquet of flowers, a stylist, or a wardrobe enhancement to make her feel truly celebrated.

For a couple's photoshoot, focus on capturing the essence of your unique bond. Pick a theme or location that reflects your shared story—a favorite hiking trail, a charming coffee shop, or even the comfort of your home. The key is to create a relaxed and genuine atmosphere so your connection shines through in every shot. The surprise lies not only in the photoshoot itself but in the joy of experiencing something creative and new together.

Planning the shoot in secret takes attention to detail. Coordinate with a photographer, secure the location, and arrange for her availability—all while keeping the plans under wraps. When the day arrives, reveal your surprise with excitement and let her know this is your way of celebrating her and the relationship you've built together. The care behind the gesture will mean as much as the photos themselves.

Once the photos are ready, share them in memorable ways. Frame her favorite shot, create an album of the session, or print a large canvas to display at home. These keepsakes become treasured reminders of a day filled with connection, effort, and affection—proof of how much you cherish the beauty of your journey together.

220

Convert Her Old Media to Digital Modern Memories

Preserving her cherished memories by converting old media like VHS tapes, DVDs, or even cassette recordings into digital formats is a caring way to honor her past. These older forms of media often hold irreplaceable moments—childhood milestones, family gatherings, or sentimental events—that can be challenging to access as technology changes. By digitizing them, you're ensuring these memories remain accessible and can be enjoyed for years to come.

This gesture is not just practical; it's deeply personal. Research reputable conversion services or invest in the necessary tools to do it yourself, demonstrating your effort and care in safeguarding what's important to her. Present the final collection in a neatly organized format, perhaps on a USB drive, an external hard drive, or even a curated cloud folder. Adding thoughtful touches, like labeling the files or creating a digital slideshow, can make the gesture even more special.

Not only does this act preserve her memories, but it also shows her how much you value her history and the moments that have shaped her life. It's a way of saying that her past is important to you too, and you want to make it easier for her to relive those beautiful memories. By bringing her old media into the digital age, you're giving her a timeless gift—one that ensures her memories remain accessible, shareable, and safe.

221

Give Her Your Undivided Attention During Special Moments

Giving her your undivided attention during special moments is one of the most meaningful ways to show your love and respect. Whether it's during an important conversation, a vulnerable moment when she's opening up, or a special date night, your full focus lets her know she's the priority in your life. In a world constantly pulling us toward phones, emails, and social media, choosing to be fully present is a powerful gesture that speaks volumes about your commitment and care.

During these times, make a conscious effort to put your phone away—not just silenced but out of sight—and resist the urge to check emails, texts, or scroll through social media. Instead, give her your full attention: maintain eye contact, actively listen, and respond with empathy and thoughtfulness. This act of presence communicates that her words and feelings matter more to you than any notification, ensuring she feels truly heard and valued.

Abstaining from distractions, especially social media, also reinforces the importance of these moments and your connection. It's not just about avoiding interruptions but about creating a sacred space where she feels cherished. By being fully present, you send the message that no external matter—no post, like, or comment—is as significant as the time you share together. These focused moments strengthen your bond and remind her that she is the center of your attention, where she belongs.

Write a Love Story Starring the Two of You

Writing a story that features the two of you as characters is a unique and imaginative way to celebrate your relationship. It's a deeply personal gesture that showcases your creativity and reflects how much you value your connection. Whether it's an epic adventure where you both save the day, a whimsical tale set in a fantasy world, or a romantic story that mirrors your real-life experiences, this narrative becomes a love letter in story form.

Incorporate meaningful details that make the story truly yours—inside jokes, favorite places, shared dreams, or qualities you admire about her. You can be as playful or heartfelt as you want, crafting a tale that captures the essence of your bond. The beauty of this gesture lies in its originality and the effort you put into weaving the story, making it a one-of-a-kind gift that speaks directly to her heart.

When you present the story, make it a special moment. Print it out, bind it like a mini-book, or read it aloud to her in an intimate setting. Sharing this story offers not only entertainment but also a deep reminder of your love and creativity. It's a lasting keepsake that celebrates your journey together and highlights the magic of being part of each other's lives, forever captured in words.

223

Treat Her to Sips at Sunset with a Personalized Tasting

Few things evoke romance like the combination of a beautiful sunset and a carefully planned tasting experience. Hosting a personalized wine, beer, or even non-alcoholic beverage tasting for her blends elegance with the joy of exploration. It's not just about the drinks; it's about creating a warm, inviting atmosphere that reflects the effort you've put into planning an unforgettable evening.

Start by considering her preferences—does she lean toward a crisp white wine, or does she enjoy a bold stout? Maybe she'd appreciate a curated selection of craft sodas or sparkling waters if she doesn't drink alcohol. Research flavors that match her tastes and arrange a variety of options. To make the experience even more special, include pairings like charcuterie, chocolates, or small bites that complement the beverages. Setting up this experience at home or at a scenic outdoor location adds a personal touch that turns an ordinary day into a unique celebration.

Incorporate interactive elements to keep the tasting engaging. Add little tasting cards where she can write down her impressions of each drink, or share fun trivia about the beverages you've chosen. This playful dynamic makes the event feel special and adds an element of learning and exploration. It's also an opportunity for meaningful conversation as you share stories, memories, or dreams that connect to the experience.

What makes this idea even more beautiful is its flexibility. You can adapt it for any occasion, whether it's a quiet date night, an anniversary, or even just a way to brighten her week. The key is in the personalization—choosing items she'll love and setting the stage to show her that every detail was chosen with her in mind. By crafting this one-of-a-kind experience, you'll create a memory that reflects your thoughtfulness and strengthens the bond you share.

224

Gift Her a Romance Token for Selfless Intimacy

Creating a coupon for a night of selfless sex is a loving and intimate way to communicate your dedication to her happiness and satisfaction. This thoughtful gesture isn't just about the physical—it's about prioritizing her desires, focusing on her needs, and ensuring that she feels completely adored and appreciated. The coupon adds a playful touch, turning your promise into something tangible and fun while conveying a deeper message of care and commitment.

The key to a night of selfless intimacy is listening and being attentive to her preferences, ensuring she feels comfortable, safe, and valued throughout. Whether it's a romantic atmosphere with candles and soft music, or simply being fully present and patient, the goal is to create a moment that revolves entirely around her. This act not only deepens your physical connection but also reinforces your emotional bond, showing her that her pleasure and well-being are a top priority.

By giving her this coupon, you're making a statement that intimacy is about more than just physical acts—it's about fostering trust, closeness, and mutual respect. It's a way to celebrate your love in its most vulnerable and personal form, leaving her feeling cherished, confident, and deeply loved. The gesture itself, and the thought behind it, will likely be as meaningful as the experience.

Learn from Past Mistakes to Avoid Repeating Them

Learning from past mistakes is an essential part of growing both individually and as a couple. Mistakes happen in any relationship, but what matters most is how you respond to them. Taking time to reflect on where things went wrong—and understanding how they affected your partner—shows maturity and a willingness to improve. By addressing these moments honestly and constructively, you demonstrate your commitment to building a stronger, more harmonious bond.

The key to this process is honest communication and accountability. Acknowledge where things may have gone wrong without defensiveness or excuses, and actively work to change behaviors or patterns that led to the issue. This isn't about dwelling on the past but using those moments as opportunities for growth. When you show her that you're willing to make adjustments for the betterment of your relationship, you foster trust and mutual respect.

By learning from mistakes, you create a foundation of resilience and understanding. This effort reinforces the idea that your relationship is a partnership where both parties are invested in improving and supporting each other. Each lesson learned and applied becomes a stepping stone toward a future filled with greater compassion, empathy, and love—a future where you're both better because of the challenges you've overcome together.

226

Cater to Her Through Better Financial Stewardship

Money can be a source of stress or stability in a relationship, and practicing sound financial stewardship shows her that you're not just thinking about today but planning for tomorrow. Managing your finances responsibly doesn't just benefit you—it's a way of demonstrating care for her security, your shared goals, and the future you're building together.

Start by being transparent about your financial habits and goals. Whether it's setting a budget, paying off debt, or saving for something meaningful, involve her in the conversation. Transparency builds trust and shows her that you're serious about creating a foundation that supports both of your dreams.

Good financial stewardship isn't just about avoiding recklessness; it's about being intentional. Approach spending with care, making decisions that align with strong values and contribute to long-term stability. While aligning with her financial values is ideal, there may be times when her approach isn't conducive to healthy habits. In these cases, it's your responsibility to lead by example. Demonstrate good decision-making by setting clear boundaries, discussing the importance of savings and investments, and showing how thoughtful financial choices benefit both of you. Leadership in this area doesn't mean being controlling—it means being a source of guidance and balance.

Lastly, prioritize learning and improving. If finances have been a challenge for you in the past, take steps to educate yourself. Whether it's reading about budgeting, seeking professional advice, or using tools like apps to track expenses, showing her that you're committed to growth reassures her that you value the stability and future of your relationship.

Better financial stewardship is a quiet yet powerful way to cater to her needs and show her that you're not just thinking of the present—you're investing in a lifetime together.

227

Delight Her with a Day of Saying Yes to Everything She Loves

Organizing a surprise "Yes Day" is a playful way to show her that her happiness is your top priority. For one whole day, commit to saying yes to her requests (within reason, of course), letting her plan activities and enjoy the freedom to call the shots. Whether it's indulging in her favorite foods, going on an impromptu shopping spree, or binge-watching her guilty pleasure shows, the day becomes all about her, filled with spontaneity and fun.

This gesture is more than just saying yes—it's about showing her that you're willing to step outside your usual routine and embrace her interests wholeheartedly. The joy and laughter that come from participating in her chosen activities create unforgettable memories and reinforce your connection. By relinquishing control for a day, you demonstrate your trust and devotion, allowing her to feel completely seen and valued.

But here's a word of caution: be ready for her creativity to shine, and prepare yourself for unexpected surprises! If she decides you're getting matching pedicures, you might find yourself selecting a polish color. Or if she has a talent for turning "yes" into unexpected adventures, you could end up singing karaoke in public or sporting something hilariously outside your comfort zone. Embrace it all—after all, the excitement lies in showing her that you're game for the fun, no matter where it takes you!

228

Celebrate Her Unique Sparkle and Everything That Makes Her Special

Taking the time to point out what makes her truly special and unique is a powerful way to show your deep appreciation and love. Everyone has qualities that set them apart, and highlighting these traits—whether it's her kindness, intelligence, sense of humor, creativity, or resilience—can make her feel seen, valued, and cherished. This isn't just about giving compliments; it's about acknowledging the qualities that make her who she is.

You can express these thoughts in various ways: through a heartfelt conversation, a handwritten note, or even a surprise list of her unique traits left where she'll find it. By articulating what you love and admire about her, you reinforce her self-worth and strengthen your bond. This affirmation is a beautiful way to celebrate her individuality and remind her how much she means to you.

229

Score Strikes and Share Laughs During Bowling and Laser Tag

Taking her bowling and playing laser tag is a fantastic way to inject energy and excitement into your date. Bowling offers the perfect blend of friendly competition and relaxed fun. Whether you're nailing strikes or mastering the art of the gutter ball, it's all about cheering each other on, sharing laughs, and maybe even creating a playful rivalry. It's a great opportunity to show off (or laugh about) your skills and keep the atmosphere lighthearted.

After bowling, step things up by diving into a game of laser tag. The rush of strategizing, dodging lasers, and sneaking up on each other adds a thrilling dynamic to your time together. The playful competition keeps the adrenaline high, while the teamwork can bring out your fun, adventurous sides. It's not just about winning but about letting loose and enjoying the thrill of the game.

Just remember to bring your A-game, but also be ready for the unexpected—some women can be incredibly competitive in the right arena. Don't be surprised if she suddenly starts pulling off perfect strikes or dominating the laser tag scoreboard like she's been training for this moment her whole life. Embrace her competitive streak, laugh through the surprises, and let the spirited rivalry add even more fun to your time together!

230

Shape Beauty Together in a Glass-Blowing Experience

Taking her out for a glass blowing experience is a creative and memorable way to spend time together while learning a unique art form. Glass blowing is an intricate process that involves shaping molten glass into beautiful pieces, and participating in a workshop or class allows both of you to try your hand at this fascinating craft. Whether you create simple ornaments, decorative vases, or custom pieces, the experience is sure to be exciting and rewarding.

This activity is not only a chance to learn something new but also a way to bond over a shared challenge. The process of working with glass requires focus, patience, and teamwork, making it a great way to connect while creating something tangible together. At the end of the session, you'll have a beautiful, handmade piece of art to take home—a lasting reminder of the fun and creativity you shared during this unique experience.

231

Help Her Glow with the Ultimate Hydrating Facial Surprise

Scheduling a moisturizing facial appointment for her is a wonderful way to show your appreciation. A moisturizing facial not only provides relaxation but also hydrates and revitalizes the skin, leaving it soft, glowing, and refreshed. It's a simple yet impactful way to encourage her to take some time for herself and enjoy a moment of pure indulgence.

Take the initiative to research and book an appointment at a reputable spa or skincare clinic that offers high-quality treatments. Surprise her with the details, ensuring the time and location work conveniently for her schedule. This effort shows that you're paying attention to her well-being and want her to feel cared for and appreciated. It's not just about the facial—it's about giving her a chance to unwind and prioritize herself.

A moisturizing facial can be a standalone gift or part of a larger plan for a day of pampering. Either way, the experience will leave her feeling refreshed, rejuvenated, and confident. And when she returns with glowing skin and a relaxed smile, she'll know that you're always thinking of ways to make her feel beautiful and valued. This thoughtful gesture is a win for her, and for the love you share.

232

Create Lasting Memories Letting Loose at an Entertainment Venue

Enjoying a night out at popular entertainment venue is a perfect way to break from the usual routine and dive into a world of fun and games. The venue's combination of arcade classics, cutting-edge gaming, and interactive experiences creates an atmosphere that's energetic and entertaining. Whether you're challenging each other to air hockey, showing off your skills in basketball shootouts, or teaming up in multiplayer games, the night is sure to be filled with laughter and friendly competition.

If there isn't a popular entertainment venue nearby, don't worry—look for one in your closest metropolitan area, as many cities nowadays have a plethora of spots that are 'poppin', lit, or buzzin'.' Look for places that offer a mix of arcade games, food, and drinks. Gaming lounges, bowling alleys with arcades, or family fun centers are great alternatives. The goal is to find a spot where you can both let loose, share some laughs, and enjoy the thrill of gaming together.

Make the night even more special by indulging in some playful rivalries—set bets for the highest scores or try to win prizes for each other. These shared moments of fun and excitement create memories you'll both treasure. No matter where you go, the experience is about enjoying each other's company in a lively and lighthearted setting that brings out the best kind of competitive fun.

233

Show Her She'll Always Be Your Number One Priority

For married couples, reaffirming to your wife that she is your number one priority is an essential part of nurturing your bond. It's easy for life's demands—work, kids, and other responsibilities—to consume your time and energy, but consistently making her feel cherished strengthens your marriage. Whether through intentional conversations, actions, or regular date nights, remind her that amidst all the roles you play, being her partner comes first. Tell her explicitly, "You're my number one," and back it up by showing up for her emotionally, physically, and mentally.

For those who aren't married but share a life together, especially with children, the message remains just as important. Let her know that while parenting and daily obligations take up much of your focus, your love and commitment to her are at the core of everything you do. Carve out time for one-on-one moments, even in the midst of busy schedules. A handwritten note, a quiet walk together, or simply holding her hand and saying, "You're still my priority," can make all the difference.

Reaffirming her place as your priority shows her that your relationship is the foundation for all you build together. It's not just about words—it's about demonstrating that her happiness, well-being, and partnership are at the center of your life. Whether married, co-parenting, or deeply committed in other ways, this consistent reinforcement strengthens your connection, ensuring she feels loved, valued, and secure in her place in your world.

234

Dive Into Her Passions and Empower Her Growth

A key part of nurturing a loving relationship is showing genuine interest in what makes her light up. Dive into her favorite pastimes, whether it's painting, yoga, gardening, or something entirely unique. Sharing these activities is not just about spending time together; it's about celebrating the things that bring her delight. By stepping into her world, you demonstrate that her interests matter to you, and you're invested in the things that shape her happiness.

Supporting her hobbies is also a way to empower her growth. Encourage her to deepen her skills, try new challenges, or even turn her passion into something more significant if she dreams of it. Whether it's cheering her on at her first art show, gifting her tools for her craft, or simply being her biggest supporter, your actions show her that you believe in her capabilities and aspirations.

Sometimes, participating in her passions can also open doors for you to bond in new ways. If she's a runner, join her on a jog. If she loves cooking, make a meal together. These moments of shared experience help you connect on a deeper level, creating memories that strengthen your partnership.

It's also important to respect the space her hobbies provide her. Some passions may be deeply personal, offering her a sense of peace or independence. In these cases, your role is to support from the sidelines—celebrating her growth and ensuring she knows you value the joy and fulfillment she finds in them.

When you make the effort to engage with her passions and support her personal growth, you're investing in her happiness and your relationship. She'll see your care and encouragement as proof of your commitment to her as an individual and as your partner. Together, you'll build a stronger bond rooted in mutual respect and shared enthusiasm for each other's interests.

Unleash Creativity with a Paint and Sip Night at Home

Planning a night of paint and sip at home is a fun and intimate way to enjoy each other's company while tapping into your creative sides. Start by gathering all the supplies—canvases, paints, brushes, and maybe even some aprons to keep things neat. Pick an image or theme for inspiration (Pinterest is a great resource), or let your imaginations flow freely. Set the mood with some great music, your favorite beverages, and snacks to enjoy while you paint.

This activity is all about connection and creativity. Whether you're trying to replicate a famous painting or just experimenting with colors, the focus is on having fun together. Laugh at your artistic attempts, encourage each other's efforts, and enjoy the process without the pressure of creating a masterpiece. It's a chance to let loose, make a mess, and see where the evening takes you.

For me, putting this together was a blast. I went out to buy the supplies, picked a fun image from Pinterest, threw on some good music, and poured some great drinks. By the end of the night, we were laughing our butts off at our "artistic" creations. The paintings might not have made it to the gallery, but the memories we made were priceless—and that's what the night is all about.

You never know who's watching and learning from your actions. After seeing me set up a paint and sip night, my son decided to do the same for his girlfriend. As men, it's not just about how we treat our significant others, but also about the example we set for the next generation. It's our responsibility to raise and mold our boys into high-value young men who know how to cherish and respect the women in their lives. Every action you take plants a seed of understanding in them, shaping their future relationships in meaningful ways.

236

Dance to the Rhythm of Love at a Music Festival

Attending a dance or music festival together is an electrifying way to immerse yourselves in live performances, celebrate your favorite genres, and bond over shared musical tastes. Whether it's a small local gathering or a globally renowned event, festivals offer an energetic atmosphere where you can dance, sing along, or simply enjoy the vibes. It's an opportunity to connect through the universal language of music, creating memories that resonate long after the final note.

Festivals often provide more than just music, with food trucks, art installations, and interactive experiences adding to the excitement. You can explore new activities, try delicious cuisines, or simply soak up the lively energy of the event. Dancing together to live music—whether it's a slow, intimate groove or carefree, wild moves—brings a sense of spontaneity and fun to your relationship, making the experience even more unforgettable.

Some popular festivals cater to different musical tastes, so you can choose one that matches her favorite genre. For jazz lovers, consider iconic events like the Montreux Jazz Festival in Switzerland, the New Orleans Jazz & Heritage Festival, or the North Sea Jazz Festival in the Netherlands. Rock enthusiasts might enjoy Glastonbury in the UK, Rock am Ring in Germany, or Lollapalooza around the globe. R&B fans could revel at the Essence Festival in New Orleans, Lovers & Friends in Las Vegas, or the Soul Beach Music Festival in Aruba. For pop, Coachella in California, Primavera Sound in Spain, or BottleRock Napa Valley are fantastic choices. Hip-hop aficionados would love Rolling Loud, Wireless Festival in London, or Made in America in Philadelphia.

No matter which genre or festival you choose, the experience of live music creates a magical, joyful outing. It's a celebration of rhythm, creativity, and connection, shared with the one you love.

237

Grow Closer While Building a Terrarium

Creating a terrarium together is a relaxing and rewarding way to connect while bringing a bit of nature indoors. A terrarium is a small, enclosed garden, usually housed in glass, that can be customized with various plants, stones, and decorative elements. This activity allows you both to express your creativity while building something beautiful and lasting that you can enjoy in your home.

Start by gathering the materials—a glass container, soil, small plants (like succulents or moss), stones, and any decorative items you want to include. As you work together to arrange the plants and design the layout, you'll enjoy the process of creating a little world of your own. The terrarium becomes a shared project that reflects both of your styles and preferences, and it's a lasting reminder of the time you spent together.

Once completed, the terrarium can serve as a unique and personal piece of decor in your home, symbolizing the growth and care that you put into your relationship. It's a simple yet meaningful activity that combines creativity, teamwork, and a love for nature.

238

Spread Joy Every Day with Words That Affirm Her Worth

Making it a habit to affirm her each day is a powerful way to show your love and appreciation consistently. Daily affirmations don't have to be grand gestures; even simple words like "You look amazing today," "I'm so proud of you," or "I love how you handled that situation" can have a profound impact. These little expressions remind her of her worth and let her know that she's on your mind, building her confidence and reinforcing the strength of your relationship.

Consistency is key to making this practice meaningful. By affirming her regularly, you create a positive and supportive environment where she feels seen, valued, and cherished. You can mix it up with spoken words, sweet texts, or handwritten notes left in unexpected places like her bag or on the mirror. The consideration behind these daily affirmations strengthens the emotional connection between you, making her feel secure and loved.

Even I forget this at times, as it's easy to get wrapped up in life, career demands, or unforeseen circumstances. However, making the effort to pause and offer her a kind word or acknowledgment amidst the chaos of life is a reminder of the love that anchors your relationship. It's not about perfection—it's about the consistent effort to let her know she's a priority, no matter what else is going on. These daily affirmations create a foundation of appreciation and love that stands strong through all of life's ups and downs.

239

Relax and Connect Over a Game of Billiards

Enjoying an evening of billiards together is a fun and laid-back way to spend quality time while engaging in a bit of friendly competition. Whether you're both seasoned players or just learning the game, playing pool offers a relaxed atmosphere where you can chat, laugh, and connect over the table. It's an activity that allows you to focus on each other, away from the usual distractions of daily life.

Head to a local billiards hall, a bar with pool tables, or even set up a game at home if you have a table. As you play, you can challenge each other, share tips, or simply enjoy the casual back-and-forth of the game. The combination of skill, strategy, and lighthearted banter makes billiards an enjoyable way to unwind together. It's a perfect date night option that blends competition with camaraderie, creating an evening that's both entertaining and memorable.

240

Feel the Thrill of Love (and Pain) with an Action-Packed Paintball Date

Taking her out for a paintball date is an exciting and adventurous way to add some action to your time together. Paintball offers a mix of strategy, teamwork, and adrenaline, making it a perfect activity for couples who enjoy a bit of thrill and friendly competition. Whether you're on the same team or playfully competing against each other, paintball provides an opportunity to work together, communicate, and share in the excitement of the game.

The experience of navigating through the course, planning your moves, and celebrating victories (or laughing off defeats) brings a dynamic energy to your date. It's an unconventional way to bond, breaking away from traditional date ideas and diving into something active and exhilarating. After the game, you can relax and reminisce about the best moments over a meal or drinks, making it a day full of fun, connection, and shared adventure.

Slide Into Good Memories with a Day at the Waterpark

Planning a day together at a waterpark is a fun and adventurous way to embrace the joy of summer while cooling off and enjoying each other's company. From the adrenaline rush of towering water slides to the peaceful drift of a lazy river, waterparks offer a variety of activities that cater to all energy levels. The shared laughter as you splash through wave pools or try to outpace each other on racing slides creates moments of pure connection and playful fun.

The beauty of a waterpark outing is that it has something for everyone. If she loves a thrill, you can hit the most exciting rides together; if relaxation is the goal, lounge by the pool with drinks and snacks while soaking up the sun. These dynamic options ensure that your day is filled with variety, catering to both your adventurous and laid-back sides. Don't forget to indulge in some classic waterpark treats like snow cones or funnel cakes to complete the experience.

Capture memories with fun photos, but also embrace the spontaneity of the day—letting the splashes and laughter take over. A waterpark day is more than just an outing; it's a chance to reconnect with your inner child, let go of life's stresses, and create joyful memories you'll both cherish. Whether it's a local waterpark or a trip to a major destination, this outing guarantees a blend of excitement, relaxation, and love.

Surprise Her with Comfort-Focused Lingerie or Sleepwear

Surprising her with comfortable lingerie or sleepwear is an attentive way to show that you care about her comfort and well-being. While lingerie is often associated with elegance and romance, focusing on items that prioritize her comfort—like soft fabrics, relaxed fits, and designs she loves—takes the gesture to another level. Think cozy boy shorts, breathable cotton bralettes, stylish joggers, or even silky loungewear that balances elegance with ease.

By selecting sleepwear or lingerie that aligns with her personal style and comfort preferences, you demonstrate not only your attentiveness but also your understanding of what makes her feel her best. This gift is about celebrating her in a way that is both practical and intimate. Whether she's wearing it for a cozy night in or just to unwind, the right choice will leave her feeling relaxed, cherished, and confident.

To make the surprise even more meaningful, consider pairing the gift with a personalized touch—like a handwritten note expressing how much you admire her. This thoughtful gesture transforms a simple piece of clothing into a reminder of your love and care, showing her that you're always thinking of ways to bring her happiness and comfort.

243

Empower Her Leadership Role at Home with Love and Respect

In a family dynamic, it's crucial to reaffirm her position as an authority figure in the home, ensuring that she is respected by the children at all times. Often, there's an unspoken stereotype that the father is the ultimate disciplinarian, while the mother's authority can be seen as secondary. This imbalance can lead to children testing boundaries with their mother or assuming they can disregard her instructions, especially when the father isn't around. As a husband, father or head of household, it's your role to set the tone in your household, making it clear that her voice carries just as much weight as yours.

Teaching your children to comply with her requests and treat her with respect isn't just about maintaining order—it's about modeling healthy family dynamics. Disrespectful behavior, hesitation, or defiance when she asks for something should be met with swift reinforcement of her authority. Addressing this directly with your children emphasizes that the home operates as a team, and she is an equal leader. This sets the expectation that her words and decisions are not to be questioned or undermined, regardless of whether you are present or not.

This practice isn't just about household management; it's a way to cater to her emotional well-being. When you stand firmly by her and ensure that her authority is upheld, you create an environment where she feels respected, valued, and supported. It eliminates the burden of feeling like she has to fight for respect, allowing her to lead confidently without second-guessing her role. Knowing that her partner has established and enforced her position as an authority figure strengthens her sense of security and reinforces the bond between you both as a united front.

This also sets an important example for your children, teaching them to appreciate the roles both parents play in their upbringing. Boys learn to respect and value the women in their lives, and girls grow up understanding that they, too, deserve respect and recognition in positions of leadership. By reinforcing her role in the home, you're not just creating harmony and structure—you're showing her and your children what it means to support, value, and uplift the woman who holds the family together.

Brighten Her Day with a Silly Selfie and a Sweet Note

Sending her a playful, silly selfie along with a sweet note is a lighthearted way to make her smile and let her know you're thinking of her. Whether you're making a funny face, wearing something goofy, or just catching yourself in a candid moment, a silly selfie adds a bit of fun to her day. Pair it with a simple, heartfelt note like, "Just thinking of you," "You make me smile," or "Can't wait to see you later," to add an extra touch of affection.

This playful gesture shows that you don't take yourself too seriously and that you're always looking for ways to brighten her day. It's a quick and easy way to stay connected, even when you're apart, and reminds her that she's on your mind. Whether she's having a tough day or just needs a little pick-me-up, a silly selfie with a sweet note is sure to bring a smile to her face.

245

Bond Over Creativity by Crafting a Homemade Gift Together

Creating a homemade gift together is more than just a project—it's an opportunity to strengthen your connection while crafting something meaningful. Whether it's a custom piece of art, a batch of homemade candles, or even a small piece of furniture, the process of working side by side fosters collaboration and shared creativity. The gift you create together becomes a symbol of your teamwork and the love you've poured into it, holding sentimental value that far outweighs anything store-bought.

To make the experience even more memorable, choose a project that reflects both of your interests or something you've been excited to try. Maybe she loves the idea of hand-poured candles, or you've always wanted to explore woodworking. Whatever the project, the real magic lies in the act of learning and experimenting together. Mistakes will undoubtedly happen, but they often lead to laughter and create moments you'll look back on fondly long after the project is complete.

The charm of crafting a homemade gift lies in the blend of effort and connection. It's not just about the finished product but about the journey of creating it together. As you collaborate and problem-solve, you'll strengthen your bond and gain a deeper appreciation for each other's strengths and creativity. Whether the gift finds a home with you or is given to someone special, it will carry the story of your shared effort and the fun you had making it.

DIY projects like these are a reminder of the importance of teamwork and quality time. In a world of instant gratification, taking the time to create something with your own hands—and doing it together—reinforces the value of patience, care, and collaboration. It's a meaningful way to express love, creativity, and the simple appreciation for being a team.

Spark Laughter and Playfulness with a Blindfold Tasting Game

Playing a blindfold tasting game is a playful and engaging way to spice up your time together while exploring new flavors. Gather a variety of foods—sweet, savory, spicy, or even quirky—and take turns wearing a blindfold as the other person feeds you small bites. The goal is to guess each food based on taste, smell, and texture, turning the simple act of eating into a fun, sensory adventure. This lighthearted activity is sure to spark laughter and create moments of surprise with every new bite.

This game isn't just about the food—it's about trust and connection. With one partner blindfolded, the other becomes their guide, encouraging a deeper level of communication and vulnerability. You can include familiar favorites to keep things comfortable or introduce exotic items for a bit of adventurous fun. It's a great way to break out of the everyday routine, connect through shared discovery, and bond over the sheer joy of the unexpected.

To make the experience even more entertaining, add a twist like keeping score for the best guesses or choosing a specific theme, such as international dishes or favorite desserts. You can even prepare drinks to complement the flavors and cleanse the palate between rounds. This sensory-filled game is simple to set up, easy to enjoy, and a creative way to laugh, explore, and create lasting memories together.

247

Chase Adrenaline and Excitement with a Supercar Experience

Scheduling a supercar high-speed racetrack experience is an exhilarating way to share an adrenaline-pumping adventure together. Whether she's a car enthusiast or just up for an exciting challenge, driving or riding in a supercar at high speeds on a professional racetrack offers a thrill like no other. You can both take turns behind the wheel or enjoy a professional driver taking you for the ride of a lifetime.

This experience combines luxury with excitement, allowing you to test your limits in some of the world's most powerful cars. The rush of speeding around the track, feeling the car's power and precision, is something you'll both remember long after the day is over. It's a unique and unforgettable way to bond over a shared love of adventure and create a story you'll both be excited to tell.

248

Share in Conversations About the Best Parts of Your Childhood

Engaging in conversations about the fun parts of your childhood is a heartwarming way to connect on a deeper level through shared nostalgia. Reminiscing about the games you played, the cartoons you loved, or the adventures you had creates an atmosphere of joy and discovery. These moments offer insight into each other's upbringing, highlighting the playful and carefree sides of your personalities that might not often come to the forefront.

Take turns sharing stories about your favorite toys, holiday traditions, or the neighborhood games you used to play with friends. You might even find similarities in your childhood experiences or uncover quirky differences that lead to lighthearted moments and meaningful exchanges. These reflections can inspire a sense of wonder and gratitude for how far you've both come, while still honoring the innocence and fun that shaped who you are today.

To make it even more engaging, consider recreating an activity from your childhood together, like building a blanket fort, playing an old board game, or visiting a place that holds special memories. Conversations about childhood not only evoke smiles and amusement but also deepen your connection by allowing you to relive those treasured moments side by side.

249

Hold Her Close During Fireworks or Stunning Scenic Views

Holding her close during fireworks or while taking in a beautiful view is a romantic and comforting way to share a special moment together. Whether it's during a fireworks display, a stunning sunset, or while overlooking a scenic landscape, wrapping your arms around her creates a sense of safety and intimacy. The beauty of the moment combined with your closeness enhances the connection between you, making it an experience that both of you will cherish.

These shared moments of awe and wonder, whether accompanied by the excitement of fireworks or the tranquility of a breathtaking view, provide a perfect backdrop for deepening your bond. The gesture of holding her close shows your affection and commitment, reinforcing the idea that you're there for her, sharing in the beauty and magic of the world around you. It's a simple yet powerful way to create lasting memories together.

250

Bonus: Possession Isn't Love— Trust Is Key to a Strong Relationship

Being possessive and controlling is like poison to what could otherwise be a flourishing relationship. It doesn't signify strength or devotion but rather reflects insecurities that can erode trust and intimacy. If another man looks at her or tries to strike up a conversation, it shouldn't provoke fear or jealousy. Instead, it should serve as a reminder that you are with someone truly special—someone unique enough to attract admiration. But it's vital to remember that, unlike a Rolex or a car, she isn't a possession to be controlled.

While it's natural to want to protect her, there's a fine line between being protective and being overbearing. Giving her the space to breathe and be her own person is a demonstration of your confidence in her and in your relationship. If she truly loves, values, and respects you, she won't entertain anyone else. And if she does, then the relationship lacked the foundation of mutual trust to begin with. Trust and respect are the bedrocks of a healthy partnership, far stronger than any attempts to control or monitor her every move.

Trust also empowers both of you to grow as individuals while strengthening your bond as a couple. When she knows she's free to be herself without fear of suspicion or accusations, she's more likely to open up and deepen the connection you share. In turn, you can focus on building a relationship rooted in mutual admiration and support rather than wasting energy on fear-based behaviors. Possessiveness breeds tension and resentment, but trust fosters love, harmony, and a sense of security that cannot be faked or forced.

As men, it's essential to evaluate how we approach relationships, especially in a world where societal pressures often encourage control and dominance. Let your confidence in yourself and your relationship be the antidote to insecurity. Love isn't about keeping someone on a leash—it's about holding space for them to thrive and choosing each other freely every day. Trust is the key to unlocking the most fulfilling and lasting partnership possible.

251

Turn Dreams into Reality by Helping Her Fulfill Her Bucket List

Helping her create a bucket list and fulfilling an item from it is a meaningful way to support her dreams and share in her excitement for life's adventures. Start by sitting down together and discussing the experiences, goals, and dreams she's always wanted to pursue—whether it's traveling to a specific destination, learning a new skill, or trying something daring like skydiving. Writing these down as a bucket list not only acknowledges her aspirations but also shows that you're invested in making them come true.

Once the list is created, choose an item to fulfill together. Whether it's something small and achievable in the short term or a bigger, long-term goal, taking the initiative to help her realize one of her dreams is a powerful gesture of love and commitment. It shows that you're not just a partner in the day-to-day but also someone who wants to see her live her life to the fullest. This experience becomes a shared memory, reinforcing your bond and adding a sense of adventure and fulfillment to your relationship.

In the process, you may also discover a newfound appreciation for her passions and perhaps even find inspiration for your own goals. Sharing these milestones fosters a deeper connection, as it allows both of you to step out of your comfort zones and grow together. Plus, watching her excitement as she checks off an item from her list is a rewarding experience in itself, proving that supporting her dreams is as fulfilling as achieving your own.

252

Savor the Craft of Local Flavors at a Brewery or Distillery

Visiting a local brewery or distillery together is a fun and engaging way to explore the craft of brewing or distilling while enjoying each other's company. These venues often offer tours where you can learn about the process of making beer, whiskey, gin, or other spirits, from the selection of ingredients to the final product. You'll get a behind-the-scenes look at the craftsmanship involved and may even have the opportunity to taste different varieties or limited-edition releases.

After the tour, you can relax in the tasting room, savoring the flavors and discussing your favorites. Whether you're both enthusiasts or just curious, this experience offers a blend of education and enjoyment in a relaxed setting. It's also a great way to support local businesses and discover new drinks that you can enjoy together in the future. The outing combines learning, tasting, and quality time, making it a memorable and enriching experience.

253

Laugh and "Howl" Your Hearts Out at a Karaoke Night Together

Attending a karaoke night together is a lively and entertaining way to let loose and enjoy each other's company. Whether you're both confident singers or prefer to stay in the background, karaoke provides a fun and supportive environment where you can sing your hearts out to your favorite songs. It's a chance to show off your vocal skills, laugh at each other's performances, and maybe even discover a hidden talent.

You can choose to sing solo, duet on a romantic ballad, or join a group for a crowd-pleasing anthem. The energy and excitement of karaoke night create a joyful atmosphere where you can connect through music and shared experiences. Even if singing isn't your forte, the focus is on having fun and creating memories together. Afterward, you can continue the night with a drink or dessert, reflecting on the highlights of the evening and enjoying the lighthearted mood.

254

Be the Rock She Can Rely On

Reliability is a cornerstone of trust in any relationship. It's not just about doing what you say you'll do—it's about showing her, day in and day out, that she can depend on you. Whether it's remembering small commitments, like picking up her favorite snack on your way home, or being present during life's bigger challenges, your actions show her that she's a priority in your life. This consistency builds security and reassures her that you're someone who won't let her down when it matters most.

Reliability also requires accountability. If you commit to something, follow through—even if it's inconvenient or challenging. My mother instilled in me at an early age that "your word is your bond." Broken promises, no matter how small, can gradually erode the foundation of trust in your relationship. If unforeseen circumstances prevent you from fulfilling a promise, communicate openly and take responsibility. By addressing setbacks head-on and making amends, you demonstrate integrity and respect for her feelings.

Being reliable extends to emotional presence. When she's dealing with difficulties, celebrating victories, or simply needing someone to listen, show up fully. Emotional availability means being attentive and empathetic, not distracted or dismissive. These moments of support aren't just about solving problems—they're about making her feel seen and understood. By consistently offering her your presence and understanding, you strengthen the emotional bond between you and create a space where she feels safe and valued.

Proactive reliability is the ultimate expression of care. Anticipate her needs by paying attention to her words and actions. If she's overwhelmed or stressed, step in and offer help before she asks. These thoughtful gestures—whether it's organizing her schedule, handling errands, or simply being there to ease her load—show her that she's not alone. When reliability becomes a habit, it creates a partnership defined by trust, stability, and unwavering support, deepening your connection and enriching your relationship.

255

Bond Over Language Learning and Unlock New Worlds Together

Learning a foreign language together is a fun and intellectually stimulating way to bond while acquiring a new skill. Whether you choose a language that's relevant to your travel goals, cultural interests, or simply one that you both find intriguing, the process of learning together can be both challenging and rewarding. It's an activity that requires teamwork, practice, and patience, all of which can strengthen your relationship.

Language apps like Duolingo, Babbel, Rosetta Stone, and Memrise make this journey accessible and enjoyable. These apps offer interactive lessons, games, and exercises you can complete at your own pace. Duolingo uses gamification to make progress fun, Babbel focuses on real-world conversational practice, and Rosetta Stone immerses you in the language for deeper learning. I've personally tried these three and found Babbel to be the most enjoyable for its practical approach and conversational emphasis. Practicing together through these platforms adds an engaging dynamic, allowing you to support and motivate each other.

You can further enhance the experience by watching movies, listening to music, or cooking dishes from the culture of your chosen language. Practicing phrases over meals or competing on vocabulary quizzes keeps the process lively and interactive. As your skills grow, you'll not only gain confidence but also create a unique bond through this shared adventure—perhaps even inspiring plans to visit a country where you can both use your newfound language skills.

256

Explore New Adventures by Discovering a Hobby You Both Love

Coming up with a new hobby or passion together is an exciting way to explore new interests and create shared experiences. Whether you both decide to try something neither of you has done before—like photography, hiking, cooking a new cuisine, or crafting—choosing a new hobby as a couple allows you to learn, grow, and have fun together. This shared pursuit can become a regular activity that brings you closer, offering opportunities to connect and create lasting memories.

Start by brainstorming ideas based on mutual interests or activities you've always wanted to explore. Once you've chosen a hobby, dive in together with enthusiasm, encouraging each other through the learning process and acknowledging your achievements along the way. The experience of discovering a new passion as a team brings fresh energy to your relationship and strengthens your connection through the excitement of shared discovery.

257

Craft Love Together Through Brushstrokes and Clay

Engaging in artistic activities together, like painting personalized ceramics or shaping clay at a pottery studio, is a wonderful way to tap into your creative sides while strengthening your bond. Whether you're painting mugs, plates, or quirky figurines, or trying your hand at molding something from scratch, the focus isn't on artistic perfection but on the joy of creating side by side. It's an opportunity to laugh at your bold color choices, admire each other's designs, and share a moment of connection that's as colorful as the paints on your brush.

These sessions are perfect for all skill levels, making them accessible whether you're a seasoned artist or someone who hasn't held a paintbrush since grade school. The beauty lies in the process: selecting pieces to work on, experimenting with patterns, and letting your imagination run free. You'll leave with personalized keepsakes—whether practical like a painted plate or sentimental like a hand-sculpted vase—that serve as lasting reminders of the fun you shared.

Pairing the artistic process with exploration can make the experience even more special. Seek out a hidden gem of a studio in a nearby town or an artsy district in your city. The journey itself adds an extra layer of excitement, offering moments to discover unique spots, enjoy a cozy café nearby, or simply savor the thrill of doing something new together. These little adventures turn a creative outing into a full-day experience you'll both treasure.

Ultimately, getting creative together is about embracing imperfection, discovering hidden talents, and celebrating each other's unique expressions. The finished pieces are meaningful, but the real masterpiece is the memory of the time spent together—laughing, learning, and deepening your connection in ways that no brushstroke could ever capture.

Have Saturday Morning Cartoons and Cereal Together

Ahh, nostalgia… Recreating the simple joy of Saturday morning cartoons and cereal is a whimsical way to step back into your childhood while enjoying some quality time together. The charm of waking up, grabbing a bowl of your favorite sugary cereal, and plopping down in front of a screen to watch beloved animated characters is timeless. Whether you're revisiting classics like Looney Tunes or Scooby-Doo, or diving into modern favorites, this activity is a ticket to pure, unfiltered fun.

Start the morning by setting the scene: comfy blankets, oversized bowls, and a spread of cereals that'll take you both back in time. From the first slurp of milk to the hilarious moments that comes with cheesy catchphrases and cartoon hijinks, you'll find yourselves reminiscing about childhood memories while creating new ones together. Share stories about your favorite characters, the excitement of getting the prize in the cereal box, or the simple delight of being carefree on a Saturday morning.

This activity is more than just cartoons and cereal—it's about slowing down, reconnecting, and indulging in life's simple pleasures. It's a reminder that sometimes the best moments are the ones where you let go of the complexities of adulthood and embrace the joy of being a kid again, together.

Sip, Watch, and Laugh While People-Watching at a Cozy Café

Man, there's nothing like kicking back at a café with a good cup of whatever you're into, soaking up the vibe, and just watching the world go by. Pick a spot that's got the right energy—maybe it's a busy corner with traffic hustling, or a chill patio where you can hear snippets of people's conversations. Order your drinks, grab a seat with a solid view, and settle in for some low-key fun while you two observe the show life's putting on.

Here's where it gets good: make up stories about the folks you see. That guy with the "smedium", super tight jeans on? Might have a yeast infection by the time he gets home. The couple holding hands but not talking? You just know he's in trouble, even if he didn't do it. It's all jokes, it's all light, and it's all about finding the fun in what's right in front of you. You'll crack up, share side-eyes, and maybe even drop a "Did you see that?" as someone walks by with their dog dressed better than you.

This isn't just people-watching—it's your time to unplug and vibe with her. Let the city or neighborhood be your entertainment for the day while you connect over the little things. Plus, who doesn't love that café life? Good drinks, good company, and a front-row seat to the everyday chaos—it's the perfect mix of chill and fun.

260

Strengthen Your Spiritual Connection with Consistent Prayer

Making it a habit to pray together is a powerful way to deepen your spiritual connection and strengthen your relationship. Whether you share the same faith or have different beliefs, setting aside time to pray or meditate together fosters a sense of unity and trust. It's an opportunity to align your hearts and minds, seeking guidance, expressing gratitude, or simply being present with each other in a sacred space. Incorporating this practice into your daily routine, such as starting or ending the day with a prayer, or setting aside specific times each week for joint prayer or meditation, can bring comfort, peace, and a stronger sense of purpose to your relationship.

By making prayer a regular part of your life together, you build a foundation of mutual support and understanding that enriches both your relationship and your individual spiritual journeys. For those who may not follow a religious path, you can create a similar habit by taking time to speak positive affirmations and intentions over each other's lives. Whether it's wishing each other peace, wellness, protection, or success, these moments of shared focus and positivity can have a powerful impact on your relationship. Expressing hopes for each other's happiness and well-being strengthens your bond and demonstrates your commitment to supporting one another in all aspects of life.

Another way to make this habit meaningful is by incorporating moments of reflection together. After praying or sharing affirmations, take a few minutes to talk about your thoughts, hopes, or challenges. These conversations can open doors to deeper understanding and give you insight into each other's hearts. It's not just about the practice—it's about how it strengthens your connection and provides emotional and spiritual alignment.

In Chapter 1, the emphasis was on taking personal responsibility to pray for your partner, demonstrating your love and leadership through individual acts of spiritual covering. This approach underscores the importance of speaking positive energy into her life and seeking guidance on her behalf. Here, the focus shifts to the power of praying together as a couple. Moving beyond individual responsibility, consistent prayer or meditation as a pair fosters a deeper sense of unity and shared purpose. This is not just about covering your partner but about aligning your hearts and minds as a team, creating a sacred rhythm that strengthens your bond. By regularly engaging in these moments together, you cultivate a connection rooted in mutual support and understanding, enriching both your relationship and your spiritual journey.

Lastly, remember that consistency is key. Life gets busy, but prioritizing this habit shows that you value your partner and the relationship you're building. Whether it's a quick prayer, a few kind words of affirmation, or an intentional pause during a hectic day, these moments of unity make a lasting impact. It's not about perfection; it's about showing up for each other, sharing the journey, and leaning into love and faith.

Celebrate Her Intelligence and Admire Her Wisdom

Acknowledging her intelligence and wisdom is a powerful way to show your deep respect and admiration for her mind. Whether she's knowledgeable in a specific field, offers insightful advice, or simply has a natural curiosity about the world, recognizing these qualities lets her know that you value her thoughts and perspectives. Compliment her on the way she solves problems, makes decisions, or shares knowledge with others.

You can express this admiration through sincere compliments during conversations, praising her for her sharp thinking or the wisdom she brings to discussions. Let her know how much you appreciate her intellect and how it enhances your relationship, making it richer and more meaningful. By celebrating her intelligence and wisdom, you reinforce her confidence and show that you're truly captivated by her mind as much as her heart. This kind of recognition not only strengthens your bond but also deepens the emotional and intellectual connection between you.

Assumptions Make Messes — Ask First, Clean Less Later

In any relationship, making assumptions can lead to misunderstandings and unnecessary conflict. Jumping to conclusions without seeking clarification risks distorting reality and misjudging your partner's intentions. By taking the time to understand her perspective, you show her that you value open communication and trust over rushed judgment.

Assumptions often stem from miscommunication or unspoken expectations. Instead of acting on what you think she means, ask her directly. For example, if she seems quiet, don't assume she's upset with you. A simple "Is everything okay?" can open a conversation and avoid unnecessary tension. These moments of clarity help strengthen your connection and prevent minor issues from escalating into larger problems.

Practicing patience is key to breaking the habit of making assumptions. It's natural to want immediate answers, but jumping to conclusions often leads to inaccurate interpretations. Give her the space to share her thoughts and feelings in her own time. By waiting and listening, you show respect for her voice and a willingness to meet her where she is emotionally.

Focusing on curiosity rather than judgment fosters understanding and empathy. Approach situations with an open mind, seeking to learn more about her perspective. For instance, if she reacts strongly to something, instead of assuming why, ask, "What's on your mind?" or "Can you help me understand how you're feeling?" This shift in approach builds trust and deepens your emotional connection.

Avoiding assumptions and seeking clarity creates a foundation of trust and mutual respect in your relationship. When she feels safe to share without fear of being misunderstood, it fosters a deeper bond and reinforces your commitment to honest communication. Together, you'll create a dynamic where open dialogue replaces uncertainty and love thrives in the space of understanding.

Let Loose and Laugh Together at a Comedy Show

Hitting up a comedy show together is a dope way to kick back, share some laughs, and vibe out in a fun atmosphere. It's the kind of night where you can both let loose, forget about the stress of the week, and just enjoy the moment. Whether it's stand-up, improv, or even an open mic night, the live comedy scene always delivers energy and surprises that'll have you laughing until your sides hurt.

Scope out a local spot or grab tickets to see one of her favorite comedians. Pair it with some pre-show eats or drinks to set the tone for the night. The jokes, the crowd, and the whole vibe make for an unforgettable time—and you'll leave with inside jokes that'll keep you laughing long after the show's over. It's the perfect way to mix things up and remind each other that life doesn't always have to be so serious.

What's great about a comedy show is that it's not just about the jokes; it's about how you both react. Whether you're cracking up together or exchanging those "did-they-really-just-say-that" looks, it's all part of the fun. Even if the jokes miss the mark sometimes, the experience of being in that space together makes it all worth it. A good laugh is one of the best ways to bond, and a night at a comedy show guarantees you'll leave feeling lighter and more connected.

264

Craft Unique Memories While Knitting a Blanket or Scarf Together

I failed miserably at this, but that doesn't mean you will. Creating a handmade knitted scarf or blanket together can still be a fun and creative way to vibe out and bond with your partner. Knitting might seem like an intimidating or slow process at first, but it's all about the journey, not just the result. Grab some soft yarn in colors you both vibe with, pick a simple pattern, and don't be afraid to laugh at each other's first attempts—you're in it for the memories.

You can tag team the project—one person knits while the other cheers them on, or you can both work on different sections to combine later. This whole process is about patience and teamwork, even if you end up with something lopsided or not quite Instagram-worthy. It's not just about the final product; it's about spending quality time together and appreciating the effort you're both putting into creating something uniquely yours.

The best part? Even if your knitting game is as weak as mine was, the laughter, teamwork, and creative energy make the experience worth it. And who knows? You might walk away with a scarf, a blanket, or even just a hilarious story about how you tried to craft and ended up turning the yarn into a tangled masterpiece. Either way, it's a win.

265

Bake Up Flavor with a Homemade Pizza Night

Having a DIY pizza-making night is a fun and creative way to bring some flavor—literally and figuratively—into your time together. Start by gathering all the essentials: pizza dough, a rich sauce, plenty of cheese, and a variety of toppings to suit your tastes. Stick to the classics like pepperoni and mushrooms, or mix it up with options like spinach, feta, barbecue chicken, or even unconventional picks like figs or hot honey.

You can each craft your own individual pizza masterpiece or team up to create one epic pie. The process of rolling out the dough, spreading the sauce, and loading up on toppings gives you time to relax, joke around, and maybe show off some culinary skills (or lack thereof). It's not about perfection—it's about the experience, the laughs, and making something together that's uniquely yours.

Once the pizzas are baked to perfection with that golden crust and bubbling cheese, the best part begins: digging in. Sit down, enjoy the delicious creations you made, and toast to a night of good eats and teamwork. Whether your pizzas turn out gourmet-worthy or a little "experimental," you'll have a blast creating something together and savoring every bite.

266

Rejuvenate Her Spirit at a Botanical Garden or Nature Reserve

Visiting a local botanical garden or nature reserve together is a peaceful and rejuvenating way to connect with nature and each other. These beautiful spaces offer a chance to explore a variety of plants, flowers, and landscapes while enjoying the tranquility of the outdoors. Whether you're both plant enthusiasts or simply looking for a serene escape, walking through lush gardens or natural trails provides an opportunity to slow down, breathe in the fresh air, and take in the beauty around you.

As you stroll through the garden or reserve, you can share your thoughts, admire the diverse plant life, and perhaps learn something new about the flora and fauna in your area. This outing is perfect for quiet reflection, meaningful conversation, or simply enjoying each other's company in a calming environment. It's a wonderful way to spend quality time together, appreciating the natural world and the peaceful moments you share.

267

Set the Mood with a Surprise Sunset Picnic

Planning a surprise picnic at sunset is a smooth move to set the stage for an unforgettable evening. Find a spot that shows off the sunset like it's on display just for you two—whether it's at a local park, by the water, or up on a hill with a view. Pack a basket with her favorite foods, drinks, and maybe even a little something sweet for dessert. Don't forget a cozy blanket and some pillows for extra comfort.

As the sky transforms with hues of orange, pink, and purple, the moment practically creates itself. Share laughs, swap stories, or just enjoy the silence while taking in the beauty of the sunset. The peaceful vibe, paired with your careful planning, will make her feel cherished and loved. Bonus points if you bring a playlist or a Bluetooth speaker to set the mood with soft tunes.

What makes this special is how effortless it feels. It's not about doing something extravagant—it's about being present, making her feel like the world stopped spinning for just a little while. The combo of a beautiful sunset, good food, and your effort? That's an evening she'll be replaying in her mind for a long time.

268

Celebrate Her Agility and Ability to Wear Multiple Hats

Recognizing her agility and versatility is a powerful way to affirm the extraordinary woman she is. Life rarely moves in a straight line, and her ability to pivot—juggling personal, professional, and emotional responsibilities gracefully—is nothing short of remarkable. Whether she's managing a demanding job, caring for family, pursuing personal passions, or doing all three simultaneously, take time to let her know you see the finesse and balance she brings to it all. It's in how she anticipates needs before they arise and transitions effortlessly between roles—leader, nurturer, problem-solver, and dreamer. Remind her that her adaptability is not just impressive; it's inspiring.

When her commitments become overwhelming, step in with encouragement and support, let her know she doesn't need to have it all figured out every moment of every day. I remember at one point in time, back when I was in high school, my mother was carrying quite the load. She worked at a department store, taught both Bible study and Sunday school at church, took late-night calls from people seeking prayer or simply needing to talk, came home from work to cook dinner every evening, drove me to basketball practice, and somehow still made it to nearly every game. I didn't fully grasp it then, but looking back, I see now the quiet power it took to manage all of that with such poise. Women like her move through life with an unspoken agility that deserves both recognition and reverence.

By celebrating her ability to manage life's many demands with intention and fluidity, you affirm her brilliance in everyday life. Whether it's with a warm embrace, words of appreciation, or a thoughtful act that eases her load, let her know her efforts don't go unnoticed. Show her she's not just maintaining balance—thriving in motion. And as she moves through life with determination and heart, remind her she's never alone. You're right there beside her—aware, grateful, and proud.

269

Tackle Procrastination Together by Helping Her Complete a Project

Helping her with a task or project she's been procrastinating on is a practical way to show your support. Whether it's organizing a cluttered space, finishing a work assignment, or tackling a home improvement project, offering your assistance can help her overcome the inertia that often comes with procrastination. Your involvement not only makes the task more manageable but also shows that you're willing to lend a hand to ease her burden.

Start by identifying the task she's been putting off and gently offer your help, emphasizing that you're in it together. You can break the project down into smaller, more manageable steps, and work side by side to complete it. The process can turn what once felt overwhelming into a shared accomplishment, and she'll appreciate your encouragement and support. By helping her finish what she's been delaying, you're not just completing a task—you're also strengthening your bond by demonstrating your commitment to her well-being and success.

270

Ignite Her Off-roading Interests with an ATV Riding Adventure

Going ATV riding is an adrenaline rush and the perfect way to switch things up with your partner. Whether you're out ripping through the sandy dunes, carving trails in the woods, or kicking up dust in open fields, it's all about the thrill and that feeling of freedom. It's a dope way to bond while both of you step out of your comfort zones and get a little wild with it.

When I hit the dunes in Yuma, let me tell you—it was like being in a real-life action movie. The sand felt endless, and every time I thought I had it down, another steep drop had me questioning my life choices. But once I got into the groove, it was straight fire. The craziest part? Watching her handle those slopes like a pro while I was over here trying not to flip. The laughs, the "did we just survive that?" moments—it's memories like that you don't forget. However, I did have a friend whose wife ate it and came up with a mouth full of sand... Don't do that one.

Find a spot that fits your vibe, whether it's a desert, a muddy trail, or a place that lets you really test those ATVs. Push each other a little, maybe have a friendly competition, but most importantly, soak up the energy and fun. When you're done, you'll have a ton of stories to laugh about, and trust me, sharing a thrill like this can bring y'all even closer.

271

Surprise Her with a DIY Basket of Snacks She'll Love

Creating a basket of her favorite snacks or treats is a personalized way to show her that you care. Whether it's a mix of sweet and savory snacks, gourmet chocolates, or healthy treats, gathering her favorite indulgences into a beautifully arranged basket is sure to make her feel special. This simple yet meaningful gesture demonstrates that you pay attention to her preferences and want to give her something that brings her joy.

You can enhance the basket by adding small, personalized touches, like a handwritten note, a favorite drink, or even a small gift that complements the snacks. Presenting her with this basket on a regular day or as a surprise during a busy week can lift her spirits and provide her with a convenient stash of her go-to treats. It's a sweet way to express your love and appreciation, offering her a delicious reminder of how much she means to you.

272

Honor Her Inner Beauty and All the Qualities That Make Her Shine

Honoring her inner beauty and admirable traits is one of the most authentic ways to show her just how much she means to you. Beyond her physical appearance, there's a depth to who she is that deserves to be celebrated. Whether it's her unmatched kindness, her sharp mind, her way of making everyone feel seen, or the resilience she shows when life gets tough, these are the things that truly set her apart. By intentionally calling attention to her inner qualities, you're letting her know you see her—not just the outside, but the soul beneath.

You don't need a grand moment to honor these traits; the small ones hit just as hard. A heartfelt "I love the way you care for people" over dinner, or a note slipped into her purse that says, "Your strength inspires me," can make all the difference. Sometimes, she might not even realize how amazing she is, and your words can be the mirror that reflects her worth. These small acts let her know she's valued for who she is, not just for what she does.

What makes this so powerful is how it deepens your connection. When she knows you're noticing the things that truly matter—the heart, the humor, the wisdom—it reinforces a love that's deeper than surface-level. Plus, this kind of honor isn't just about her hearing it; it's about showing her that who she is at her core makes her irreplaceable in your life. And when you do it with sincerity, it'll make her feel like she's won the lottery in love.

273

Upgrade Her Ride with Thoughtful Accessories

Gifting her accessories for her vehicle is an easy way to show you care about her comfort, style, and safety on the road, especially if you're a guy who loves cars the way I do. Whether she loves adding a personal flair to her ride or appreciates practical upgrades, there are countless options to enhance her driving experience. Consider items like customized seat covers, stylish steering wheel wraps, or even fun air fresheners that reflect her personality. These small touches can make her car feel like an extension of herself, adding charm and individuality to her daily commute.

For the practical-minded, look into high-quality accessories that keep her car organized and functional. Trunk storage bins, seatback organizers, and phone mounts are perfect for someone who values efficiency and convenience. You might also consider gifting an emergency roadside kit, ensuring she's well-prepared for unexpected situations. These thoughtful additions not only make her life easier but also demonstrate that you're thinking about her safety and comfort.

For a truly unique touch, you can mix a bit of style with utility by opting for customized items, like a monogrammed keychain, a personalized license plate frame, or even LED interior lights that create an inviting ambiance. Whatever you choose, tailoring the gift to her preferences shows how much attention you've paid to her tastes and needs. The time and effort you put into selecting these accessories will leave her feeling cared for every time she steps into her car.

And if you're lucky enough to share your love of cars with her, why not take it to the next level by exploring performance upgrades for her vehicle? Whether it's a sleek new set of tires, upgraded suspension, or a performance exhaust system, these enhancements can elevate her driving experience while indulging her enthusiasm for the road. Sharing the process of researching and selecting the perfect upgrade can make it even more special—an experience that reflects your shared passion.

274

Relax and Connect While Listening to Music on a Rainy Day

Do you remember back in the day when Quiet Storm came on the radio, and everything just felt smoother, calmer, and more intimate? Those were the moments when the world slowed down, and the music spoke to your soul. Recreate that vibe with her on a rainy day, letting the sound of raindrops and the mellow tunes set the perfect tone for a cozy, stress-free experience. Find a playlist of soulful R&B, soft jazz, or chill acoustic tracks, and let the music take you both to a place of pure serenity.

This isn't just about the music—it's about the vibe you create together. Dim the lights, light a candle, or just curl up on the couch with a blanket. Share a quiet conversation, reminisce about old memories, or let the music fill the silence while you soak in the peace of the moment. Whether you're sipping on a warm drink or just sitting close, the combination of soothing music and the rain will make everything feel a little more magical.

And don't be afraid to throw in some classics that make the moment nostalgic. Spin a Marvin Gaye track, slide in some Anita Baker, or let Luther Vandross remind you both of the timeless beauty of love and connection. The rain, the music, and her by your side—it's a recipe for a memory that feels like it belongs in its own love song.

275

Hit the Bullseye with a Memorable Night of Axe Throwing

Planning a night out for axe throwing is an exciting and unconventional way to spend time together while trying something new and adventurous. Axe throwing has become a popular activity, offering a mix of fun, competition, and a chance to test your skills. Whether you're both first-timers or have some experience, the thrill of hitting the target and the playful competition make for a memorable evening.

Many axe throwing venues provide a relaxed and social atmosphere, where you can enjoy food and drinks while taking turns throwing axes. It's an opportunity to cheer each other on, share laughs, and maybe even engage in a friendly rivalry. The experience is both invigorating and entertaining, making it a perfect way to break out of the ordinary and create lasting memories together. After the session, you can continue the night with dinner or drinks, reflecting on the highlights of your unique and action-packed date.

276

Enjoy a Night of Jenga and Drinks Together

Enjoying a night of Jenga and drinks together is a fun and lighthearted way to bond over some playful competition. Jenga's simple yet challenging gameplay makes it perfect for an evening of laughter and suspense, especially when paired with your favorite drinks. Whether you're enjoying a glass of wine, cocktails, or opting for alcohol-free beverages, the combination of a tipsy (or not) atmosphere and the precarious balancing act of Jenga adds an extra layer of excitement to the game.

As you take turns carefully removing blocks and stacking them higher, the anticipation builds, making each move more thrilling. The game naturally invites conversation, teasing, and shared laughter, creating a relaxed and enjoyable environment. It's an ideal way to unwind together, whether you're looking for a casual date night or just a fun way to spend an evening at home. The mix of drinks and Jenga brings out the playful side of your relationship, making it a night full of smiles and connection.

277

Praise Her for Her Willingness to Help Sustain a Peaceful Home

Creating a peaceful home doesn't just happen—it takes intention, effort, and a lot of heart. When she's doing her part to make your home a sanctuary, whether through her patience, considerate nature, or the way she handles day-to-day stress, it's important to let her know you see her efforts. A simple "thank you" for her calming presence or the way she deescalates tension can go a long way in making her feel appreciated for the quiet but essential work she puts in to make your house feel like home.

Let her know how much it means to you that she strives to maintain harmony. Maybe it's how she keeps her cool in heated moments, her knack for smoothing over misunderstandings, or the effort she puts into creating a warm and inviting environment. By praising her for these qualities, you not only affirm her contributions but also inspire both of you to continue working toward a household that feels safe, supportive, and filled with love.

Even if things aren't always smooth sailing, your recognition can encourage her to keep striving for peace—and it might even inspire you to step up your own efforts. Harmony in a home isn't just one person's responsibility, but acknowledging her role sets the tone for a collaborative partnership where both of you commit to fostering a space of love and mutual respect.

278

Discover Hidden Wonders While Exploring a Nearby Nature Trail

Exploring a nearby nature trail together is a refreshing way to step away from the stresses of daily life and reconnect with each other. Whether you're strolling through dense woods, following a riverside path, or wandering across open fields, the natural surroundings provide a calming backdrop for meaningful conversations and quiet moments. This simple yet enriching activity allows you to share in the beauty of the outdoors while enjoying each other's company, free from the distractions of screens and schedules.

As you walk, take time to notice the details around you—the rustling of leaves, the patterns of sunlight breaking through the trees, and the occasional sight of wildlife. Bring along a small snack or a thermos of your favorite drink to enjoy at a scenic spot along the way. These shared moments in nature offer the chance to slow down, breathe deeply, and truly be present with each other. It's an opportunity to bond not just through conversation, but by sharing the simple joy of being surrounded by natural beauty.

Nature trails often reveal hidden gems, from breathtaking views to secret pockets of serenity that feel like they're just for you. Whether you're tackling a new trail or revisiting a favorite spot, each adventure offers the chance to create lasting memories together. Exploring nature as a pair not only strengthens your connection to the world around you but also deepens your bond as you navigate the trail side by side, sharing in both the tranquility and the adventure of the journey.

279

Preserve Her Culinary Traditions with a Personalized Recipe Box

Creating a personalized recipe box filled with family recipes is a meaningful way to celebrate your shared culinary heritage and keep treasured dishes alive for future generations. Start by gathering recipes from both of your families—whether it's handwritten notes from a grandparent, favorite dishes from your childhood, or new recipes you've created together. Organize these recipes in a beautiful, personalized recipe box, adding a special touch with customized dividers or labels.

This recipe box not only serves as a practical collection of beloved meals but also becomes a keepsake that carries the stories and memories associated with each dish. As you cook together, you can add more recipes to the collection, making it an ever-growing testament to your shared love of food and family traditions. Presenting this personalized recipe box to her shows thoughtfulness and appreciation for your culinary journey together, creating a lasting gift that can be passed down through the generations.

280

Celebrate Her Uniqueness by Highlighting What Makes Her Special

Celebrating what makes her unique is about letting her know you see and cherish her for who she truly is. Maybe it's her infectious laugh, her off-the-wall creativity, or the way she's always the first to help someone in need. Taking the time to acknowledge these traits isn't just about compliments—it's about recognizing the little things she might not even realize stand out. Whether it's a quiet moment where you point out her strengths or a loud declaration of pride when she accomplishes something big, celebrating her individuality reinforces her sense of self-worth and your appreciation of her.

You can turn this into something meaningful by tailoring your celebration to what makes her tick. If she loves to paint, surprise her with a custom art kit. If she's a foodie, plan a dinner featuring her favorite dishes. The goal is to highlight her unique qualities in a way that shows you've paid attention and value them deeply. These acts not only make her feel seen but also create shared moments that honor what makes her different from anyone else.

By embracing her quirks and unique traits, you're not just boosting her confidence—you're deepening the connection between you. When she feels celebrated for being her authentic self, it sets the tone for a relationship that's grounded in mutual respect and genuine love. And trust, it'll mean the world to her knowing you appreciate all the little things that make her who she is.

281

Learn How to Eat "Dessert"... the Right Way

In any close relationship, prioritizing her satisfaction is not just a matter of thought—it's essential. When it comes to intimacy, stepping away from pride and embracing a mindset of learning can transform your connection. Understanding what she loves, particularly in terms of oral pleasure, involves open, honest conversations. Ask her what feels good, what excites her, and what she'd like to explore. These chats might feel awkward at first, but they're crucial to deepening your intimacy and showing her that her needs matter to you.

Don't stop at conversation—take action by investing time into truly learning. There are countless guides, tutorials, and resources available to help you improve your skills and gain insight into what works best. Be open to trying new things, taking cues from her reactions, and—most importantly—communicating throughout the process. Every effort you make reflects your commitment to her happiness and your desire to grow as a partner.

Approaching this with humility and enthusiasm not only ensures her pleasure but also strengthens your bond. She'll feel valued, knowing you're willing to put in the work to meet her needs. The journey to mastering "the right way" can be playful and exploratory—embrace it as an opportunity to connect, build trust, and create a level of closeness that enhances your relationship in every way.

… 282 …

Write a Song for Her… and Sing It

Writing a song for her and singing it is one of the most heartfelt ways to express your love. Whether or not you're musically inclined, the effort of creating lyrics that reflect your journey together, the qualities you admire in her, or how she makes you feel will mean the world to her. Your song doesn't have to be a chart-topper; it's the thought and emotion behind it that counts. Even a simple tune paired with honest lyrics can capture the essence of your relationship and show her just how much she means to you.

Performing the song is where the magic happens. Choose an intimate setting—whether it's in your living room, a backyard under the stars, or during a quiet moment on a date night. Singing the song, no matter how polished or raw it sounds, adds vulnerability and sincerity to the gesture, making it even more memorable. Her reaction to hearing something so personal and unique will show you why this effort was so worth it.

If songwriting feels like uncharted territory, don't stress. Nowadays, there are countless resources available online to help get the creative juices flowing. From apps that generate chord progressions to lyric-writing guides, you can find tools to assist in shaping your song. Even collaborating with a musician or using karaoke-style backing tracks can help you create something special. No matter how you get it done, presenting her with a song you've written just for her is a gift she'll never forget.

283

Celebrate Your Love Story by Creating a Movie Reel of Special Moments

Nothing captures the essence of your love story quite like a carefully crafted video that brings your shared journey to life. Whether it's a movie reel of your most cherished moments or a heartfelt video expressing how much she means to you, this gesture blends creativity and sentiment. Videos have a unique way of preserving emotions, great laughs, and love in a format you can revisit for years to come. Taking the time to create something this personal sends her a clear message: your love story matters, and you treasure every moment of it.

Start by gathering the pieces of your shared journey. Dig through your photos, videos, and keepsakes to find those moments that represent the highlights of your time together—your first date, that road trip where you got lost but laughed the whole way, or even the candid shots that capture her genuine smile. Pair these visuals with her favorite songs or music that holds special meaning to both of you. The right soundtrack turns your collection into a masterpiece of memories that she'll cherish.

Elevate the video by making it truly personal. Add spoken or written messages throughout, sharing your thoughts and feelings. Use this platform to express gratitude for her presence in your life, recount moments that stand out as milestones, or articulate how she's shaped your dreams for the future. Whether you narrate it yourself or overlay the video with heartfelt captions, these touches transform it from a simple video into a heartfelt tribute.

To present it, plan an unforgettable "premiere night" that reflects the care and creativity behind the video itself. Transform your living room into a private theater, complete with her favorite snacks, cozy blankets, and candles to create a warm, inviting atmosphere. Alternatively, use this creation to elevate a special occasion—

like an anniversary, her birthday, or even a random day to remind her how much she means to you. The surprise of watching it together will make her feel cherished and create a lasting memory.

A video like this is more than a gift—it's a tribute to your love story. It shows her how much you value your time together, celebrates the highs of your relationship, and honors the moments that define who she is to you. Over the years, it becomes a keepsake you can both revisit to relive the chuckles, milestones, and shared moments that have shaped the life you're building together.

284

Show Excitement when She Dresses for Special Occasions

If she's fine as chinchilla whiskers, you've got to let her know it! When she steps out dressed to the nines for a special occasion, it's your moment to show how much you admire her. Whether she's rocking a stunning dress, a sleek pantsuit, or a bold new style, make sure she knows you see and appreciate every detail. Hit her with genuine compliments, like how the outfit brings out her eyes, or how the color pops against her skin tone. Your words can make her feel like the queen she is.

It's not just about compliments—your energy should match the effort she's put into looking her best. Smile big, tell her to do a spin, or even pull out your phone for a mini photoshoot. If you're about to head out, proudly walk beside her like you've just won the lottery, because, let's be honest, you kind of did. This reaction doesn't just affirm her beauty but shows that you're proud to have her by your side.

And don't fake it—women can smell insincerity like last week's cologne. Your admiration should be authentic and come from noticing the little things she's done to shine, whether it's her makeup, her jewelry, or even her choice of shoes. By doing this, you're not just hyping her up for the night; you're reminding her that she's always a showstopper in your eyes. It's about making her feel loved, confident, and ready to own the evening.

Express Pride in Her Career and Business Achievements

If you two are truly in it for each other, then praising her and expressing pride in her achievements isn't just about catering to her—it's about nurturing your relationship as a whole. A woman who knows her partner admires her ambition and celebrates her success will feel valued and supported in ways that go beyond the workplace. Whether she's smashing corporate goals, running her own business, or excelling in her craft, your acknowledgment tells her that you see her effort and stand proudly by her side.

Some men struggle with the idea of a woman outshining them in career or earnings, letting ego get in the way. But let's be real—ego won't pay bills or build a strong foundation. In fact, insecurity in the face of her success can make you look small in her eyes and shrink your own blessings in the process. A confident man sees her growth as an extension of their shared success, knowing that when she wins, you both win. Celebrating her achievements loudly and proudly doesn't diminish your worth—it enhances your bond and shows that you're mature enough to rise above pride for the greater good of your partnership.

Don't stop at words. Make it a habit to act on that pride with gestures that match her effort. Surprise her with something thoughtful when she hits a milestone, be her biggest advocate in front of friends and family, or simply tell her how much you admire her resilience and drive. Showing her that you're in her corner, rooting for her victories, creates a love built on mutual respect and shared goals. And when she knows you're her loudest cheerleader? That's a foundation no ego can ever shake.

286

Never Be the One Walking Farthest from the Curb

This one might seem like a small thing, but it speaks volumes about how much you value her safety and comfort. When walking together on the sidewalk, always position yourself between her and the curb. It's a timeless gesture of care and protectiveness that shows you're attentive to her well-being. Whether it's shielding her from splashing puddles, reckless drivers, or even stray cyclists, this simple move communicates that her safety matters to you without needing to say a word.

Beyond being a classic act of chivalry, it's about consistency. When you make it a habit, it tells her you're always thinking about her, even in the smallest ways. It's not just about shielding her physically—it's a symbolic act that says, "I've got you." And let's be honest, no one wants to be the guy she has to nudge to switch sides because you're absentmindedly walking closest to the street.

There's nothing worse than seeing a couple in public where the man's on the inside, leaving her next to traffic like an afterthought. Don't be that guy. Step up—literally—and make it second nature to take the side closest to the road. It's such a simple gesture, but it reinforces respect, care, and the unspoken promise that you're always there to protect her. It's these little things that make the biggest difference.

287

Assess Items That Might be Worn Out and Seek Ways to Upgrade Her

Taking the initiative to assess items in her life that might be worn out and upgrading them is a proactive way to show that you care about her comfort, convenience, and overall well-being. Whether it's something small, like a pair of shoes that have seen better days, or something bigger like an outdated tech device, recognizing when something needs an upgrade and stepping in to make a change shows you're paying attention. It's about making her life easier, more efficient, and more enjoyable.

For example, if you notice her business laptop is moving slower than cold syrup on a winter's day, or her handbag is barely hanging on by a thread, take the initiative to surprise her with a replacement. Maybe it's a faster, more efficient laptop that helps her get things done or a fresh, stylish bag that will elevate her look. Upgrading these items shows her you see the little things that matter and want to make her life smoother and more enjoyable.

By doing this, you're not just supporting her emotionally, but also practically. Whether it's a high-tech gadget, a comfy new set of sheets, or something else she uses every day, these thoughtful upgrades show you're actively helping improve her daily experience. It's a way to show that you're invested in her success, comfort, and happiness—whether at work, at home, or on the go.

And let's be real—when her drawers are faded and raggedy with the homemade "ventilation holes" or that pair of leggings has been through more stretches than a yoga class, it's time to swap them out. A fresh set of cozy, comfortable underwear, or an upgrade to her workout gear, can make a huge difference in how she feels every day. These little things show you care about her comfort from head to toe—and let her know you're invested in making sure she feels good in every way.

288

Plan a "Romantic" Water Day with a Water Fight

A "romantic" water day with a playful water fight is a fun, lighthearted way to spend time together, especially when the sun's blazing. Grab some squirt guns, water balloons, or just hose each other down in the backyard. It's not about who wins, but about enjoying the moment—laughing, teasing, and maybe even getting drenched in the process. A water fight taps into that playful, carefree side of your relationship, giving you both a chance to let go and just have fun.

Once the water fight winds down, you can shift gears into a more relaxed, romantic vibe. Wrap up in towels or a cozy blanket, and chill out by the pool or on the grass. The sun might still be shining, but the energy will have shifted from playful chaos to a calm, intimate moment. This is the perfect time to share quiet conversation, reminisce about the day, or simply enjoy the peaceful feeling of being together.

By the end of the day, you'll have turned a simple water fight into a cherished memory. It's about balancing fun with romance and showing each other that even the simplest activities—like a water fight—can bring you closer and keep your relationship exciting. Whether you're soaked or sun-kissed, you'll both remember how fun and meaningful it was to just be in the moment together.

289

Unwind and Connect with Music and Ambiance at a Chill Lounge

Taking her to a lounge with smooth R&B or live jazz is the perfect way to cater to her senses and create an intimate, relaxing experience. Pick a spot with the right vibe—dim lighting, plush seating, and great music, where you can both unwind and just enjoy the moment. Let her know you're there for her by choosing a place that matches her style, where she can feel like the center of attention without any distractions. The smooth melodies and cozy atmosphere create a space for deeper connection, allowing her to let go of stress and enjoy a night focused on the two of you.

As the night goes on, order her favorite drink or suggest a new one she might love, making sure to always cater to her preferences. Take in the music and the vibe, but make it about her—listen closely, laugh together, and share moments of intimacy that will make her feel cherished. Whether it's complimenting her on how she looks or reminiscing about memorable moments in your relationship, this is a time to show her you appreciate her not just with words, but by truly being present.

The beauty of this kind of night is that it doesn't require grand gestures; it's about making her feel special in the little moments. The music, ambiance, and the relaxed energy of the lounge allow you to focus on her needs—whether that's giving her space to relax or engaging her in meaningful conversation. It's a way of showing her that you're paying attention to her desires, creating a night that's all about enjoying her company and making her feel like the queen she is.

"You Don't Have to Lie to Kick It"— Lies Break What Love Creates

There was once a song by 2Pac that said, 'You don't have to lie to kick it.' Those words carry a timeless truth: in relationships, honesty is the key to building genuine connection. You don't need pretense or deceit to win her heart—authenticity and trust will always mean more.

In today's society, dishonesty has become increasingly normalized. From "white lies" told to spare feelings to outright deception often portrayed as clever or justified, misleading others has taken root as a cultural norm. While this might seem harmless in some contexts, dishonesty in a relationship can erode trust faster than almost anything else. To truly cater to her and build a healthy partnership, you must commit to honesty—not just in the big things, but in the everyday interactions that form the foundation of your connection.

People often lie or withhold information out of fear—fear of conflict, rejection, or judgment. It might feel easier to avoid a difficult conversation than to face the discomfort of being vulnerable. Others lie to maintain control or protect their image, thinking that the truth might expose flaws or weaknesses. However, these justifications are short-sighted. Dishonesty doesn't just harm the person being misled; it creates a wall between you and your partner, preventing real intimacy and connection.

I believe true honesty requires courage and self-awareness. It means being willing to have uncomfortable conversations and owning your actions, even when it's difficult. This doesn't mean being brutally honest to the point of insensitivity, but rather communicating with transparency and care. When you share openly—your fears, mistakes, or even unpopular opinions—you show her that you trust her enough to handle the truth and value her enough to give it.

The benefits of honesty far outweigh the perceived safety of dishonesty. When you consistently tell the truth, you create a relationship where she feels secure and valued. She knows she doesn't have to question your words or second-guess your intentions. This foundation of trust allows your connection to flourish, making room for deeper emotional intimacy and mutual respect.

Honesty is a choice you make every day, and it's a gift that strengthens your bond in profound ways. By committing to truthfulness, you honor her, yourself, and the relationship you're building. In a world where dishonesty is often excused, choosing honesty sets you apart and shows her that she's worth the effort it takes to build a love rooted in trust and authenticity.

291

Ease Her Week by Preparing Her Clothes Ahead of Time

Offering to prepare her clothes for the week ahead presents a great opportunity to lighten her load and make her week more manageable. Taking the time to iron or steam her work outfits ensures she's ready to tackle her day without the stress of last-minute wardrobe preparation. This small act can significantly smooth out her mornings, especially when she's balancing a busy schedule or multiple responsibilities.

Beyond its practicality, this gesture reflects your attentiveness and willingness to help where it matters. By handling a task she might not have time for, you show that you're invested in her well-being and eager to support her in whatever ways you can. It's about recognizing her needs and stepping in to make her life a little easier.

This act also speaks volumes about your care and commitment. It's not just about the task itself but about demonstrating that you're a partner who values her time and wants to contribute to her sense of preparedness. By easing her stress in this simple yet impactful way, you strengthen your bond and show her that you're always there to support her.

292

Plan a Romantic and Adventurous Ski Resort Weekend

Planning a romantic ski resort weekend is the perfect way to combine adventure and relaxation in a cozy, wintery setting. Whether she's an experienced skier or a beginner, a weekend at a ski resort offers beautiful mountain views, exciting slopes, and opportunities for cozy moments by the fire. After a day on the slopes, you can both unwind with hot cocoa, enjoy a dip in a hot tub, or relax in the warmth of the resort's spa. These intimate moments allow you to connect, let go of the stresses of daily life, and simply enjoy each other's company in an unforgettable setting.

The trip doesn't have to be all about skiing—many resorts offer a variety of activities for couples. Snowshoeing through glistening forests, taking a scenic sleigh ride under the stars, or even trying a winter horseback ride can add a unique touch to your getaway. If skiing isn't your thing, you can always enjoy the beauty of the snowy landscape, curl up in a cozy lodge, or sip warm drinks by the fire. These simple pleasures, paired with great company, can create a magical, romantic atmosphere that's ideal for deepening your connection.

For the ultimate romantic ski weekend, choosing the right destination can transform the experience into something truly unforgettable. Classic spots like Aspen or Vail in Colorado offer world-class slopes, luxurious accommodations, and a lively après-ski scene. For something quieter and more intimate, consider Whistler in Canada or Lake Tahoe in California, where breathtaking views and serene mountain retreats create a cozy, inviting atmosphere.

If you're looking to venture beyond the U.S., explore renowned international destinations like Chamonix in France or Zermatt in Switzerland, both famous for their stunning Alpine landscapes, sophisticated resorts, and gourmet dining.

For a unique twist, Niseko in Japan offers incredible powder snow, hot springs, and a blend of traditional and modern amenities that create a one-of-a-kind ski experience. These international locations bring an exotic charm to your weekend getaway, combining adventure with cultural exploration.

For a more exclusive and secluded experience, destinations like Stowe in Vermont or Jackson Hole in Wyoming deliver top-tier skiing and picturesque, less crowded resorts where you can unwind and reconnect. Whether you choose a local gem or an international hotspot, these destinations offer the perfect balance of adventure, relaxation, and romance, making them ideal for creating lasting memories together.

293

Team Up for Fun During a Local Group Scavenger Hunt

Participating in a local group scavenger hunt is an exciting and interactive way to bond while working together as a team. Many cities host organized scavenger hunts that involve exploring landmarks, solving puzzles, and completing challenges alongside others. It's a unique opportunity to uncover new parts of your city, connect with fellow participants, and enjoy a bit of friendly competition as you collaborate to complete the hunt.

This activity blends adventure, problem-solving, and physical movement, offering a mix of excitement and accomplishment. The challenge of deciphering clues and racing against time or other teams adds a sense of urgency and fun that keeps you both engaged. Each successful find or completed task becomes a shared victory, building teamwork and creating unforgettable moments.

Beyond the hunt itself, the shared experience of navigating unfamiliar scenarios and cheering each other on strengthens your connection. Whether you win or simply enjoy the journey, the scavenger hunt becomes a memorable adventure that brings a sense of accomplishment to your time together.

Indulge Her in a Dessert-Only Date Night for Pure Sweetness

A dessert-only date night is a deliciously fun and indulgent way to connect and enjoy each other's company. Skip the savory courses and dive straight into a night filled with your favorite sweets. You can visit a local bakery or dessert bar for a tasting experience, sampling everything from rich chocolate cakes to delicate pastries, or you can stay in and create a spread of homemade treats, like brownies, cookies, ice cream sundaes, or decadent chocolate fondue. The goal is to make the entire evening revolve around the simple joy of dessert, letting you both indulge without distractions.

To make the night even more interactive and fun, try experimenting with new dessert recipes together. You could bake a cake from scratch or create custom sundaes with an array of toppings like sprinkles, fresh fruit, caramel, and whipped cream. Another idea is to set up a dessert buffet at home, complete with various toppings, sauces, and mix-ins. This creates an interactive atmosphere where you both get to customize your desserts to your own tastes, sparking a sense of playfulness and creativity in the process.

The best part about a dessert-only date is its carefree vibe—there's no pressure to be formal, just pure enjoyment of each other's company and the sweet treats in front of you. Whether you're laughing over a chocolate lava cake or sharing bites of a cheesecake, the evening will be filled with moments of sweetness, not only in the desserts but in your connection as well. It's a fun, light-hearted date idea that gives you both the chance to indulge, laugh, and create memories while focusing on the joy of being together.

295

Share Youthful Moments Together at a Nearby Car Show

Visiting a car show together is a unique way to connect, whether you're both car enthusiasts or just looking for a fun outing to explore something new. Car shows offer the chance to see rare classics, luxury models, and futuristic concept cars up close. As you walk through the displays, you can discuss your favorites, snap photos of standout designs, and learn interesting facts about the vehicles on display. It's a laid-back but exciting environment that gives you plenty to talk about while appreciating the craftsmanship and creativity behind the cars.

Many car shows also include interactive activities, like live demonstrations, restoration workshops, and even the chance to test drive high-end or specialty cars. These elements make the experience even more dynamic, allowing you both to engage with the automotive world in a hands-on way. Whether it's admiring a pristine '69 Mustang, drooling over a Lamborghini Aventador, or checking out the latest EV technology, there's something at a car show for everyone to enjoy.

Some popular shows to consider include Concours d'Elegance for luxury and vintage cars, SEMA (Specialty Equipment Market Association) for cutting-edge automotive tech, Hot Import Nights for custom imports and a nice party scene, and Goodguys Rod & Custom Shows for hot rods and muscle cars. If you're near major cities, check out events like the LA Auto Show, Detroit Auto Show, or the Chicago World of Wheels. These big-name events often feature stunning displays and unique attractions. No matter the venue, a car show is a great way to enjoy a day of fun, style, and exploration together.

296

Drop the Hints— Speak Your Heart Without the Games

Passive-aggressive behavior often feels like a safer way to express negative emotions, but it can create confusion, resentment, and distance in a relationship. Instead of addressing concerns directly, this approach buries them under sarcasm, subtle digs, or silence, leaving your partner to guess what's really wrong. Replacing passive-aggression with honest and thoughtful communication is essential to building trust and understanding.

Passive-aggression typically stems from fear of conflict or rejection. It can feel easier to hint at a problem than to openly discuss it. However, this indirectness often exacerbates the issue, as she may misinterpret your actions or words. Instead of building connection, it creates unnecessary tension. Acknowledging this pattern and committing to direct communication shows maturity and respect for her feelings.

Healthy communication starts with self-awareness. Take a moment to reflect on why you feel upset or frustrated before speaking. If you catch yourself being sarcastic or making an offhand comment, pause and consider how to reframe your thoughts into honest, constructive feedback. For example, instead of saying, "I guess I'll just do everything myself," try, "I feel overwhelmed and could use some help with this task." This approach invites collaboration rather than defensiveness.

Listening is just as important as speaking honestly. When you create an environment where both of you feel safe to share without judgment, it reduces the temptation to resort to passive-aggression. Acknowledge her perspective, even if it differs from yours, and seek to understand rather than win the conversation. This mutual respect fosters healthier dialogue and strengthens your bond.

By replacing passive-aggression with open and direct communication, you create a relationship that values honesty and trust. She'll appreciate your willingness to address challenges thoughtfully, and you'll both benefit from the clarity and connection that comes with authentic conversation. Over time, this shift will not only resolve conflicts more effectively but also deepen the emotional intimacy you share.

297

Every Queen Deserves a Fairytale Moment

Taking a horse-drawn carriage ride is a romantic and timeless way to share an unforgettable evening together. Whether it's through a scenic park, a charming downtown area, or a festive holiday setting, the gentle rhythm of the carriage provides a peaceful escape from the usual pace of life. Wrapped in a cozy blanket, you can relax, listen to the soft clip-clop of the horse's hooves, and enjoy the beauty of the world passing by.

This enchanting experience evokes a sense of nostalgia and elegance, transporting you to a time when romance was about savoring simple, meaningful moments. It's the perfect opportunity for heartfelt conversation or simply soaking in each other's presence in a serene and intimate setting. The slow pace and quaint charm of the ride create an atmosphere that feels both special and serene.

A carriage ride is more than just a date; it's a way to infuse your evening with a touch of magic. Whether it's a new experience or a cherished tradition, it offers a unique and memorable way to celebrate your bond. With the world moving at a slower pace, the moment becomes all about the connection you share, making it a night to treasure.

Fill a Gratitude Jar Together to Celebrate Shared Moments

Starting a gratitude jar together is a wonderful way to cultivate appreciation for each other and the moments you share. Begin with a jar and small slips of paper, and regularly write down things you're grateful for—whether it's a kind gesture, a shared laugh, or a simple moment that brightened your day. Over time, the jar becomes a collection of heartfelt reflections, showcasing the love and positivity that define your relationship. This practice not only highlights what makes your connection special but also serves as a gentle reminder to celebrate the little things that make life meaningful.

When the jar is full or during special occasions, take time to read the notes together. Reliving these expressions of gratitude allows you to reflect on your shared journey and the many ways you've supported and cared for each other. It's a practice that reinforces the positive aspects of your relationship and encourages you both to focus on the blessings in your life. By turning this simple activity into a shared tradition, you create an ongoing source of connection and inspiration that deepens your bond.

299

Be Vulnerable About the Things You Struggle With

Opening up about the things you struggle with is a powerful way to strengthen your bond and show your commitment to becoming a better partner. Vulnerability isn't always easy, but being honest about areas where you fall short—whether it's communication, patience, or balancing work and personal life—shows that you care about her happiness and the health of your relationship. By admitting where you want to improve, you demonstrate self-awareness and a genuine desire to grow.

These conversations don't just strengthen your connection; they also create a space where she feels safe to share her own struggles and aspirations. Mutual vulnerability fosters understanding and encourages both of you to approach challenges as a team. Let her know that your goal isn't just self-improvement for the sake of it, but to make her life better and the relationship stronger. Acknowledging these struggles isn't a sign of weakness—it's an act of love and accountability.

Approach these discussions with humility, leaving pride at the door. As men, we're often conditioned to bottle things up or "fix" problems silently, but true growth comes from transparency. Being honest about where you need to improve—whether it's managing anger, becoming more attentive, or simply being present—can inspire her confidence in your willingness to evolve. This level of honesty not only makes her feel valued but also reassures her that you're invested in building a relationship based on trust, growth, and mutual care.

300

Bonus: Physical Abuse Has No Place in Her Life

Physical abuse has no place in any relationship, especially one that is meant to be built on love and mutual respect. Hurting her physically is not only a violation of trust but also a betrayal of the very essence of what love represents. Love is about care, protection, and nurturing—not control, harm, or intimidation. If you claim to love her, raising a hand against her is a contradiction of that love. No matter how intense a situation may become, violence is never the answer.

Resorting to physical abuse is a sign of weakness, not strength. It reflects the poorest form of manhood—a cowardly and destructive impulse. True strength lies in self-control, in choosing kindness and understanding over aggression. If you have children, the impact of such behavior is magnified. When you hit her, you not only hurt her but also expose your children to an environment of fear and instability. They learn by watching, and if they see violence, they will internalize it as part of how relationships work. What kind of legacy are you leaving if your actions teach them fear instead of love, respect, and protection?

Abuse doesn't just leave physical scars; it damages her emotional well-being, self-worth, and sense of security. It creates an atmosphere of fear and erodes the foundation of trust in your relationship. Even if apologies follow, the harm caused by such behavior lingers, making it harder to rebuild the bond you've broken. Abuse strips her of the safety and peace she deserves in her life and her relationship, leaving her to navigate the lasting pain of your actions.

If conflict arises, there are countless healthier ways to address it. Communication, patience, and compromise are the tools of a strong relationship. When challenges feel overwhelming, seek professional help or mediation to find productive resolutions. Turning to violence only escalates problems, while healthy conflict resolution builds trust and deepens your bond. Respect her enough to address issues constructively and show her that she is worth the effort to do things the right way.

Above all, understand that love cannot coexist with fear. A relationship built on respect, care, and kindness offers a safe space for both partners to grow and thrive. She deserves a life where she feels valued and protected—not one where she has to question her safety. Physical abuse has no justification, no excuse, and no place in her life—or in yours. True love empowers and uplifts; it does not harm or diminish.

Perhaps you grew up in a home where domestic violence was common or come from a family where such behavior has been normalized for generations. This is your opportunity to break the chains of that cycle. Acknowledging the influence of your past doesn't excuse abusive behavior, but it does provide a starting point for change. Be courageous enough to seek professional help—not only to heal from the wounds of your upbringing but also to learn healthier ways of handling conflict and expressing emotions. Breaking free from this pattern can transform your relationships and set a positive example for future generations.

301

Climb a Lighthouse or Scenic Overlook for Stunning Views

Visiting a nearby lighthouse or scenic overlook is a beautiful way to spend time together while taking in breathtaking views. Whether you're climbing to the top of a historic lighthouse or enjoying the panoramic view from a hilltop or coastal overlook, these locations offer a serene and romantic atmosphere. It's the perfect spot to share quiet moments, take photos, and appreciate nature's beauty.

The sense of adventure, combined with the peaceful environment, allows for meaningful conversations or simply enjoying each other's company while being surrounded by natural wonders. This outing provides a chance to disconnect from the busy world and reconnect with each other in a stunning setting.

302

Curate a Sentimental Keepsake Box Full of Memories

Collecting a box of keepsakes is a heartfelt way to capture the essence of your relationship and show her how much the little things mean to you. Fill the box with sentimental items that symbolize key moments in your journey together—ticket stubs from your first movie date, a pressed flower from an anniversary bouquet, or small mementos that remind you of shared adventures. These items may seem simple, but together they tell the story of your love and the meaningful moments you've experienced as a couple.

Make it a tradition to revisit the box together, pulling out items and reliving the memories attached to them. Whether it's a laugh over a silly trinket or a heartfelt reflection on a handwritten note, this ritual strengthens your bond by keeping your shared history alive. It's a powerful reminder of how far you've come and the love that's grown between you.

This gesture isn't just about preserving the past—it's about making her feel seen and valued. Taking the time to curate these keepsakes shows that you cherish the details of your relationship and the impact she's had on your life. By focusing on moments both big and small, you let her know that everything she brings to your partnership is appreciated and worthy of being remembered.

303

Make Today Count by Achieving What Was Once Out of Reach

Is there something she's been longing for but couldn't make happen because of past limitations? Whether it was a lack of financial means, time constraints, or personal hesitation, life's obstacles can sometimes put her wishes on hold. But now that circumstances have shifted—whether it's improved finances, a more flexible schedule, or personal growth—you have the chance to bring those dreams to life. Doing today what you couldn't yesterday is a powerful way to show her how much you care and how far you've come.

Think about what she's expressed wanting in the past: a dream vacation she's mentioned, an item she's had her eye on, or even a gesture like becoming more patient or attentive. Fulfilling these wishes now shows not only that you've been listening but also that you value her happiness enough to revisit what couldn't happen before. It's about acknowledging the moment, seizing the opportunity, and making good on what may have felt impossible back then.

This chapter is especially written for men who have been in their relationships for years and might have gotten comfortable with just being present. While being there is important, taking action to address those long-standing desires shows that you're not complacent—you're still actively invested in her happiness. The gesture speaks volumes about your willingness to evolve for her sake, showing her that you're constantly striving to give her the best version of yourself. It lets her know that her dreams and desires are just as important now as they were then—and that you'll always work toward making them come true, no matter how long it takes.

304

Sweep Her Off Her Feet
—Literally—
with a Passionate Lift and Kiss

If you're physically able, picking her up and sharing a long, passionate kiss is a gesture that combines physical intimacy with emotional depth. This isn't just about the kiss—it's the act of physically lifting her, which symbolizes strength, support, and a playful kind of affection. It's the kind of move that can take her by surprise, making her feel cherished and special in the moment. Whether it happens after a heartfelt conversation, in the middle of the kitchen, or just because you felt like it, it creates an unforgettable experience.

The long kiss itself sets this apart from ordinary gestures. It's not a quick peck or a casual moment; it's about slowing down, holding each other close, and letting the world around you fade. It gives you both a chance to focus solely on your connection—physically and emotionally—making it a powerful way to express love and deepen intimacy. The lift adds an extra layer of vulnerability and trust, reinforcing the bond between you in a way that words can't.

Unlike previous chapters that might focus on kisses or physical closeness, this gesture adds a dynamic twist by incorporating movement and spontaneity. Picking her up is an act of confidence and intention, making it more than a simple expression of love. It's a moment that says, "I see you, I love you, and I want to sweep you off your feet—literally and figuratively." It's not just a kiss; it's an embodiment of romance, care, and passion wrapped into one memorable action.

305

Share Trust (and Maybe Laughter) by Letting Her Style Your Hair

Letting her shave or style your hair is a unique and intimate way to bond, especially if it's something you've never let anyone else do. Whether she's trimming your beard, lining you up, or trying out a simple hairstyle, it's more than just grooming—it's about trust. You're allowing her to take control of something as personal as your appearance, and that vulnerability can strengthen your connection. Plus, it can turn into a lighthearted moment that brings you closer through laughter and teamwork.

For the men who are serious about their hair—and fiercely loyal to their barbers—this might feel like treading on sacred ground. If you're the type to have your barber on speed dial or feel like you're cheating just by looking at someone else's clippers, this can be a test of your nerves. But think of it as an adventure. Worst-case scenario, you're wearing a hat for a few days; best-case, she surprises you with skills you didn't know she had. And hey, if it doesn't work out, you've got an epic story for your next visit to the barber.

At the heart of this gesture is the opportunity to laugh, connect, and let go a little. It's not about perfection—it's about letting her in and sharing a playful experience together. Whether she aces the lineup or you both end up cracking up at the results, the memory will be priceless. Just keep the guard on the clippers and the mood light, and you'll be good to go. I guess this one's easy for me to recommend since I've been bald for quite some time. . . . Good luck!

306

Explore an Intimate Store Together for New Adventures

Visiting a local intimate store together is a bold and adventurous way to deepen your connection and explore new dimensions of your relationship. Whether you're there to find something playful, romantic, or educational, this experience is about stepping into a space where open communication and trust take center stage. Walking through the store side by side gives you the chance to share thoughts and ideas, discover each other's preferences, and find ways to spice things up in a way that feels comfortable for both of you.

This outing is more than just shopping—it's about fostering a sense of curiosity and excitement in your relationship. Laugh together as you explore new possibilities, ask questions, and consider things you may never have thought about before. Whether you leave with a new purchase or simply enjoy the experience of being playful and open, the act of exploring together helps build intimacy and breaks down barriers around conversations about your desires.

For those who might feel hesitant, remember that this is an opportunity to share a unique moment together and reinforce the trust between you. A trip to an intimate store can be lighthearted, educational, and even empowering when approached with the right mindset. It's not about pressure or expectations but about creating an environment where you can openly and respectfully explore what makes your relationship stronger, closer, and more exciting.

307

Include Her in Major Decision-Making Moments

Including her in major decision-making moments is an essential way to demonstrate that you see her as an equal partner in your relationship. Whether the decisions are about finances, career changes, moving to a new city, or any other big life choice, inviting her input ensures that you're both aligned in your goals and values. When she sees that you genuinely care about her perspective, it reinforces her importance in your life and shows that you respect the shared nature of your journey together.

Patience is key in these discussions. Major decisions often come with stress, differing opinions, and moments of uncertainty. Taking the time to listen to her thoughts without rushing or dismissing them fosters trust and allows for more meaningful dialogue. Showing patience also ensures that you're making well-considered decisions that reflect both of your needs and aspirations. These moments of collaboration strengthen the foundation of your relationship by highlighting your ability to navigate challenges as a team.

Remember, this is about building a partnership where both of you feel heard and valued. Even if her views differ from yours, embracing her input creates a sense of unity and mutual respect. Including her in these decisions isn't just practical—it's a way to show her that you see your relationship as a partnership rooted in love, patience, and a shared vision for the future.

308

Improve Your Perspective of Her Capabilities

Improving your perspective of her capabilities starts with recognizing that your partner is more than capable of excelling in whatever she sets her mind to, whether it's in her career, personal goals, or the shared responsibilities of your life together. It means shedding outdated beliefs or societal stereotypes that may have subtly shaped your expectations. Viewing her as an equal partner who is resourceful, intelligent, and resilient allows you to fully appreciate her contributions and support her as she pursues her dreams.

This shift in mindset strengthens your relationship by building mutual respect and trust. When you openly express faith in her capabilities, you empower her to embrace her strengths and feel confident in tackling challenges. It's not just about words of encouragement—it's about actively demonstrating that you believe in her abilities by asking for her input, celebrating her successes, and showing that you value her talents. This creates an environment where she can flourish both within the relationship and in her individual pursuits.

This approach also has a ripple effect beyond your relationship. By demonstrating these values, you set an example for the younger generation, challenging cycles of limiting beliefs. Young men who see this will grow up understanding the importance of uplifting their partners, while young women will learn to seek relationships built on respect and encouragement. Changing this perspective isn't just about your relationship; it's about reshaping cultural expectations and fostering a future where women are cherished, valued, and supported as equals.

309

Glide Across the Water on a Ferry to a Nearby Island Escape

Taking a ferry ride to explore a nearby island is a perfect way to mix relaxation with adventure. The ferry ride itself offers a sense of escape as you glide across the water, taking in picturesque views and feeling the breeze on your face. It's an opportunity to pause, enjoy the moment, and anticipate the fun that awaits on the island. Whether you're planning a full day of exploration or just a few hours of unwinding, the ferry ride is a soothing prelude to your adventure.

Once you arrive, the island offers endless possibilities. Depending on your destination, you might hike scenic trails, lounge on beautiful beaches, savor local delicacies, or shop at quaint island boutiques. It's an exciting chance to break from routine, immerse yourselves in a different environment, and create lasting memories together. The mix of exploring new surroundings and sharing the day's experiences fosters connection and adds a sense of spontaneity to your relationship.

Some of my favorite popular cities with ferry rides include Seattle, Washington, where you can visit Bainbridge Island; San Francisco, California, with ferries to Sausalito or Angel Island; and New York City, where you can take the Staten Island Ferry. Other noteworthy spots include Boston, Massachusetts, for trips to the Boston Harbor Islands, and Vancouver, British Columbia, with ferries to Vancouver Island. These locations offer diverse experiences and scenic views, making them perfect for an unforgettable island adventure.

310

Challenge Each Other in a Mystery Ingredient Cooking Showdown

Turn your kitchen into a lively culinary arena with a cooking challenge featuring mystery ingredients. This activity is a creative and exciting way to bond, as you both flex your cooking skills—or embrace the chaos if neither of you are seasoned chefs! Start by picking a few random ingredients from your pantry or take turns surprising each other with items you've secretly purchased. The goal is to craft a dish using all the mystery ingredients, no matter how odd the combination.

The unpredictability of the challenge guarantees laughs and keeps the energy high. Whether you're trying to figure out how to incorporate gummy bears into a savory dish or turning canned tuna into a gourmet masterpiece, the process pushes you both to think outside the box. Work as a team to combine your culinary ideas or compete to see whose dish reigns supreme. Either way, the kitchen will be filled with laughter, playful banter, and maybe a bit of friendly competition.

To add structure, you can set a time limit, bring in a judge (kids or friends make great ones), or even record your challenge for fun memories. If you need inspiration, try themes like "breakfast for dinner," "international flavors," or "dessert fusion." At the end, sit down together to taste your creations—whether they're Instagram-worthy or hilariously disastrous. The focus is on spending quality time, embracing spontaneity, and turning an ordinary evening into an unforgettable shared experience.

311

Cultivate a New Mindset About Life Together

Shaping a new perspective on life as a couple is one of the most profound ways to deepen your connection and create a thriving relationship. It's not just about shared goals but about aligning your attitudes toward challenges, successes, and personal growth. This process begins with honest conversations about what truly matters to both of you—your values, aspirations, and even fears. By reflecting together on what you want out of life, you can identify ways to support each other in becoming the best versions of yourselves.

For her, this shared mindset shows that you value her thoughts, dreams, and emotional well-being. It caters to her by making her feel seen and heard, ensuring that her desires and aspirations are as important as your own. It's a way of demonstrating that you're not just building a life for yourself but for both of you. This shared journey tells her that she has a partner who is fully invested in creating a fulfilling and harmonious life together, where her happiness and growth are prioritized.

Cultivating this mindset means recognizing that change doesn't happen overnight. You might stumble, fall back into old patterns, or face external pressures that test your resolve. The key is to commit to the journey, not the immediate results. Even if you only take small steps—like pausing to celebrate little victories or rethinking how you approach daily frustrations—it's the effort and intention that matter most. And if it feels like a one-time experiment? That's okay. At least you'll have tried together, and even that attempt will bring you closer.

Ultimately, adopting a new mindset as a couple isn't just about what you gain individually—it's about what you create together. It's about shaping a life where both of you feel supported, inspired, and deeply connected. Whether it's finding joy in the little things or navigating big dreams hand in hand, this shared outlook becomes a cornerstone of your relationship, ensuring that no matter where life takes you, you're in it together.

312

Turn Your Evening into One of Discovery with DIY Science Experiments

Transform your evening into a playful and brainy adventure by hosting a home science experiment night. It's a fantastic way to bond while tapping into your inner child and exploring the wonders of science together. Gather easy-to-find materials for fun experiments like baking soda volcanos, making glow-in-the-dark slime, or building a simple circuit with household items. If you need inspiration, online tutorials and science kits can help you set up experiments that are entertaining, interactive, and safe for beginners.

The joy of this activity lies in the shared excitement and discovery. Watching reactions bubble over or figuring out why something worked—or hilariously didn't—encourages collaboration and conversation. For an added twist, turn it into a competition to see who can create the most creative or successful experiment. Whether you're laughing at a messy failure or marveling at a surprising result, the experience brings out your playful sides and keeps the energy light and enjoyable.

And let's be clear—this isn't an invitation to start up an illegal chemistry operation! You're crafting childhood nostalgia and bonding moments, not cooking up a "meth"odology that will land you and your lady behind bars. Stick to the baking soda and vinegar; it's a lot more fun when your experiments don't require a legal defense team.

313

Do Something Different and Take a Pottery Class Together

Taking a pottery class together is an immersive and rewarding experience that combines creativity, fun, and a touch of teamwork. As you sit side by side, learning to shape and mold clay on a spinning pottery wheel, you'll not only create unique pieces but also share moments of laughter and discovery. Whether it's your first attempt or you've dabbled in pottery before, the process of working with your hands, learning techniques, and navigating the occasional messy mishap creates a lighthearted atmosphere where you can enjoy each other's company while embracing something new.

Beyond the fun of the experience, pottery teaches patience and teamwork as you encourage each other to perfect your pieces. The tangible result—a bowl, mug, or even a quirky abstract sculpture—serves as a lasting reminder of your time together. Every time you see or use your creations, you'll recall the joy and connection you felt while crafting them. This creative outing isn't just about making pottery; it's about making memories and strengthening your bond through a shared artistic journey.

314

Wander Through the Beauty of a Botanical Garden or Arboretum

Visiting a botanical garden or arboretum is a serene and romantic way to escape into nature's vibrant beauty while spending quality time together. Walking hand in hand through lush gardens filled with colorful blooms, towering trees, and soothing water features creates a tranquil environment that encourages connection and relaxation. As you explore, you'll discover exotic plants and flowers, each with its own story, offering opportunities to share curiosity and learn together. The peaceful surroundings make it easy to pause, take a deep breath, and appreciate the calming influence of nature.

The experience goes beyond the visuals; it's about the atmosphere of stillness and the quiet conversations that flow naturally in such a setting. Some botanical gardens or arboretums even have themed sections, such as Japanese tea gardens or desert landscapes, adding variety to your exploration. The serene environment is perfect for meaningful moments, whether you're sitting on a bench watching butterflies or marveling at the intricate beauty of a rare orchid. Visiting these green havens allows you to reconnect with nature—and each other—while leaving the hustle of daily life behind.

315

Build and Fly a Kite Together for a Little Outdoor Fun

Building and flying a kite together is a fun, creative way to spend quality time outdoors while embracing a bit of childlike wonder. Start by choosing a simple kite design or, if you're feeling adventurous, go for something more intricate that matches your personalities. As you assemble the kite, you'll find yourselves laughing, problem-solving, and collaborating to bring your creation to life. This process isn't just about building a kite; it's about strengthening your bond through teamwork and shared creativity.

Once your masterpiece is complete, take it to a park, beach, or open field where the wind can take it sky-high. Watching your kite soar through the air brings a unique sense of accomplishment, especially knowing it's something you built together. And if the kite crashes more than it flies, that's just another opportunity for laughter and playful competition as you figure out how to keep it steady. The experience of flying a kite taps into the simple, carefree joys of childhood, creating lasting memories in the process.

Now, I'll admit, my last kite-building adventure was a comedic disaster. Despite my best efforts, the kite refused to stay airborne. Still, the shared frustration and humor made it a day to remember. So even if your kite turns out to be more "crash and burn" than "soar and glide," the experience is worth it. The laughter and bonding that come from trying something together—and maybe failing spectacularly—make it an activity I wholeheartedly recommend.

316

Refresh Her Favorite Sneakers to Show You Care About the Details

Cleaning her shoes and sneakers is a maintenance-friendly gesture to show you care, especially if she's a sneakerhead or simply takes pride in her footwear. Gather the necessary supplies—soft brushes, cleaning solution, a microfiber cloth, and even some fresh laces if needed—and give her favorite kicks a proper refresh. This gesture demonstrates your attention to detail and your willingness to help her maintain the things she values. It's not just about removing dirt; it's about preserving the style and longevity of something that represents her personality and interests.

If she's a true sneaker enthusiast, take the time to learn about her collection and the proper techniques for cleaning specific materials, whether it's leather, suede, or mesh. Brands like Reshoev8r, Jason Markk, and Crep Protect offer high-quality cleaning products that make the process easier and more effective. Cleaning her shoes can spark conversations about her favorite pairs, limited editions she admires, or the stories behind her collection. The act of caring for her sneakers shows that you're invested in her passions, turning what might seem like a mundane task into a meaningful way to bond and cater to her individuality.

317

Bounce Into Fun and Soreness at a Trampoline Park Date

A night at a trampoline park is the perfect way to combine energy, fun, and connection in a lighthearted environment. From bouncing side by side to launching into foam pits, this outing offers a playful break from routine that encourages great laughs and shared excitement. Challenge each other to trampoline basketball, show off your flips (or hilariously failed attempts), or team up for an obstacle course. The sheer energy of jumping around together creates a carefree atmosphere where you can bond over fun and fitness in a completely unexpected way.

Trampoline parks often offer unique experiences like dodgeball arenas, ninja warrior courses, and even glow-in-the-dark sessions, making it easy to tailor the night to your vibe. The physical activity also releases endorphins, boosting your moods and creating a sense of accomplishment as you tackle challenges together. Whether you're competitive or just looking to bounce off the stress of the day, a night at the trampoline park fosters a sense of playfulness that strengthens your connection and creates memories worth jumping for.

Spice it Up with a Bucket List of Places to Make Love

Creating a bucket list of places to make love is an exciting way to infuse your relationship with adventure and spontaneity. Sit down together and let your imaginations run wild, brainstorming locations that feel meaningful, romantic, or thrilling. From classic spots like under the stars or in front of a fireplace to adventurous ideas like a secluded beach, a cozy cabin, or a quiet corner of a scenic park, the possibilities are endless. This isn't just about the physical act—it's about embracing new experiences that add spark and variety to your connection.

This shared activity is also an opportunity for open and honest communication about fantasies and desires. Discussing what excites both of you fosters a deeper understanding of each other's preferences and keeps the relationship vibrant. The anticipation of crossing items off the list adds a playful, long-term goal that keeps the chemistry alive. It's about creating moments that aren't just intimate but also unforgettable, woven with spontaneity and trust.

It's important to remember that as time goes on, it's easy to get comfortable or even complacent, especially after being together for years. A bucket list like this serves as a reminder to prioritize your love life and keep the flame burning. Keeping things fresh and adventurous in your intimacy shows that you're still invested in the relationship, ensuring that the passion and excitement you had in the beginning continue to grow. Reigniting that spark not only strengthens your bond but also reinforces that your love is worth the effort, every single day.

While creating an exciting bucket list of places to make love can add spontaneity and thrill to your relationship, it's crucial to prioritize privacy and be aware of the laws in your location. In many countries, engaging in sexual activity in public spaces can lead to serious legal consequences, including arrest, as it is often considered public indecency or a disturbance. To ensure that your intimate experiences remain enjoyable and free of legal risk, it's important to choose private or secluded locations where you can be undisturbed. Always be mindful of local laws and respect the privacy of others, ensuring that your moments of intimacy are both discreet and within legal boundaries. Unless, of course, you're looking to create some jailtime memories to share together. But hey, I also understand some of you appreciate the most extreme thrills in life. Go get it, Tiger!

319

Plan a Family Gathering to Reconnect Her with Loved Ones

Arranging a family gathering for her is a heartfelt way to show that you value the people she loves and want her to feel connected to them. Whether it's a dinner at a cozy restaurant, a backyard barbecue, or even a themed potluck at home, taking the lead in planning makes all the difference. Think about what would make her feel special—a menu filled with her favorites, a playlist of nostalgic tunes, or a casual setting where everyone can simply relax. By handling the details, you allow her to fully enjoy the occasion without the usual stress that comes with organizing such events.

For those who might struggle with tolerating certain family members, it's perfectly natural to feel some hesitation. Your feelings about the dynamics are valid, and it's okay to acknowledge that some relationships may be challenging. However, remember that this day is about her joy and creating a space where she feels surrounded by love. If you approach the event with an open mind, even for just a few hours, you'll demonstrate not only your support for her but also your commitment to doing what matters most to her. Focus on the fact that your effort—whether big or small—can make a meaningful impact on her well-being.

That said, this doesn't need to become a regular event if it doesn't work for you. Maybe hosting her family isn't something you'd do every year, and that's okay. What matters is that you've tried. Even if this gathering ends up being a one-time effort, she will see how much you care about her happiness and her relationships. Sometimes, showing up for her just once in this way can mean more than you realize, leaving a positive impression that lasts long after the event is over.

Ultimately, this is an opportunity to connect with her on a deeper level by supporting what brings her joy. Whether you walk away feeling like it was a success or a challenge, the fact that you made the effort will not go unnoticed. You've shown her that you're willing to step outside your comfort zone for her sake, and that speaks volumes about your dedication to her happiness. At the end of the day, the most important takeaway is that she'll know you tried—and sometimes, that's more than enough.

320

Delight Her with Thoughtful Gifts of Her Favorite Girly Essentials

Surprising her with her favorite girly items—like lashes, hair care products, makeup, or skincare—is a simple gesture to show that you pay attention to the little things that make her feel her best. These items are more than just products; they're tools that help her feel beautiful, confident, and ready to take on the world. Whether it's a top-tier makeup palette, a high-end curling iron, or a nourishing hair mask, choosing products that cater to her preferences is a meaningful gesture that says you appreciate her self-care rituals.

If you're unsure of what to get, consider brands like Fenty Beauty for makeup, Olaplex or SheaMoisture for hair care, and Laneige or The Ordinary for skincare. Sephora gift sets, MAC lipsticks, or even a subscription to a beauty box like Ipsy can also hit the mark. Pay attention to the products she already uses, or subtly ask what's on her wishlist—she'll notice the effort you've put into finding the perfect gift just for her.

Beyond the products themselves, this gesture reflects your care and attentiveness. It's not just about the tangible items but the understanding that she deserves to feel pampered and valued. By gifting her these personal items, you remind her that her happiness and confidence are priorities in your relationship—and that you're more than willing to invest in her feeling her absolute best.

321

Remember Diamonds Are Still a Girl's Best Friend

Diamonds have stood the test of time as a symbol of love, commitment, and unmatched elegance, making them a meaningful gift for any special occasion. Whether it's a pair of diamond earrings, a dazzling necklace, or a stunning bracelet, giving her diamonds is a timeless way to show your appreciation and celebrate her beauty. These pieces go beyond material value, often becoming cherished keepsakes that hold emotional significance.

For many men, buying diamonds is a milestone—whether it's for an engagement ring, a wedding band, or a special anniversary gift. Understanding the "4 Cs" of diamonds—Cut, Color, Clarity, and Carat weight—is essential when selecting the perfect piece. The cut affects how brilliantly the diamond sparkles, while the color ranges from clear to faint hues, with colorless diamonds being the most prized. Clarity refers to the presence of inclusions or flaws, and carat weight determines the size of the diamond. Striking a balance between these qualities based on your budget ensures you find a piece that is both beautiful and meaningful.

It's also crucial to purchase diamonds from reputable jewelers who provide certified stones. Brands like Tiffany & Co., Cartier, and De Beers offer impeccable quality, while stores like Blue Nile or James Allen provide excellent options for those shopping online. Always ask for a certificate from trusted organizations like GIA (Gemological Institute of America) or AGS (American Gem Society) to ensure you're getting an authentic and accurately graded diamond.

This chapter is four paragraphs because most men will find themselves buying diamonds at least once in their lives, whether for an engagement, a wedding, or as a romantic gesture. Learning about diamonds not only helps you make a thoughtful purchase but also shows that you're willing to invest in something that holds material and sentimental value. Choosing the right diamond jewelry demonstrates your understanding of her tastes, creating a gift that's as radiant as your relationship.

Uncover Hidden Gems Together at a Local Market or Bazaar

Exploring a local market or bazaar together is a vibrant and engaging way to spend quality time while uncovering hidden gems. Markets often feature an array of unique items, from handmade jewelry and artisanal crafts to fresh produce and delicious street food. As you navigate the colorful stalls, you'll have the chance to discover treasures that reflect her tastes or pick out something meaningful to commemorate the day. The lively atmosphere, filled with the sounds of music and chatter, adds an exciting energy to your outing.

This experience is more than just shopping—it's about immersing yourselves in the local culture and connecting over shared discoveries. Trying out local delicacies, admiring intricate handiwork, or finding quirky antiques sparks conversations and creates cherished memories. Whether you're in search of the perfect keepsake or simply soaking in the ambiance, a day at the market is a relaxed and enjoyable way to strengthen your bond while supporting local artisans and vendors.

Paddle Through the Rapids on a Canoe or Kayak Journey

Taking a canoe or kayak trip on a nearby river is a peaceful and adventurous way to spend quality time together. Gliding through calm waters or tackling light rapids gives you both a chance to work as a team, find your rhythm, and enjoy the beauty of nature. Whether you're spotting wildlife, soaking in the lush scenery, or simply appreciating the gentle sway of the water, it's a refreshing escape from the hustle of everyday life. The adventure creates shared memories, laughter, and plenty of moments to connect while paddling in sync.

And yes, safety matters—but let's keep it real. If one of you panics at the thought of tipping over in a spot where the water barely covers your knees, just remember: it's only a teaspoon of water, not Niagara Falls. Wear a life vest anyway, because it'll save you from embarrassment when the lifeguard fishes you out like a soggy breadstick. Keep the mood light and bring a sense of humor—because even if you're not expert paddlers, the trip will be unforgettable (even if it's because someone panics at a rogue ripple).

324

Step Up—Lead with Love and Confidence

Indecisiveness can quietly erode the strength of a relationship. When you avoid making decisions or hesitate to take the lead, it can leave your partner feeling unvalued or burdened with having to shoulder the responsibility alone. While collaboration is key in a healthy partnership, there are moments when what she needs most is for you to step up with confidence and provide direction. Taking the initiative shows her that you're not only invested but also capable of navigating life's challenges together.

Being decisive doesn't mean ignoring her input or making choices without consultation—it's about finding balance. Listen to her needs and preferences, but don't shy away from taking the lead when the situation calls for it. Whether it's planning a date night, making financial decisions, or navigating a tough moment, stepping forward with clarity and conviction signals your commitment to the partnership. It tells her, "I've got us."

For those who struggle with indecision, start small. Take charge of everyday choices, like picking a restaurant or suggesting an activity. Gradually build your confidence by learning to trust your instincts. Remember, leadership isn't about perfection; it's about effort and intention. Even if the decision you make isn't flawless, your willingness to act and guide will be appreciated far more than prolonged hesitation.

At its core, decisiveness in a relationship is a form of care. It reduces stress, builds trust, and strengthens your connection. By stepping up with love and confidence, you create a sense of stability that allows both of you to thrive. Let her see that you're willing to lead—not because you have to, but because you want to, for the sake of the life you're building together.

325

Roll, Bounce, and Glide Together with a Roller Skating Date

This is a good way to bust your ***—at least I did a couple of times when I tried to get fancy on 'em. Going roller skating together is a hilarious and energetic way to spend quality time. Whether you're at an old-school indoor rink with dope vibes or gliding around a smooth outdoor trail, skating brings out your playful side. Holding hands while you skate (or trying to!) is both romantic and practical—especially if one of you isn't quite ready for the skating Olympics.

The music, movement, and upbeat atmosphere make roller skating an excellent way to break free from the ordinary and let loose. You'll find yourself laughing at each other's fancy footwork, near-misses, and, yes, even those unplanned tumbles. The shared experience of navigating the rink together, whether it's graceful or clumsy, strengthens your bond and guarantees a good time.

And don't worry if you're not a pro—nobody looks cool while flailing to avoid a wipeout. Just embrace the chaos, enjoy the fun, and be ready to laugh when someone (probably you) ends up hugging the floor. By the end of the session, your cheeks will hurt from smiling, your legs might ache a little, but the memories will be worth every stumble and slide.

Grant Her the Gift of a Day of "Nothingness"

Give her a day where the agenda is as blank as the sky on a clear summer afternoon. No chores, no obligations, no expectations—just a complete escape from responsibility. Let her spend the day however she pleases, whether that means lounging on the couch in her favorite pajamas, binge-watching her go-to show, or taking a guilt-free nap in the middle of the day. You handle everything—meals, errands, or even the kids—so she can fully immerse herself in the bliss of doing absolutely nothing.

This day of "nothingness" is not just about giving her time off; it's about creating an environment where she feels cared for and free to recharge. Sometimes, the best way to connect isn't through grand plans or activities but by simply existing together without pressure. Lay back, share a few laughs, or just sit quietly, enjoying each other's presence. These moments of stillness and simplicity often remind you both of what matters most—being fully present and at peace with each other.

327

Let Her Sleep in While You Tackle the Morning Chaos

Give her the ultimate luxury: uninterrupted sleep. Take charge of the morning chaos by wrangling the kids, handling breakfast, and keeping the household calm so she can indulge in some much-needed rest. Whether she's been up late tending to the kids, working long hours, or just dealing with life's endless demands, giving her a quiet, stress-free morning is a small act of care with a huge impact. Let her drift back to sleep without worrying about alarms, screaming toddlers, or requests for waffles—this is her time to recharge.

While she's calling hogs, take the opportunity to bond with the kids. Whether you're watching cartoons, making pancakes, or tackling a quick chore, the goal is to handle it all so she wakes up to a home that's not only peaceful but also running smoothly. By stepping in and giving her this break, you're showing her that you see and appreciate all the work she does and that her well-being matters just as much as anyone else's in the house.

When she finally emerges from her restful sanctuary, she'll be greeted with a calm environment and maybe even breakfast waiting for her. This gesture doesn't just cater to her need for rest—it also strengthens your partnership, showing her that you're fully invested in sharing the load and ensuring she feels supported and loved. Plus, the kids get a chance to appreciate her absence, making them all the more excited when she's ready to rejoin the fun.

328

Surprise Her with a Spontaneous Financial Gift

There's nothing quite like the thrill of being surprised with a random financial gift, whether it's a well-placed envelope, a stylish bag, or even a stack of cash. This gesture goes beyond material value—it shows her that you're thinking about her needs, goals, and desires. Whether she chooses to use the money for shopping, travel, or investing in her own business or personal pursuits, you're giving her the freedom to treat herself or work toward something meaningful. The surprise element makes it even more exciting, as it's a thoughtful and spontaneous way to express your support.

Surprising her with a financial gift, no matter the amount, shows that you recognize her aspirations and want to contribute to her happiness and success. It's not just about the money itself but the underlying message: you believe in her dreams and want to empower her to achieve them. Whether she uses it to indulge in something she loves or invest in her future, this thoughtful act of generosity leaves a lasting impact, reinforcing your commitment to her happiness and growth.

329

Fold Together: Learn the Art of Origami

Learning to create origami together is a creative and calming way to spend quality time while tapping into your artistic sides. Origami, the ancient Japanese art of paper folding, requires focus, patience, and attention to detail—all skills that can strengthen your connection as a couple. Whether you start with simple shapes like paper cranes or challenge yourselves with more intricate designs, this activity allows you both to work together and encourage each other along the way.

As you fold and create various shapes, you'll enjoy moments of laughter, concentration, and shared accomplishment. Each finished piece is a symbol of teamwork and creativity, and the process itself fosters a deeper connection. The beauty of origami lies in its simplicity and elegance, making it a relaxing and meaningful experience that leaves you with tangible keepsakes of your time spent together.

330

Dive into Her World: Learn About What She Loves

Taking the time to educate yourself on topics she's passionate about is an awesome way to show that you value her and the things that light her up. Whether it's understanding the nuances of her favorite book genre, exploring the details of her craft hobby, or diving into her advocacy for a social cause, this effort proves that you're invested in her world. It's about more than just nodding along—it's a chance to engage meaningfully in her interests and demonstrate your respect for what's important to her.

Not only does this effort lead to deeper conversations, but it also creates opportunities for shared experiences. Imagine discussing her favorite author's works over coffee or joining her in a workshop to learn her favorite skill. These moments become more than just time spent together; they're about fostering connection through curiosity and care. When you take an active interest, you're reinforcing that her passions aren't just her own—they're a part of your relationship's fabric.

In my own journey, diving into her interests opened unexpected doors for me. What began as an attempt to understand her industry turned into a newfound entrepreneurial interest of my own. This isn't just about showing support—it's about expanding your horizons, growing closer as a couple, and perhaps even discovering something that could enhance your life as well. It's a win-win when your curiosity leads to connection and personal growth.

Keep Chivalry Alive: Always Open the Door for Her

Back in the day, when knights were galloping around in shiny armor, opening a door for a lady was as essential as knowing how to wield a sword. Why? Because women often wore elaborate gowns with enough fabric to upholster a couch, making it impossible to easily navigate doors. While the gowns are long gone, the gesture of opening a door remains a timeless sign of respect and care. It's not just an old-fashioned move—it's a universal way to say, "I've got you."

Today, opening the door for her isn't about assuming she can't do it herself (she definitely can)—it's about showing that you want to. Whether it's the car door, the entrance to a restaurant, or even the front door at home, these small acts of attentiveness convey that you're mindful of her comfort. It's a moment of intentionality that says, "You're important to me," without needing to use words. Plus, it's a classic move that shows you value courtesy in your relationship.

This simple habit keeps the spark alive by bringing a touch of romance to the everyday. Each time you step ahead to open the door, you're giving her a reason to smile and reminding her of your care. And if she's ever in heels, juggling bags, or simply not in the mood to wrestle with a door handle, your gesture becomes not just considerate but genuinely helpful. In an age of swiping and tapping, a bit of real-world chivalry speaks volumes.

332

Don't Skimp...
Give Her the Best in All You Do

Giving her the best isn't about extravagance—it's about effort, intention, and pride in what you do for her. As men, the way we prioritize ourselves often reflects how we view our worth. If you're stepping out of the house looking fly in designer threads while she looks like Celie from The Color Purple, it's time to reassess. Your partner should reflect your pride in her, not just in how she looks but in how she feels when she's with you. If you're giving yourself top-shelf treatment while handing her leftovers, you're sending the wrong message about her value in your life.

Some men weren't taught better, and that's understandable—but ignorance is not an excuse to stay stagnant. It's time to ask yourself, "Am I giving her my best, or am I giving her what's convenient?" Don't put yourself in the finest while settling for the cheapest options for her. Don't take her to sleazy, budget hotels when you'd demand more for yourself. Giving her the best is about consistency in showing that she's as much of a priority as you are to yourself.

This extends beyond material things—it's about putting real effort into what you do for her. When you make the extra effort to find a special gift, plan a beautiful evening, or ensure she feels pampered and appreciated, you're showing her she's worth the care and consideration. It's not about impressing others or competing with anyone else—it's about making sure she knows she's valued, celebrated, and loved. When she walks beside you, she should feel as cherished and confident as you feel stepping out in your best.

If you're not used to this mindset, don't be discouraged. Change starts with small, intentional steps. Elevate how you treat her, how you show her she matters, and how you prioritize her needs. Over time, these efforts will transform the way she experiences your love. The goal isn't perfection; it's progression. When she sees that you've taken pride in doing right by her, she'll know that she's not just your partner—she's your queen, and queens deserve nothing less than your best. Right?

333

Have a Goofy Night Face Painting Each Other

Having a night of face painting together is a fun, creative, and lighthearted way to connect. Grab some non-toxic face paints and let your imaginations run wild as you paint each other's faces with colorful designs. Whether you go for something silly, artistic, or themed, the process allows for silly moments, playful interaction, and an opportunity to let your inner child come out.

As you paint each other, you can take turns coming up with creative ideas or challenge one another to try different themes. The best part is that it doesn't have to be perfect—just enjoy the process and the memories you're creating together. At the end of the night, you'll both have vibrant, funny, or beautiful designs that remind you of the joy in simply being present and playful together.

334

Have an Indoor Nerf Gun War Together

An indoor Nerf gun war is the perfect way to let loose and have some fun while unleashing your playful side. Armed with Nerf guns, foam darts, or even foam balls (now available in some Nerf models), you can transform your home into a lively battlefield. Set up forts with pillows, use furniture as obstacles, or even designate certain rooms as safe zones. The goal is simple—let the friendly competition and hysterical moments begin. Whether you're ducking behind corners, sneaking through hallways, or going for the perfect shot, it's all about having fun together in a stress-free, lighthearted way.

To make the game even more interesting, you can add challenges, create objectives, or keep score to see who comes out victorious. It's a great way to break the routine and enjoy some excitement indoors, with the added benefit of some physical activity. The best part is that the foam darts or balls are soft and safe, making it easy to engage in some friendly rivalry without any risk. Whether you're playing in teams or going head-to-head, an indoor Nerf gun war brings out your inner child and creates joyful memories you'll both cherish.

335

Take a Scenic Drive and Escape into Nature

Taking a scenic drive through the countryside is a simple yet meaningful way to slow down and reconnect with your significant other. The rolling hills, endless fields, and tranquil beauty of nature provide a perfect backdrop for quality time together. Whether the two of you are deep in conversation or enjoying comfortable silence, the open road creates a serene atmosphere to bond without the usual distractions of daily life. It's a moment to appreciate each other and the world around you, creating memories as you go.

The drive becomes even more memorable when you include small stops along the way. Visit charming small towns, capture stunning views at scenic overlooks, or enjoy a roadside picnic with your favorite treats. These spontaneous detours add a sense of adventure to the trip, transforming a simple drive into a shared experience filled with lighthearted moments and exploration. It's an opportunity to appreciate the journey itself and savor the joy of spending time together.

This kind of outing is an antidote to the rush of modern life. With no rigid schedule or destination, you can focus entirely on each other while immersing yourselves in the peaceful rhythms of nature. It's a reminder that sometimes the best moments are the simplest ones—just the two of you, the open road, and a horizon full of possibility.

336

Craft Beauty Together: Take a Flower Arranging Class

Taking a flower arranging class together is a creative and hands-on way to enjoy each other's company while learning something new. In this class, you'll get the chance to explore different flowers, colors, and textures, creating your own beautiful bouquets. The process of selecting and arranging flowers allows you both to tap into your artistic sides and share ideas on how to create the perfect arrangement. It's a fun, relaxing activity that lets you work side by side, encouraging collaboration and creativity.

Beyond the class itself, flower arranging can become a meaningful skill that you can use to bring fresh beauty into your home. Each bouquet you make becomes a symbol of the time you spent learning together. Plus, you get to leave with a beautiful arrangement that you created as a team, adding a personal touch to the experience. Whether you're making floral centerpieces for a special occasion or just enjoying the simple pleasure of working with flowers, this activity strengthens your bond through shared creativity.

337

Roll and Feast with DIY Sushi Night at Home

Having a DIY sushi night at home is a fun and interactive way to explore new flavors together while showing off your culinary creativity. Gather fresh ingredients like sushi-grade fish, vegetables, rice, and seaweed, and work together to roll your own custom sushi creations. Whether you're making classic rolls like California or spicy tuna, or experimenting with unique combinations, the hands-on nature of sushi-making encourages teamwork and bonding.

Setting up your kitchen as a sushi bar allows for a playful and relaxed atmosphere, where you can laugh, learn, and enjoy the process. You can even challenge each other to see who can create the most creative or delicious roll. Once you've completed your sushi masterpieces, sit down together and enjoy the fruits of your labor, pairing your rolls with sauces, wasabi, and soy sauce. It's an adventurous and tasty way to spend the evening, making both the preparation and the meal enjoyable and memorable.

But let's be real—if you end up with rice all over the floor, lopsided rolls that fall apart, or seaweed wraps that look like they've been pre-chewed, don't stress. Just laugh it off, pack up the chaos, and head to your nearest grocery store to buy some pre-made sushi. The fun is in trying, and as long as you enjoy the night together, even failed sushi is a win!

338

Plan a Special Intimate Night of "Hide 'n Go Get It"

LET'S GO! . . . Ok, maybe I was a little too excited about this chapter . . . Planning a special night of "Hide n Go Get It" is a playful and intimate way to inject excitement into your relationship while rediscovering each other in a fun and lighthearted manner. The game, a more grown-up version of hide-and-seek, allows you both to enjoy the thrill of searching for each other in the privacy of your home. Dim the lights or use candles to set a romantic atmosphere, and let the playful chase begin. The anticipation of hiding and being found adds to the excitement, making the evening a mix of fun and sensuality.

This grown-up twist on a childhood game is a perfect way to shake up your routine and keep the spark alive. The mix of laughter and flirtation will remind you both that intimacy doesn't always have to be serious—it can be spontaneous and filled with joy. Whether you're hiding in the closet, under the table, or trying not to laugh while crouched behind the couch, the playful energy will add a new layer of closeness to your relationship.

And let's face it, the best part of this game isn't in the hiding but in the finding. By the time the "seeker" catches their prize, you'll both be laughing, energized, and ready to shift the game into something a little more romantic. It's a fun way to explore each other and create a night full of memories you'll both smile about for days to come.

339

Create a Popcorn Paradise with Flavored Kernels

Surprise her with a personalized gift basket filled with an assortment of uniquely flavored popcorn. Whether you buy pre-made flavors or create them from scratch at home, you can include a variety such as buttery, caramel, chocolate, cotton candy, or cheddar. For an extra personal touch, package each flavor in its own bag, tied with colorful ribbons that add a creative flair. The effort you put into choosing or making each flavor shows that you're thinking about her preferences and are willing to go the extra mile.

Making the popcorn yourself adds even more charm to the gesture, as you can experiment with flavors and even tailor the seasoning to her tastes. Whether you plan this gift for a cozy movie night or just as a fun snack surprise, the basket is sure to bring a smile to her face. It's not just about the popcorn—it's about the time and care you've put into creating something special just for her.

For those who want to DIY, hop online and find some easy-to-follow popcorn recipes—there are endless options for savory, sweet, or gourmet creations. From adding melted chocolate and crushed candies to trying bold spices like smoked paprika or ranch seasoning, the process is simple and fun. With a little creativity and inspiration, you can craft a unique and delicious gift that's just as enjoyable to make as it is to give.

340

Challenge Her to a Coloring Book Contest

Challenge her to a fun and creative coloring book contest to bring out both your inner artists. Choose a couple of adult coloring books with themes that you'll both enjoy, like intricate mandalas, animals, or floral designs. Gather your favorite coloring tools—whether it's crayons, markers, or colored pencils—and set up a cozy space to start the competition. The relaxed pace of coloring creates a calm atmosphere, while the challenge adds an element of playful fun.

As you color, the contest opens the door for lighthearted banter, giving you a chance to cheer each other on or poke fun at the more "abstract" attempts. Decide on criteria for judging—like creativity, color coordination, or boldness—and either evaluate each other's work or enlist a third-party judge (even if it's the family pet "choosing" a winner). No matter who claims victory, the real prize is the time spent bonding in a stress-free, colorful way.

When you're done, you can keep the artwork as a cute reminder of the day or turn the pages into something fun like bookmarks or framed mementos. Whether you're seriously competing or just enjoying the process, the activity fosters connection, creativity, and joyous time together, making it a perfect way to mix relaxation with a dash of friendly rivalry.

… 341 …

Learn How to Make Homemade Ice Cream Together

Learning how to make homemade ice cream together is a sweet way to bond while getting creative in the kitchen. From sticking to your favorite flavors to experimenting with mix-ins like crushed cookies, fresh fruit, or even candy, the process is a blend of fun, teamwork, and indulgence. Whether you decide to use an ice cream maker or keep it simple with a no-churn recipe, this activity lets you craft something delicious while enjoying each other's company.

The beauty of a no-churn recipe is that it's ridiculously easy and doesn't require any fancy gadgets—at least for me it didn't. Whip 2 cups of heavy cream until it's thick and fluffy, then fold in 1 can of sweetened condensed milk along with whatever flavors or mix-ins you're feeling—cookies, fruit, candy, you name it. Pour it into a loaf pan, toss it in the freezer for about 4-6 hours, and let the magic happen. While you wait, why not whip up some toppings like a rich chocolate drizzle or a fruity syrup? If you're feeling extra, bake some cookies so you can turn your ice cream into the ultimate dessert sandwich. It's all about adding your own flavor—literally and figuratively.

Once your homemade ice cream is ready, set the mood for the ultimate taste test. Grab some bowls, pile on the toppings, and dig in together. Whether it's perfect or a little experimental, the point is you made it as a team. This shared experience of creating something sweet (and savoring it afterward) is not only delicious but also a playful reminder of how fun it is to try new things together. Plus, let's be real—there's nothing quite like the joy of saying, "We made this!" with a spoonful of your custom ice cream in hand.

342

Relieve Her Stress by Covering a Major Expense

One of the most meaningful ways to show your support is by stepping in to pay off a significant bill or expense that she's been wanting to or struggling to handle. Whether it's an unexpected medical bill, student loans, or something as practical as a car payment, helping her financially in this way lifts a huge burden off her shoulders. It shows that you're not just invested in her emotionally but also in her financial well-being, offering relief in an area that can often be a source of stress.

This gesture speaks volumes about your desire to support her beyond the day-to-day and reinforces your commitment to her success and peace of mind. It's a powerful way to show that you're paying attention to her needs and are willing to help alleviate any financial pressure. While this act is about money, the message behind it—of care, partnership, and shared responsibility—will strengthen your bond and give her a renewed sense of security.

When you look at the big picture, stepping up to handle a significant expense is more than just a momentary solution—it's an investment in your shared future. If you're functioning as a cohesive unit or striving to build one, removing financial stress from her plate helps you both focus on long-term goals. A bright future requires a solid foundation, and acts like this show her that you're all-in for the partnership you're building together. Ultimately, this isn't just about helping her; it's about creating a thriving relationship where you're both supported and set up for success.

343

Keep Her Inspired with a Personalized Magazine Subscription

Surprise her with a simple gift by getting her a magazine subscription that reflects her passions and interests. Whether she loves fashion, fitness, travel, cooking, or even niche hobbies like gardening or photography, this subscription will give her something to look forward to every month. It's a personalized gift that keeps on giving, allowing her to dive into articles, tips, and stories tailored to her favorite topics. Each issue will provide her with inspiration, knowledge, and a sense of enjoyment as she explores the subjects that bring her joy.

The beauty of gifting a magazine subscription is that it shows you're attentive to what she cares about, reinforcing that you're supportive of her interests. It's also a fun way for her to relax and unwind, whether she's curling up with the latest issue after a long day or flipping through it on the weekend. With every new delivery, she'll be appreciative of your purchase (at least in the moment), creating a sense of ongoing connection and consideration. It's the perfect balance of indulgence and practicality, showing that you appreciate and encourage her passions.

344

Create and Laugh: Produce a Funny Movie Together

Producing a funny short film together is a creative and entertaining way to bond while letting your imaginations run wild. Start by brainstorming a silly or lighthearted movie plot as a team, incorporating wacky characters or outrageous scenarios. To add an extra layer of fun, write each other's lines in secret, making sure neither of you knows what you'll be saying until it's time to act. This improvisational aspect will keep things spontaneous and hilarious as you react to each other's unexpected dialogue.

Once you've recorded your scenes, take some time to edit the footage, add music or sound effects, and produce a short film that captures your playful energy. Not only will this activity give you plenty of laughs along the way, but the finished product will also be a memorable keepsake you can watch and enjoy together for years to come. It's the perfect way to combine creativity, humor, and connection into an unforgettable shared experience.

Or, if you're both in one of "those" moods, you could take a different approach and create "that kind of movie"—a more intimate, private one, just for the two of you. If you're feeling playful and adventurous, it could be a unique way to celebrate your connection in an entirely different light. After all, it's your moment, your movie, and your love story—no matter the genre. Just be sure to handle it with trust and care, making it a fun and meaningful experience for both of you.

345

Respect Her Boundaries and Foster a Space of Trust

Every strong relationship is built on mutual respect, and one of the most significant ways to show respect is by honoring her boundaries. These boundaries may involve personal space, emotional limits, or areas of her life where she needs autonomy. Disregarding these boundaries—whether intentionally or unintentionally—can lead to feelings of mistrust, frustration, and even resentment. By respecting her limits, you demonstrate your commitment to fostering a healthy and trusting partnership.

For me, I've had to stay mindful of the space needed when she's not ready to share because I'm naturally a fixer. It's in my nature to want to solve problems and make things better, but I've learned that sometimes, she doesn't need a solution—she just needs time and understanding. It takes me a while to truly get attached to someone at this point in my life, so when I do, I feel a strong desire to protect her heart, even if I've said or done something that may have disappointed her. Respecting her boundaries means giving her the room to process at her own pace, even when my instincts push me to step in and fix things right away.

Start by understanding her boundaries. These aren't just rules—they're expressions of her comfort and needs. If you're unsure what they are, ask her directly and listen with an open mind. Recognize that boundaries may differ depending on her experiences and personality, and respect her need for personal space, emotional processing, or independence. Respecting boundaries also means reflecting on your actions. Are you interrupting her quiet moments? Pushing her to share when she's not ready? Overstepping in areas where she's asked for space? Being mindful of these behaviors can help you course-correct and build a dynamic where she feels seen and respected.

Finally, be patient. Boundaries are not static—they can evolve as trust deepens and your connection grows. By consistently showing her that you honor her needs, you're creating a foundation of safety and understanding. This not only strengthens her confidence in the relationship but also deepens the bond you share. Respect is the ultimate form of love, and honoring her boundaries is a powerful way to show it. When she feels that her limits are valued, she'll know she's in a relationship where her individuality is celebrated, and her trust is cherished.

346

Deepen Your Intimacy with the Wisdom of the Kama Sutra

Reading the Kama Sutra together is a great way to deepen your intimacy while exploring new facets of your relationship. This ancient guide offers more than just physical positions—it also encourages emotional connection, mindfulness, and mutual respect in your intimate life. As you go through the book together, take the time to discuss what appeals to both of you, sharing thoughts and desires in a safe and open space. This shared exploration strengthens communication and fosters a deeper understanding of each other's needs.

The experience is not just about trying something new physically but about creating a stronger emotional bond through exploration, trust, and respect. By engaging with the book as a couple, you enhance both your physical connection and emotional intimacy, making your relationship more fulfilling. It's a playful, yet meaningful way to connect on a deeper level while also embracing openness and fun.

Approach this journey with sensitivity and an open mind, ensuring that your partner feels entirely comfortable and heard. Instead of pressuring her to try anything outside her comfort zone, focus on creating an environment where she feels safe to explore and express her boundaries freely. The goal is to make it a mutual discovery that strengthens trust and builds excitement for new shared experiences. When handled with care and respect, this can be a liberating and empowering journey for you both.

347

Be Mindful to Get Her the Help She Needs

One of the most loving things you can do for her is to ensure she has the help she needs, whatever the situation. Life is demanding, and no one can do it all alone. If she's juggling kids and needs a break, but you're not available to step in, don't hesitate to hire a reliable sitter. Giving her time to breathe and recharge is a gift that shows you value her well-being. If there's a task at home that she can't handle and you're not exactly a handyman—because let's be honest, not everyone is—hire a professional to take care of it. It's not about your ego; it's about making her life easier and showing her that you're attentive to her needs.

Sometimes her needs are smaller but just as meaningful. If she's short and struggling to reach the top shelf or has to stand on tiptoes to see over the countertop, don't just laugh (at least out loud)—get her a stool that's both sturdy and stylish. These small gestures may seem minor, but they add up to a bigger picture of care and thoughtfulness. They show her that you see her struggles, no matter how big or small, and are willing to step up to make her life better.

If she's going through a tough time emotionally—whether it's stress, depression, or a situation that feels overwhelming—be proactive in helping her find the support she needs. You don't have to be her therapist or fix all her problems, but you can be her partner in finding someone who can. Research therapists, counselors, or support groups that align with her needs, and encourage her to take that step. If she's in need of spiritual guidance and you're not in a place to offer it yourself, help her connect with a pastor, parishioner, or spiritual mentor who can provide the wisdom and comfort she's seeking. Your willingness to help her find these resources speaks volumes about your dedication to her well-being.

Meeting her needs isn't about solving everything on your own; it's about recognizing when to call in reinforcements. When you make an effort to lighten her load or support her through challenges, you're showing her that she doesn't have to carry it all alone. Whether it's hiring a sitter, finding a therapist, or simply getting her a stool to make life easier, your actions communicate that you care deeply about her happiness and peace of mind. At the end of the day, your proactive mindset and commitment to her needs will strengthen your relationship and remind her that she's truly cherished.

348

Preserve Her History: Restore a Treasured Photo

Surprise her with a beautifully restored photo that carries deep sentimental value. Look for an old or damaged picture that holds significant meaning—perhaps a beloved family portrait, a snapshot from a once-in-a-lifetime trip, or an early photo of the two of you. By choosing a photograph that reflects cherished memories, you're acknowledging the moments that have shaped her life and your relationship. Seek out a professional restoration service, either locally or online, to bring the image back to its original glory.

Once the photo is restored, present it in a way that makes it even more special. You could frame it elegantly, create a shadow box with other mementos from the time the photo was taken, or incorporate it into a personalized gift like a scrapbook or a photo album. Placing the restored image somewhere prominent in your home is a lasting reminder of the love and memories that define your bond. It's more than just a picture; it's a testament to the beauty of the moments you both treasure.

This thoughtful gesture goes beyond material value—it's a way of honoring her history, family, and the journey you've shared together. Restoring an old photograph shows that you not only pay attention to what's meaningful to her but that you also value preserving the past to celebrate the present. It's an act of love that highlights your effort to keep those memories alive, reinforcing the foundation of your relationship with care and appreciation.

349

Explore More: Take a Multi-City Flight Together

Planning a multi-city flight together is an exhilarating way to explore the world and make memories in multiple destinations on a single trip. Instead of limiting yourselves to just one city, you can craft an itinerary that takes you to a variety of places, each offering its own unique culture, cuisine, and adventures. This kind of trip keeps things fresh and exciting, as every stop brings new sights, sounds, and experiences to share. It's a perfect way to infuse your travels with variety and spontaneity, ensuring that every day feels like a fresh chapter in your journey together.

The planning process itself can be a bonding experience. Sit down together to map out your dream route, researching must-visit spots, hidden gems, and experiences in each city. Whether you're hunting for the best local eats, iconic landmarks, or unique activities, collaborating on the details builds anticipation and helps you both feel invested in making the trip extraordinary. From sightseeing during the day to reflecting on your adventures over dinner, each city adds a new layer to your shared story, creating a trip filled with both exploration and connection.

Contrary to what you might think, a multi-city trip doesn't have to be complicated or break the bank. With budget-friendly airlines, flight deal websites, and travel platforms that specialize in multi-city routes, it's easier than ever to find affordable options. Many major airlines offer discounted multi-stop itineraries, while dedicated services like Skyscanner and Google Flights help uncover hidden deals across the globe. By being flexible with your dates and destinations, you can craft an unforgettable journey that's both adventurous and surprisingly cost-effective.

350

Bonus: Commit to Being the Best Version of You

Committing to being the best version of yourself is one of the greatest gifts you can give to your relationship. This involves an ongoing journey of personal growth, encompassing emotional, mental, and physical improvement. When you actively work on becoming more self-aware, emotionally intelligent, and physically healthy, you bring stability and positivity into your partnership. Your personal growth isn't just about bettering yourself—it directly impacts your ability to nurture and sustain a thriving relationship. Striving to be your best ensures that you're showing up as a reliable, attentive, and loving partner, setting the foundation for a strong, lasting bond.

For those guided by faith, remember that God has already equipped you with the tools and qualities necessary for greatness. Becoming the best version of yourself is about aligning with His purpose for you and allowing His wisdom to guide your actions. Through prayer, self-reflection, and humility, you can strengthen your character and better fulfill the role you're called to play in her life. This spiritual journey not only brings you closer to God but also enhances your ability to lead, love, and support her in a way that aligns with His design for a flourishing relationship.

It's important to recognize that this journey isn't about perfection—it's about progress. Whether you're improving your communication, developing healthier habits, or learning to better manage stress, each small step contributes to your overall growth. Being intentional about your self-improvement inspires trust and admiration, showing her that you're committed to growing not just for yourself but for the relationship as a whole. It also sets an example of accountability and dedication, encouraging her to feel secure and motivated in her own journey of growth.

Ultimately, committing to being the best version of yourself strengthens the partnership you're building together. It's a declaration that you value the relationship enough to consistently put in the work to be a better man. This act of dedication enriches not only your connection but also your shared future, ensuring that your relationship continues to thrive on mutual growth, respect, and love. It's a promise to her—and to yourself—that you're fully invested in being a partner she can count on and grow with.

351

Balance the Books of Love and Labor

As a man with a demanding career that requires frequent travel, I understand how difficult it can be to juggle professional obligations with the needs of your relationship. The pressures of work can feel all-consuming at times, but I've learned that maintaining balance is essential—not only for the sake of my household but also for keeping the spark alive in my relationship. No matter how busy life gets, it's crucial that she always knows she's my priority.

Intentional planning is my secret weapon. I rely on my calendar, not just for work tasks but for relationship reminders, too. I schedule surprise deliveries—flowers, her favorite treats, or thoughtful gifts—and leave handwritten notes behind before I travel. These gestures show her that even when I'm away, she's never far from my thoughts. It's about finding ways to bridge the physical distance and remind her that she's deeply valued.

During trips, I make an effort to stay connected through video calls, where we can laugh, share our days, or simply see each other's faces. Sometimes, I'll call using my deep voice just to flirt and make her smile. Keeping the spark alive isn't always about grand gestures; it's about the little moments of joy and affection that reinforce the bond we share. These small but consistent efforts remind her that distance is temporary, but our connection is constant.

Open communication is another cornerstone of this balance. I share the realities of my career—the successes, the challenges, and the long-term goals—so she understands my world and feels like an integral part of it. When she knows the "why" behind my busy schedule and sees the effort I make to prioritize her, it builds trust and strengthens our partnership. She's not just part of my life—she's the foundation that keeps me grounded.

Balancing the demands of work and love takes intention, creativity, and consistency. As men, we may face immense pressures, but we have a responsibility to ensure our relationships thrive. By planning ahead, staying connected, and finding ways to keep the spark lit, we can create a life where our ambitions and our love complement each other. Success in both areas is not just achievable—it's deeply fulfilling.

Gift Her a Personalized Greeting from Her Favorite Celebrity

Imagine her surprise and excitement when she receives a personalized greeting from her favorite celebrity! This thoughtful gift is unique, memorable, and guaranteed to make her feel incredibly special. Many celebrities now offer custom video messages through reputable platforms, such as Cameo and Memmo, where you can request a personalized shoutout. Whether it's a birthday, anniversary, or just because, a message from someone she admires will be a moment she'll cherish.

The joy of receiving this heartfelt greeting isn't just about the celebrity—it's also a reflection of the time and effort you put into finding something meaningful for her. This gift shows that you know her well and care enough to make her feel celebrated in a way that's tailored to her interests. It's a unique surprise that will leave her smiling and will likely become a memory she treasures for years to come.

353

Support Local Creativity by Attending a Theater Production

Attending a local theater production is a wonderful way to enjoy an evening of culture, creativity, and live entertainment together. Community theaters often feature a variety of performances, from classic plays and musicals to original productions by emerging playwrights. By supporting local theater, you not only enjoy a unique and intimate experience but also show appreciation for the talent and hard work within your community.

Sharing the thrill of live performance allows you both to connect over something new, whether it's a thought-provoking drama, a lighthearted comedy, or a musical extravaganza. Discussing the show afterward can lead to engaging conversations about the characters, storyline, or even the actors' performances. This outing provides a refreshing change of pace, letting you both escape into a world of storytelling, artistry, and shared experience.

For a truly memorable evening, look for productions of well-loved classics like The Phantom of the Opera, Hamilton, or Les Misérables, which are sure to impress with their storytelling and musical scores. Alternatively, seek out critically acclaimed modern hits like Dear Evan Hansen or Hadestown for something fresh and innovative. If your local theater offers more intimate performances, productions like Our Town or The Glass Menagerie can bring a sense of nostalgia and emotional depth. No matter the choice, attending a live performance is bound to leave you both inspired and with lasting memories.

354

Romance on Ice: Go Ice Skating Together

Going ice skating together is a fun and romantic way to enjoy each other's company, whether you're experienced skaters or trying it for the first time. Bundle up in warm layers, lace up your skates, and head to a local rink or an outdoor ice-skating area if it's in season. The activity naturally encourages lighthearted moments—laughing at near-falls, holding hands for balance, or racing each other around the rink. Even if you both spend more time wobbling than gliding, the shared experience is what makes it special.

After skating, take a break and cozy up with some warm drinks like hot cocoa, mulled cider, or even a spiked coffee if the rink offers refreshments. This time to relax and talk gives you both a chance to soak in the wintry ambiance and reflect on the fun you had together on the ice. Whether it's a quiet moment by a fire pit or at a nearby café, the post-skating ritual adds a warm, intimate touch to the outing.

For an extra layer of charm, seek out venues that offer festive atmospheres, like rinks with twinkling string lights, holiday music, or scenic outdoor settings. Iconic spots like Rockefeller Center in New York City, Millennium Park in Chicago, or even a local pond transformed for the season can elevate the experience. Ice skating together is a delightful mix of playfulness and romance, making it a perfect way to create memories while embracing the magic of winter.

355

Keep it Simple by Spending Time Feeding Ducks at a Local Lake

Spending time feeding ducks at a local lake is a charming way to escape the daily grind and enjoy a peaceful moment together in nature. Bring along duck-friendly snacks like oats, halved grapes, or birdseed (since bread can harm their health) and settle by the water to watch the ducks paddle gracefully or waddle toward you for treats. The simplicity of this activity allows you both to slow down and immerse yourselves in the calming rhythm of nature while sharing quiet laughter and conversation. It's a refreshing and lighthearted way to step outside of your routine.

This outing also provides the perfect opportunity to deepen your connection as a couple. With no distractions, you can fully focus on each other while appreciating the serene setting around you. Whether you're reminiscing about shared memories or enjoying the tranquility in comfortable silence, the experience of feeding ducks together becomes a moment of mindfulness and bonding. It's a small but meaningful escape that lets you connect not only with each other but also with the beauty of the natural world.

356

Embrace Nature with a Weekend Camping Trip

This really isn't my thing, at all. I'm not one with nature, and the thought of sleeping outside isn't exactly on my bucket list. But I've done it, and let me tell you, if I can survive a weekend in the wild, you can too! Planning a weekend camping trip is a great way to break free from the daily grind and embrace some quality time together in the great outdoors. Whether you opt for a serene lakeside campsite, a cozy spot in the woods, or a mountain retreat, camping brings a sense of peace and adventure. Picture hiking scenic trails, trying your hand at fishing, or simply sitting by the campfire roasting marshmallows and laughing about the day.

Camping's simplicity is its charm—it strips away the noise of modern life and gives you a chance to connect on a deeper level. Without the interruptions of phones, emails, or daily stressors, you can focus on each other and the shared experience of being immersed in nature. From pitching a tent to cooking meals over an open flame, the teamwork involved strengthens your bond and adds a sense of accomplishment to the trip. Plus, those quiet moments by the fire under a blanket of stars? Unbeatable.

If you're nervous about the whole "roughing it" part, don't worry. There are plenty of ways to ease into camping, like choosing a site with amenities or even glamping, if tents aren't your style. The goal isn't to become the next wilderness survivalist but to create memories with your partner in a setting that lets you slow down and appreciate the simple joys of life—together. And hey, if the tent starts looking like a Rubik's Cube during setup, at least you'll have something to laugh about for years to come.

357

Chase Serenity by Taking Her to a Waterfall or Natural Springs

Visiting a local waterfall or natural springs is a beautiful and refreshing way to spend the day together while connecting with nature. Pack a picnic, bring comfortable shoes, and set out on a scenic adventure to explore the sights and sounds of rushing water and lush landscapes. Whether you hike to a hidden waterfall or relax by the clear pools of a natural spring, the experience provides a serene escape from the routine, offering a chance to unwind in each other's company.

The peaceful surroundings and gentle sounds of flowing water create a calming atmosphere where you can chat, relax, or simply take in the view. It's a perfect setting for meaningful conversations or quiet moments, allowing you both to recharge and feel grounded in nature. Exploring these natural wonders together not only brings tranquility to your day but also helps build a sense of connection through shared adventure.

For popular destinations, consider iconic spots like Multnomah Falls in Oregon, Havasu Falls in Arizona, or Hamilton Pool Preserve in Texas. If you're near the East Coast, explore Niagara Falls in New York or Anna Ruby Falls in Georgia. For those in the Midwest, Tahquamenon Falls in Michigan is breathtaking. Wherever you are, a little research can uncover hidden gems in your region, ensuring that your day spent exploring waterfalls or springs will be as memorable as it is picturesque.

358

Support Her Soul... Give Her Spiritual Encouragement

Providing spiritual encouragement is a meaningful way to support her inner well-being and show that you're deeply invested in her personal journey. If you both share a religious faith, offering her an uplifting verse or teaching that aligns with her challenges or aspirations can provide a comforting reminder of divine support. Sending her a heartfelt text with a scripture or sharing a moment of prayer together reinforces her strength and sense of purpose. For example, a passage like "I can do all things through Christ who strengthens me" (Philippians 4:13) can resonate during times of doubt or difficulty, offering hope and reassurance that both her faith and your love are steadfast pillars in her life.

Even if you don't share her spiritual beliefs, you can still offer encouragement in ways that affirm her personal growth and resilience. Positive affirmations, secular quotes, or even your own words of encouragement can make a profound impact. Consider sharing sentiments like, "You are capable of handling anything life throws at you, and I believe in you every step of the way." What matters most is that the message feels genuine and aligns with what she needs to hear in the moment. Taking time to notice her struggles or aspirations and offering encouragement tailored to her journey shows your love, care, and dedication.

Incorporating spiritual encouragement into your relationship fosters a deeper emotional and intellectual bond. Whether it's attending a faith-based event together, meditating in tandem, or simply reflecting on shared values, these moments create space for meaningful connection. Encouraging her spiritually strengthens her confidence and brings a sense of peace that reflects in your shared life. By nurturing her spiritual side, you're showing her that you're a partner who values her inner growth as much as her external achievements.

Remember, spiritual encouragement isn't about perfection but about presence. Whether you're reminding her of her potential, standing with her in prayer, or simply sending her a quote that made you think of her, your consistent gestures affirm her worth. Life's challenges often feel lighter when shared, and your willingness to support her spiritually, emotionally, and mentally reinforces the strength of your bond and her ability to navigate life with grace.

359

Plan a Day of Extreme Sports (e.g., Skydiving, Bungee Jumping, Ziplining)

Planning a day of extreme sports is an electrifying way to break from routine and inject your relationship with adventure and excitement. Activities like skydiving, bungee jumping, or ziplining offer a unique combination of adrenaline and awe as you challenge yourselves to conquer the elements. Sharing these moments of heightened emotion and exhilaration builds a powerful bond as you're stepping out of your comfort zones together to create memories you'll both talk about for years. Whether it's the feeling of free-falling through the sky or soaring over treetops, these experiences allow you to embrace the thrill of living in the moment.

Extreme sports also foster trust and teamwork in a way that's hard to replicate in everyday life. Encouraging each other to take the leap—literally—strengthens your connection as you both lean on each other for courage and support. The thrill of these adventures can transform nerves into laughter and fear into triumph, giving you both a shared sense of accomplishment. Plus, the unique setting of such activities sparks deep conversations about facing fears and overcoming challenges, adding layers of emotional growth to the physical adventure.

If skydiving or bungee jumping feels like too big of a leap (pun intended), ziplining is a fantastic entry point into the world of extreme sports. Many adventure parks and resorts offer guided tours that combine adrenaline-pumping ziplines with stunning views of forests, mountains, or canyons. For example, you can zip through the lush treetops of Costa Rica, glide over the cliffs of Colorado, or explore adventure parks closer to home. No matter what activity you choose, the shared adrenaline and happiness of achieving something daring together will leave you both feeling exhilarated and even more connected.

360

She's Gotta Have Bras, Man...

Many men don't realize that women, on average, own only 5 to 10 bras—but often rely on just 3 to 5 of them as their regular, go-to options. Because bras are essential but pricey, it's common for women to make do with a few well-worn bras, sometimes kept far past their prime. Additionally, budget-friendly bras may lack the support, durability, and comfort that higher-quality bras offer, which can make a huge difference in daily comfort and confidence. Good bras are more than an accessory—they're an investment in her comfort and well-being.

Show her you care by learning her bra size (check her current favorites or ask if she's open to a professional fitting) and choosing a few high-quality bras that match her style and needs. Focus on trusted brands known for comfort and fit, and don't get hung up on the price tag—a well-made bra lasts longer, provides better support, and is often crafted with high-quality fabrics that make it breathable and comfortable all day. Whether you go for her usual style or try something new, this thoughtful gift shows that you value her comfort and are willing to invest in what makes her feel her best.

361

Immortalize Her Memories with a Custom 3D Hologram Photo Cube

Surprise her with a custom 3D hologram photo cube, a stunning and innovative way to preserve a cherished memory. By transforming a special photo—whether it's from a milestone moment, a favorite trip, or a meaningful snapshot of your relationship—into a three-dimensional hologram, you create a keepsake that's as artistic as it is sentimental. The intricately etched crystal captures depth and detail, making the image appear dynamic and alive as it reflects light from every angle. It's a one-of-a-kind gift that blends modern technology with heartfelt emotion, perfect for highlighting moments that mean the most to both of you.

This custom photo cube is more than just a decorative piece; it's a daily reminder of the love and memories you share. She can place it on her desk, dresser, or a special corner at home, where it will serve as a constant source of joy and inspiration. The elegance of the design and the uniqueness of the hologram make it a timeless keepsake, showing that you've put thought and care into giving her something meaningful. Whether for a birthday, anniversary, or just because, a 3D hologram photo cube elevates the art of gift-giving into a deeply personal gesture she'll treasure for years to come.

362

Keep a Spirit of Gratitude and Continue to Seek Wisdom

Practicing gratitude and seeking wisdom not only enriches your life but also strengthens your relationship in meaningful ways. Begin each day with a conscious effort to be thankful for the love, health, and lessons life brings you both. Gratitude shifts focus to the positives and reminds you to value the relationship you share, even in the face of challenges. If you follow a faith, spiritual texts encourage a spirit of thankfulness. For instance, 1 Thessalonians 5:18 from Christianity teaches, "Give thanks in all circumstances; for this is God's will for you in Christ Jesus." In Islam, gratitude is also emphasized in Surah Ibrahim 14:7: "If you are grateful, I will certainly give you more." Similarly, Hindu scriptures like the Bhagavad Gita stress contentment and gratitude for life's gifts, while in Buddhism, gratitude is a core practice that cultivates mindfulness and joy in the present moment.

Wisdom, like gratitude, is celebrated across major faiths. The Jewish Proverbs 4:7 states, "Wisdom is the principal thing; therefore, get wisdom: and with all thy getting get understanding." Islam encourages its followers to continually seek knowledge and better themselves, with the Prophet Muhammad saying, "Seeking knowledge is an obligation upon every Muslim." Hinduism's texts often discuss gaining wisdom through reflection and self-discipline, and Buddhism calls for continuous learning as part of the Eightfold Path. For those who do not follow a specific faith, this pursuit can take the form of reading, mindfulness, or meaningful discussions. These practices help build self-awareness and emotional intelligence, allowing you to grow as an individual and a partner.

If faith isn't part of your life, the principles of gratitude and wisdom are equally applicable through secular practices. Mindfulness encourages daily acknowledgment of life's positives, promoting mental clarity and emotional balance. Journaling gratitude and engaging in critical reflection on past decisions foster resilience and growth. By committing to these habits, you create a relationship where love, support, and understanding flourish, benefiting you both. A focus on self-awareness and continuous learning enriches your ability to nurture her emotionally and navigate challenges as a team.

No matter your path, keeping gratitude and wisdom at the forefront of your life sets a tone of positivity and openness that will ripple through your relationship. It's about creating a foundation of mutual respect, growth, and support, ensuring she feels valued and secure. Together, you can build a partnership grounded in these timeless principles, paving the way for a fulfilling and enduring connection.

363

Be Willing to Learn How to Love Her... According to HER Needs

Learning to love her in a way that truly meets her needs requires humility, effort, and a willingness to put aside ego. As life brings new challenges and opportunities, both of you will grow and change. The love that sustains your relationship must adapt as well. Open communication is key—ask her to share what she needs from you at this stage of her life, and listen with an open heart. This act of learning how to love her, in her language and on her terms, reflects deep respect for who she is and who she's becoming. It's an ongoing journey, but one that strengthens your connection and shows her your commitment to growth.

The timeless words from 1 Corinthians 13:4–7, "Love is patient, love is kind... It always protects, always trusts, always hopes, always perseveres," serve as a guide for cultivating a love that meets her needs. These verses remind us that love requires understanding, patience, and kindness—not just in grand gestures, but in everyday actions. It's about protecting her heart, trusting her intentions, and holding hope for your future together. When you approach loving her from this perspective, you foster an environment where she feels secure, valued, and deeply cherished.

Recognize that learning to love her according to her needs is not just a gift to her but also to your relationship. This journey of growth teaches you both to prioritize understanding over assumptions and connection over routine. Whether she needs more emotional support, encouragement, or shared laughter, your willingness to learn creates space for your love to thrive. By embracing this process, you create a bond that not only weathers life's changes but flourishes through them, making your relationship an ever-evolving testament to true partnership.

Bonus: Be Genuine in How You Love Her

True love begins with authenticity. It's not about putting on a show for others or projecting a false image of your relationship. Genuine love is built on consistency, demonstrated by how you treat her when no one else is around. Whether you're sharing a quiet moment at home or navigating life's challenges together, your actions should reflect the same care, respect, and devotion in private as they do in public. A love rooted in authenticity doesn't falter when the spotlight is off; it thrives because it's real, not performative.

When you're genuine, she can trust in the stability of your love, knowing it isn't swayed by external validation or the opinions of others. Be the same partner to her whether you're in the comfort of your home, with friends, or in a crowded room. This means showing respect in your words, valuing her input, and demonstrating your commitment through both small gestures and significant actions. Genuine love isn't conditional or performative—it's steady, unwavering, and sincere, no matter the circumstances.

Being genuine in your love creates a foundation of trust and emotional security, allowing her to feel fully cherished for who she is. It's not about grand gestures or hollow words; it's about showing up, being honest, and making her feel respected and supported every day. This kind of love isn't just about her; it also transforms you, making you a better, more grounded partner. When you're real in your actions and intentions, your love becomes a source of strength and inspiration for both of you, creating a relationship that stands the test of time.

365

Commit to Better Days, a Better Life

As you reach the end of this journey, take a moment to reflect on how far you've come and the ways you've grown. Committing to better days and a better life isn't about grand, one-time gestures—it's about choosing, every day, to show up for her and for your relationship. This commitment means carrying forward the values and actions you've cultivated here, turning them into enduring habits that bring joy, stability, and growth to your shared life. Each day is an opportunity to nurture your bond, improve yourself, and build a relationship that thrives in both good times and challenging ones.

Better days don't come from perfection; they come from progress and intention. It's about choosing to listen more, love harder, and be the partner she can rely on. By consistently showing her that she's valued and loved, you create an environment where both of you can flourish. This isn't just about her—it's about creating a shared vision of the life you both want, filled with mutual respect, laughter, and the pursuit of dreams. Together, you can build a foundation so strong that no obstacle can shake it.

Let this commitment be your north star, guiding you toward a relationship that brings out the best in both of you. Keep the fire alive by celebrating the small wins, learning from mistakes, and continuing to grow. The life you build together is not just a reflection of your love but also a testament to your resilience, dedication, and the choice to invest in each other every single day. Here's to better days, a brighter future, and a love that grows stronger with time.

Conclusion

You've made it to the end! You've mastered 365 ways to cater to her, right? Just kidding—this is a lifelong journey, not a checklist. My hope is that you feel equipped, inspired, and ready to infuse your relationship with love, thoughtfulness, and meaningful connection. This book wasn't just about grand gestures or fleeting moments of romance; it's about helping you become the best version of yourself, not only for her but for your own personal growth. Love is a practice—a daily commitment to showing up, learning, and nurturing your bond. Now, the real work begins: taking what you've learned and making it a consistent part of your life.

Along the way, you've likely encountered moments that pushed you out of your comfort zone. Maybe you felt the joy of reigniting a spark, the satisfaction of seeing her smile, or even the humility of trying something new that didn't go quite as planned. These experiences are what growth looks like. They're reminders that love is built not on perfection but on consistent effort. Each moment you spend learning, improving, and giving is a brick in the foundation of a lasting relationship.

Becoming the man you're called to be—a man who embodies love, patience, and consistency—is a journey that will never truly end. Every day brings new challenges and opportunities to grow, not just as her partner but as a man striving to create a life filled with purpose and connection. Even during tough times when love feels like hard work, remember: true love is about perseverance, showing up when it counts, and valuing the bond you've built together.

I encourage you to share this book with others. If it's helped you create a more fulfilling relationship or inspired you to be a better partner, imagine the impact it could have on someone else. Recommending this book isn't just sharing tips; it's passing on a roadmap for love, growth, and transformation. When we empower each other with tools for better relationships, we create a ripple effect that strengthens families, friendships, and communities. There's no better gift than helping someone else improve their life.

As you move forward, know that you're not alone in this journey. There will be times of joy and moments of struggle, but with intention, love, and the willingness to grow, you have everything it takes to nurture a thriving partnership. This book was designed to guide you, not as a rulebook, but as a resource to inspire and challenge you along the way. Keep revisiting it, trying new ideas, and reflecting on how far you've come.

Finally, thank you for taking this journey. Your commitment to love, growth, and connection is what makes this world a better place. The small, thoughtful acts you bring into your relationship each day have the power to create something extraordinary—a bond built on trust, joy, and unwavering support. Here's to the life you're building together and the endless possibilities that come with love nurtured every day. Blessings to you in your journey!

Sincerely,
Duke

Reflections Journal: Your Journey of Growth and Love

You know what? After finishing this book, I felt like something was missing—like the need to reflect, journal, capture thoughts, and process everything. It's not enough to just read the book, and it's not all about grand gestures. I really want you, as the reader, to discover ways to create lasting connections and memories.

This journal is just the starting point—a space to reflect on what you've learned, set intentions for your relationship, and truly capture the essence of time with your partner along the way.

Use these pages however you'd like. Write down takeaways from the book, set personal and relationship goals, write love notes to your partner, or track the changes you're making in your life. The goal is to be purpose-driven, to grow, and to celebrate the love you're building—one moment at a time.

Need a prompt to get started? Try one of these:

- What are three small ways I can be more intentional in my relationship?

- What's one lesson from this book that I will start applying today?

- How has my understanding of love and partnership evolved while reading this book?

- What's a meaningful moment I've shared with my partner recently, and how did it make me feel?

- What's one habit I can develop to consistently show appreciation for my partner?

Now, woosah, grab a pen and a nice, refreshing beverage, and start writing—because your love story is still being written. And when you're done on this page, click the QR code to keep the momentum going!

SCAN ME

About the Author

DEVOLIS NEWBURN is the acclaimed author of *365 Ways a Year to Cater to Her*, a transformative guide designed to empower men to cultivate deeper, more meaningful relationships through consistent, intentional actions. With over 25 years of reflection and life experience, Devolis brings a wealth of insight into how thoughtful gestures and daily practices can create lasting emotional connections.

Devolis's journey began in a traditional household where love was often viewed through the lens of duty and responsibility. Watching the dynamics around him, he realized that while providing and protecting were important, they were not enough to nurture the emotional and spiritual needs of a partner. Fueled by a desire to break the cycle, he embarked on a lifelong mission to redefine love as a practice rooted in empathy, attentiveness, and celebration of a partner's individuality.

His thoughtful approach to relationships is informed not only by his personal growth but also by years of observing and listening to others. Devolis's writing offers men a blueprint for building partnerships that thrive on mutual respect, shared values, and daily acts of love. From small gestures like handwritten notes to life-changing practices like fostering open communication, his book provides practical, heartfelt solutions for men at all stages of love.

Beyond his work as an author, Devolis excels as a senior IT executive, blending analytical problem-solving with creative thinking. His professional success is a testament to his ability to balance technical precision with visionary leadership—qualities that also shine through in his writing.

When he isn't inspiring readers or excelling in his career, Devolis enjoys exploring the world with his family, attending professional sports events, and cheering on his favorite teams—the Philadelphia Eagles and the New York Yankees. He also has a passion for high-performance vehicles and car shows, frequently participating in events that celebrate craftsmanship and attention to detail.

A proud member of Kappa Alpha Psi Fraternity, Inc., Devolis is deeply committed to service and philanthropy. He is a strong advocate for women's rights and actively participates in initiatives that support those in need, including programs that provide meals for the underserved and assistance for military veterans. His dedication to giving back reflects his belief in leadership through action, ensuring that his impact extends beyond personal relationships and into the broader community.

Devolis's belief in intentional living extends beyond relationships to every aspect of his life. Whether traveling, pursuing hobbies, or engaging with his readers, he consistently seeks to inspire connection, growth, and empowerment. Through his writing and personal journey, Devolis offers men a path to not only transform their relationships but also become the best versions of themselves.

Book Group Discussion Questions

This book was written to challenge men to step beyond traditional roles and embrace intentionality in love—but the real growth happens in conversation, accountability, and action. As a group, take time to listen, reflect, and challenge each other. Be open to different perspectives, and don't be afraid to push beyond your comfort zone. This isn't just about relationships, it's about who we are as men.

Understanding Love & Intentionality

1. What does "catering to your partner" mean to you? How is it different from just being a good partner?

2. The book emphasizes daily actions over grand gestures. Why do you think small, consistent efforts have a greater impact?

3. Which action or chapter resonated with you the most? Why?

Masculinity & Leadership in Relationships

4. What are some traditional ideas of masculinity that this book challenges?

5. How do you balance strength and vulnerability in a relationship?

6. What does it mean for a man to also be submissive in marriage? How does mutual submission play a role in a healthy partnership?

Growth & Accountability

7. How has this book changed the way you see your role in a relationship?

8. What's one thing you've learned from this book that you will commit to applying in your relationship or future relationship?

9. How can men hold each other accountable for being intentional partners?

10. How has this book challenged you to reassess your spiritual growth?

11. If a younger man asked you for relationship advice, what's one lesson from this book you would share with him?

Final Thought: Again, this group discussion is about more than just discussing ideas—it's about action. At the end of your conversation, challenge each other to apply something from the book. Commit to accountability and consistency. Trust me when I tell you that great days are ahead!

Bonus Challenge: Show Your Love in Action

So, you've made it through the book—but now it's time to bring it to life. I want to challenge you to record a short video with your partner sharing how this book has impacted your relationship. What's changed? What stood out to you? What small (or big) things have made a difference?

This isn't just for me; it's for you, your partner, and maybe even another man who needs to see what leading with love looks like.

Here's how to join the challenge:

1. Record your video. Keep it real, honest, and from the heart.

2. Post it on social media and tag me @FYCreativeMedia so I can see it.

3. Use the hashtag #StrongMenLoveStrong to inspire other men to step up.

That's it. No pressure. Just an opportunity to capture your journey and celebrate the love you're building. Looking forward to seeing what you share!

Acknowledgements

I'd first like to thank God for giving me the experiences, life lessons, vision, and courage to write this book. It has been a journey, but without my Creator, I know this book would not exist.

To my beautiful queen, my wife, Constance: Thank you for supporting me in pushing this book to completion. I am also ever grateful for you for welcoming my growth over the years and giving me the space to strive and press forward in becoming the best husband and father I can be. I love you.

To my mother: Thank you for your unconditional love and support. When others doubted me, you told me I could. When I felt that love was absent in life, you reminded me that God was still present and encouraged me never to change because of negative circumstances. I am truly blessed to have the best mother God ever created. I love you.

To my close friends, I am grateful for our years of friendship and meaningful dialogue. Rindy, Brooke, Tesha, Tessa, LaNee, and Jenny—thank you for years of enlightening conversations from a woman's perspective. To LeVar, Brent, Donta, James, Ricky, Bear, Mac, and Tanny—thank you for mature perspectives, great laughs, and for being excellent accountability partners.

To my kids, thank you for leaving me alone while I wrote this book. You are my world, and I'm proud to be your father.

Lastly, to everyone I've had the pleasure of meeting and getting to know over the years—in some way, shape, or form, I have taken something valuable from our connection. You all are truly appreciated.

Thank You for Reading!

Your journey to building stronger, more meaningful relationships starts here, but it doesn't have to end with this book. Here's how you can take the next steps:

1. **Stay Connected**

   Visit www.fycreativemedia.com to explore more resources, tips, and tools designed to help you thrive in your relationships and personal growth.

2. **Join the Community**

   Sign up for my exclusive newsletter to receive:
   - Bonus content and relationship tips.
   - Free downloads like "The Ultimate Relationship Checklist for Men."
   - Updates on upcoming books and events.

3. **Share Your Feedback**

   If this book inspired you, I'd love to hear your thoughts! Please leave a review on Amazon, Goodreads, or your favorite retailer's website. Your feedback helps others discover the book and embark on their own journey to love and intentionality.

4. **Spread the Love**

   Share this book with friends, family, or anyone who might benefit from its insights. Together, we can create a world filled with stronger, healthier relationships.

Follow Me on Social Media

Stay up-to-date with the latest content and connect with me at:
- Instagram: @fycreativemedia
- Facebook: @fycreativemedia
- Twitter: @fycreativemedia
- Threads: @fycreativemedia

Let's grow together!

SCAN ME

www.ingramcontent.com/pod-product-compliance
Lightning Source LLC
Chambersburg PA
CBHW052027030426
42337CB00027B/4892